CW01313835

Sailing through Life:
Ninety-three years of adventure

Nick Coates

Book designed by Mitzi Moore and Pamela Valentine
Cover designed by Pamela Valentine

Copyright © 2024 Nick Coates
All rights reserved.

Unless otherwise noted, photos are from the family and friends of Nick Coates.

ISBN: 9798324020910

DEDICATION

There are good ships and there are wood ships, the ships that sail the sea. But the best ships are friendships, and may they always be. Irish Proverb

This book is dedicated to my many friends and family who shared my life and these adventures.

ACKNOWLEDGMENTS

I am grateful for several essays from Neligh Coates, Sr., my father, and my good friend, Bob Myers.

Many thanks to Pamela Valentine and Mitzi Moore who made the printing and publishing of this book possible. Thanks too, to Catherine Fishman who edited and organized the essays that are posted on Coates Adventures, https://www.coatesadventures.com/.

Lastly, I want to recognize my faithful guide dog, Hercules, who is supposed to be retired. He continues to lead me safely and to point his nose at the door knob when we return home.

CONTENTS

Introduction 1
FAMILY HISTORY 3
    Jefferson Coates 5
    William Coates 7
    The Origins of the Name Neligh 9
    Olive Coates—My Mother 11
    A Collection of Stories by Neligh Coates Sr. 18
    Neligh Coates Sr.'s Patents 40
PERSONAL LIFE 43
    Playground 45
    The Little House 48
    The Big House 52
    From Troublemaker to Stand-Up Citizen 54
        Early School Days: Mischief 54
        Boarding School 58
    My Year in England 61
    School in England 70
    High School 75
    My College Years 77
    Love at First Sight: Robbie Gibbon 82
    A Love like Friendship: Betty Byers 87
    When the Lights Went Out 90

MY WORLD OF BUSINESS ... 93
Clipper Manufacturing Company: A Tale of Invention and Innovation ... 95
My Development and Real Estate Career (Aspen and Beyond) ... 102
Realty Business: Coates, Reid & Waldron ... 106
Mexico: It All Began at the Oceana Bar ... 108
Trust and Betrayal ... 111

CHARACTERS ... 115
Art Weidman ... 117
Buddy Melges: My Sailing Hero ... 119
David McCullough ... 124
Debbi Fields: One Positive Cookie ... 126
Fritz and Fabi Benedict: The Ultimate Partners ... 129
Hal Russell: One-of-a-Kind ... 134
The Hefner Brothers and Friends ... 138
Jim Briggs: Larger than Life ... 141
Joe Ross: The Unconventional Half Cherokee ... 145
Lee Lyon: Friend and Fellow Adventurer ... 149
Lynn Bolkan: A Unique, Brilliant Individual ... 153
Paul Koontz: Over 70 Years of Friendship ... 156
Pierre Baruzy: The Crazy French Man ... 159
Ron Miller and Diane Disney: Silent Partners ... 161
George Waring ... 164

ADVENTURES ... 167

Baja Adventures 169

Barking Dog 172

Bullfighting 174

Cuba 177

Diving: A Family Passion 179

Dolphin Delight, Tehuantepec, and Sea Turtles............. 184

Eating Rat 186

George's 35th Birthday 188

Lake Powell and The Grand Canyon 190

The Friendship Cruise 193

Monarch Butterfly Wonderment...................................... 195

Morocco: Marrakesh, the Market, the Volkswagen 198

A New Year's Eve to Remember in Guatemala 203

The Panama Canal 205

Pig Roast 208

Robberies 211

Swimming with Sharks... 214

Wanderlust.. 217

Whale Watching 221

WATER, AIR, AND LAND 225

Water 227

The Beginning of My Sailing Days 228

Learning to Race 231

Winter Sailing— Frostbite and Freez'n Fun............. 234

Racing Days... 237

Big Butterfly 240

National Racing 243

Ocean Racing 245

The Missouri Yacht Club 248

Boats and Ships 251

Powerboats 251

Sailboats 253

Ships 258

Cruising 259

Not For Sissies 259

Our Early Cruising Life 265

The Expectation 270

The Maiden Voyage 276

More Sailing Adventures 282

Land 285

Yachts on Wheels 285

Vans, Convertibles and a 50-year Model A Infatuation
....290

Air...294

I Can Fly! 294

Mexico, Real Estate, and Gonzo Gordo 300

More Airplane Adventures 302

Midwest Hospitality 303

Aspen 304

Hot Air Balloon Racing 304

THE MENAGERIE 309
Growing Up at the Lake 311
Kids Need a Pet.. 314
The Feathered Ones... 318
Jeff's Exotic Animal Ventures.................................... 319
Picnicking with Llamas 319
Wallaby at a Cocktail Party.................................... 321
Reindeer and Movies 321
Alice and Claudio 324

THOUGHTS, MEANDERINGS, AND CONTRIBUTIONS 325
Lucky to be Blind? 327
Hercules my Guide Dog... 329
Marijuana: A Gateway Drug? 332
When the Door to Opportunity Opens, Walk Through It! 334
Memorable Moments... 337
The David... 337
Windsurfing in Panama 337
The 9/11 attack, December 11, 2001 338
Pearl Harbor, December 7, 1941 338
Roosevelt dies April 12, 1945 338
Kennedy assassinated, November 2, 1963 338
My Musical Life 340
Death Penalty 342

Where Was I? 343
   The Bombing of Pearl Harbor, December 7, 1941 ..343
   V-day, the end of World War II, September 2, 1945343
   First Moon Landing, July 20, 1969..............................344
   September 11, 2001 344
Epilogue...345
NOTES..346
ABOUT THE AUTHOR...349

Introduction

I have been fortunate to live a life full of enriching work and incredible experiences. Thus, I have taken on the task of writing a series of essays hoping to pass on tales of adventure, history, and lessons learned to my great-grandchildren and future generations.

I was born into a family line consisting of a Civil War hero and a phenomenal inventor and businessman. The **Family History** section details prominent figures of the Coates family, including the story of Clipper manufacturing, my father's extremely successful saw company. A version of my father's story in his own words can be found in this section.

My **Personal Life** details my early years as a young man, including experiences of love and becoming a father.

Everyone meets people they feel are unique; I am sure that I have met more than my share, so I wanted to write about them not only to share new perspectives and insights but also to keep them clear in my mind. I hope you will enjoy reading about this wonderful group of courageous, witty, diverse, sometimes provocative individuals found in the **Characters** section.

I have been fortunate to have had many wonder-filled experiences. I now realize that many of my adventures will fade from memory and that some of the sites no longer exist. You can read all about that in the **Adventures** section.

Having spent the summers of my youth at the family lake house, I developed a love for sailing early on in life. That love would prove to be lifelong and was supplemented with a passion for all types of boats. The **Water, Air, Land** section is about everything from my first dinghy to the infamous Pea Green Princess.

Come with me on my adventures and meet the wonderful characters I have known.

I hope you enjoy my stories.

Cheers,

Nick Coates
San Antonio 2024

FAMILY HISTORY

Jefferson Coates

Image: Public domain

Jefferson Coates 1843 - 1880

Without question my hero is my great-grandfather, Jefferson Coates. Jefferson was born August 24, 1843, in Boscobel, Wisconsin. On his 18th birthday he enlisted in the Wisconsin 7th Volunteer Army, which became known as the famous Iron Brigade. * He was wounded at the Battle of South Mountain but recovered in time to be on the front lines for day one of the Battle of Gettysburg. He fought that day with such valor that he was awarded the Congressional Medal of Honor, the highest award for valor in action.

During that battle he was shot through both eyes by a musket ball called a minié ball** and was blinded. For three days he laid on the battlefield in no man's land while the front line continuously moved back-and-forth over his position. At one point a Confederate soldier tried to steal his boots but was.

stopped by a Confederate officer. The officer reprimanded the soldier for ungentlemanly conduct, propped my great-grandfather in the shade of a tree and gave him some water. In return, even though gravely wounded, Jefferson shared his coffee with the officer.

When the battle finally ended, the Union troops came to recover their wounded. They did not realize Jefferson was alive until another wounded soldier said he had heard my great-grandfather groaning. Jefferson was carried to the temporary field hospital at Seminary Ridge. He miraculously survived despite the crude medical procedures of those days. Then he was quickly transferred by rail to the Army Hospital in Philadelphia and here he recovered from his wounds. Once ambulatory, he learned to read braille and the art of making brooms at the Philadelphia School for the Blind.

Jefferson returned to his native Wisconsin. Undeterred by his handicaps and his poverty, he married Rachel Drew, an attractive and ambitious young lady. They traveled by horse-drawn wagon to homestead in Nebraska on land the government provided for returning veterans.

In Nebraska, Jefferson and Rachel built a sod house*, farmed and raised four kids. Jefferson even served on the local school board. Sadly this brave man died at age 37, not from the shot through the eyes, but from the 19-year long festering South Mountain bayonet wounds.

Being blind myself, I was fascinated by what Jefferson Coates was able to accomplish as a blind man in the 1860s when none of the wonderful aids we have today were available. I did not want his story to be forgotten so I hired a professional writer to write a book to tell his story. *Memory of Light* by Mollie Cox Bryan is available on Amazon.

William Coates

Nick with his Grandfather

Five more hours of sitting, but exciting and hair raising! We had finally arrived at the Grand Canyon and we were riding mules to Phantom Ranch at the bottom of the canyon, along the Colorado River. The trail is like a shelf just wide enough for a mule and its rider, on one side is the sheer rock wall and on the other side is the drop-off. I held tight.

I have only hazy recollections of my grandfather, William Coates. I remember him as a kindly gentleman who lived in California with his second wife, Bo, who wasn't a family favorite. Because of the distance, I did not see a lot of Father Coates, as he was called, while growing up, but I do have embarrassing memories of that trip I took with him when I was eight or nine. He took me by train from Kansas City to see the

Grand Canyon and I'm surprised he did not kill me on that trip. On reflection, I would not have blamed him if he had.

I remember traveling on the train for hours and Father Coates pointing out the treeless rippling plains and grain elevators, missions and pueblos, mountains and deserts, all of which I did not see as he could not tear me away from my comic book.

The mules delivered us safely to Phantom Ranch where Father Coats had rented a cabin for the night and, while he was reading and having cocktails, I was busy along the river collecting frogs, lots of frogs, which I hid in his bed. Grounds for murder? At least justifiable homicide.

It's not hard to understand that special connection between grandparents and grandchildren when you see grandparents offering that extra measure of patience for a child bursting with energy.

In later years I appreciated his patience after I took my grandkids on trips to Disney World, down the Grand Canyon, to Alaska, etc. They were not always perfect, but they looked like saints compared to me.

The Origins of the Name Neligh

I was named Neligh Coates Jr. after my father who, for some unknown reason, was named after a town in Nebraska—perhaps he was conceived there.

Naming the town "Neligh" almost didn't happen.
John D. Neligh, a former Representative of the Nebraska Territory Legislature and an inventive brick maker from West Point, Nebraska, traveled with William B. Lambert, and John B. Thomson to Antelope County in 1872. "They were impressed by the Elkhorn River, bordered by cottonwood trees, and an uninhabited valley filled with clumps of green and gold grasses swaying in the August breeze." Neligh decided that the valley area was an ideal town site, and he went to Omaha to buy the land.

The Omaha & Northwestern Railroad had already chosen the property for a future town and depot location. "Fortunately, a careless clerk failed to check the railroad's choice of town locations, allowing Neligh to purchase the 500-acre tract for $6 per acre. His friends encouraged him to name the town Neligh."
After the Homestead Act passed, widespread settlement across Nebraska led to an increased need for flour mills and sawmills. John D. Neligh immediately arranged to build a brick flour mill and a dam across the Elkhorn River. He also installed machinery for a sawmill. The fledgling town prospered as did John Neligh.
Located in the middle of Antelope County, Neligh became the center of Antelope County government. Major improvements in milling occurred with each new owner of the Neligh Mill, and unlike mills in some neighboring towns, it survived the

Great Depression, operating for over seventy-five years. Now the Neligh Mill, still fully equipped with vintage machinery, is an area tourist attraction.

Neligh is the only town in the U.S. with my name.

Olive Coates—My Mother

Olive Coates with Nick and his sisters

Beside every great man is a great woman.

I have struggled with Mom's essay, struggled to make her real. I struggled to show how good she was, how intelligent, how kind and dedicated. She accomplished so much, often ahead of her time. She was a college graduate and a journalist with a column in the Kansas City Star in the 1920s, a devoted wife and business partner, a life-coach and stalwart companion who helped construct a house, a loving mother who fostered learning and independence in her children, a world traveler, a negotiator in international business arrangements, and a doting grandmother.

Emily Olive Todd was born July 15, 1904, in Fayetteville, Arkansas, the youngest of three girls. Her sisters were Rose, eight years older, and Mir, four years older. Their mother, Angie Cope McMurry Todd, died November 19, 1913, when

Mother was only nine years old. Her father, Charles McKendree Todd, was separated from her mother and had very little influence on the girls' upbringing. When their mother died, he married another woman, Aunt Ida, and moved to Houston. Mom was essentially raised by her two older sisters who were determined that she would get the education and advantages they never had.

Although born in Fayetteville, Mom and her sisters lived in Nowata, Oklahoma, until their mother's death in 1913, when the girls briefly moved to Kansas City, then to Shelbina, Missouri, where they lived with their Aunt Fan. Aunt Fan was very strict and very religious. She lived in a big, drafty house heated by a single potbelly stove. She had no running water. There was a well for water, icy cold water in winter, and an outhouse for a toilet.

While they were not Catholic, Rose and Mir saw that Mom went to St. Mary's Academy in Leavenworth, Kansas. The nuns greatly influenced her personality and her character. Mom never forgot them and kept in touch with her favorites until they died.

Mom attended Rice University in Houston for one year, then transferred to the University of Missouri in Columbia where she was a member of Phi Mu Sorority and earned a degree in journalism. Mom met Dad while she was at the University. He was selling construction materials and driving a truck. The story is that Mom was the only college girl who would ride in his truck and romance bloomed. They were married November 19, 1928. I was born on March 27, 1931, and my brother, Todd, was born four years later. Sadly, this was before antibiotics and Todd died of strep throat when only a year old.

The newlyweds were thrown into the jaws of the Great Depression. Yet somehow, they managed to buy a lot on Lake

Lotawana just as the dam was finished and the lake was starting to fill. Having no funds for building on their lot, they decided to construct their first house themselves. And they did it with not one hour of outside labor. You can read more about the project in my essay, "The Little House."

Everything changed in March 1937 when I became a big brother. My sisters, Carol and Jean, were twins but the farthest thing possible from identical twins. They dressed alike yet could not have been more different in appearance and temperament. It happened that my folks had purchased a cabin cruiser for use on Lake of the Ozarks that year and they appropriately named it the Carol Jean. I was proud to be a big brother and sometimes referee as the twins would get in the occasional scrap. Jean seemed to be the more dominant twin and I remember having to rescue Carol after Jean put her in their big toy box and sat on the lid so Carol couldn't get out. The girls were a wonderful addition to the family and certainly livened things up at our house.

Energetic, productive, and insightful Mom had her own social column in the Kansas City Star. With the help of her sister Mir, she did all the necessary ancestry research to become a member of the DAR (Daughters of the American Revolution) where she was active in their civic projects. She even found time to work as a volunteer nurse's aide, a Candy Striper, at a local hospital.

Apparently, my father who was very hard-working was also extremely shy and Mother was instrumental in building his confidence. Just one small example of her lifelong dedication to helping and supporting him.

I wish I had listened more closely and paid better attention. Mom was an excellent typist and tried to impart the value of learning to type properly to me. She even sent me to typing school and I did okay but, foolishly, did not stick with it and have been sorry ever since. She also thought that speed-reading was important and sent me to classes at Evelyn Woods to learn the art. I went through the motions to please her, but I did not follow through. Another opportunity foolishly missed.

Mom loved the crystal-clad pianist, Liberace,[4] but dad was not a fan. I remember accompanying her to the President Hotel a few times to see him perform. I loved watching her eyes dance with excitement as he played.

When I was a child, Mom made Jell-O, which came in many flavors and colors. She would pour the liquid into molds that, when set, shimmered on our dinner table. Family meals were fairly traditional – turkey at Thanksgiving and Christmas and a beautifully prepared roast beef for special occasions. Whenever she made cookies or cake, she would always leave a little in the bowl as a special treat for me to enjoy in the raw form.
Mom was a big believer in scouting and was religious about seeing that I got to my Cub Scout meetings. She was also very active when I was old enough to join the Boy Scouts. She sent me to scout camp and worked hard pushing me to earn the merit badges necessary to become an Eagle Scout. At the Eagle Scout presentation, a speaker commented that behind every one of us Eagle Scouts there was a dedicated mother, and it was certainly true in my case.

I was a slightly above average student in grade school then I slipped down a bad path when I entered Southwest High School. I thought I had a major in sports and a minor in girls. Southwest classes were large enough that I could get passing grades with minimal effort, and I am ashamed to admit, I was involved in more than my share of vandalism. A streetcar line ran down Main Street, not far from home, and my friend, Richard Miller, and I would wait by a streetcar stop. When the car stopped, we would run behind it and pull the rope controlling the lever that connected the car to the overhead power line. This, of course, threw the streetcar into complete darkness, forcing the conductor to come out to reconnect the line. If we were brave enough, we would do it a second time! My mother never knew or I'm sure she would have straightened me out.

We were Lake people. Mom and Dad took great delight in having me show off for their guests by diving off our dock and swimming underwater to the dock on the opposite shore, which was close to 100 yards away. Mom liked to stroll along the sea wall and fish for bluegill.

When I was 15, I somehow talked my parents into buying me a motor scooter. We lived in Missouri, just a few blocks from the Kansas line. In Kansas, the legal driving age was 14, but 16 was the law in Missouri. One night the police pulled over six of us underage drivers and told us to follow them to the police station. I got the smart idea to escape and pulled off on a side street, turned off my lights, and hid in a dark driveway so the chasing police did not see me. Our whole family left early the next morning for a weekend on the family cruiser at the Lake of the Ozarks. No phones, no communication of any kind and we returned too late on Sunday for me to call any of my friends. On Monday, the homeroom phone rang, the teacher looked at me and said I was needed in the principal's office. The jig was up – my friends had ratted on me. I wasn't as afraid of the police as I was of disappointing my mother.

Mother was an outstanding cook. My sister, Jean, has a scrapbook full of handwritten thank you notes from Mother's dinner guests. Candlelight, delicious food beautifully presented, refreshing drink, and stimulating conversation were Mother's recipe for many great dinner parties for both local and out-of-town guests. I have fond memories of mom's warm smile as she welcomed her guests.

This was before the days of television when dinners were a family occasion. There was one rule – you did not have to eat everything, but you had to at least try everything. I learned to eat a lot of exotic things, but I still can't stand squash. Christmas was always a huge celebration at our house. The excitement began with a beautiful, seven-foot, lush, green Christmas tree covered in twinkling lights gracing our living room and dozens of packages underneath. It was tough for us kids to wait until Christmas morning to open the presents, however that was the rule and no exceptions. If we were lucky it snowed on Christmas Eve. Finally, presents were opened one at a time with photographs of every important opening. To add to the festivities, my sisters were always dressed alike.

When it became obvious that I was not motivated enough to get the education Mom believed I deserved at Southwest High, she strongly suggested I go to a private school, and she thought it would be best for me to get out of the temptations of Kansas City. For once I listened and the next fall, I was off to Hightstown, New Jersey, the Peddie School, and a complete transformation of my educational future. I did well enough at Peddie that I won a fully paid scholarship for a year of school in England. As long as I was in the U. S., we could talk every week or so by phone but once I arrived in England that practice stopped. I don't think there was even a phone for students to use and, at that time, international phone calls were prohibitively expensive, so I didn't talk to my parents for the entire year. My time at Haileybury College is the subject of another essay.

Rarely has there been a couple who worked so closely together in every aspect of their lives. When Dad first started his business, Mom was his secretary, accountant, mail clerk, and even helped with the building of some of the first machines. As the business grew, she offered advice and counsel. When overseas factories were started Mom traveled with Dad constantly and was instrumental in charming the individuals they selected as foreign partners. They traveled for business and they traveled for pleasure. Mom was an expert at planning detailed itineraries. I have memories of her meandering through her scrapbooks and recounting their adventures. I think her favorite of all the sites they visited was the exquisite Taj Mahal, the crown of all palaces, which was the purpose of two trips. She had told me so much of its wonders that the Taj Mahal was a "don't miss" site on our trip to India and I was able to truly appreciate what I had been told. Mom and Dad also made possible a number of travel adventures for my son, Jeff: twice to Africa and extensive cruises of the San Juan Islands on their cabin cruiser, the Carol Jean.

Mother became a smoker at a time when not many women had taken up the habit. She kept it from my grandfather, William Coates, although when he did find out, he was so fond of her that he forgave her. Mom was one of those people who had a cigarette and a Coca-Cola first thing every morning. I was in Aspen when I got the call that Mother was in the hospital with severe breathing problems. It was a terrible experience to sit by her bed and hear her trying to get a breath. She passed away the next day, November 19, 1977. We thought my father was doing fine as a widower, but the loss of his partner was too much for him and he took his life just over a month later

A Collection of Stories by Neligh Coates Sr.

Neligh Coates, Sr.

A lot of people think I have lived in Kansas City all my life, but I was born in Plattsmouth, Nebraska. My folks later moved to Enid, Oklahoma and I was seven or eight years old when we came to Kansas City.

While we were living in Enid, Dad took me out to see an airplane fly which at that time was something we had never seen. We went out to a pasture where hundreds of people had turned out to watch. We saw the pilot take off and when he came in to land, he flew low over the crowd. Everyone ran in every different direction, they were so afraid. Later on I learned that the pilot was Mr. Cessna, who later started the Cessna Aircraft Company, now located at Wichita. Kansas.

I used to have a little "fix-it" shop, repairing irons, lamps and small appliances.

Sailing through Life: Ninety-three years of adventure

Later on I started to build radios, the old original crystal sets, and I sold many of them to the neighbors.

At one time, the Jones Store Company had a contest for the best crystal set costing less than $1.00 to make. I won the prize of $50 and if I remember correctly, I gave this set to Jean.

I was always keenly interested in ice skating; in fact, I would sometimes skate from early morning until late in the evening. At some point, I decided to go into the skate sharpening business. I fixed a jig to hold the skates even with the grinding wheel and with this set up, I could sharpen a pair of skates in ten minutes.

I worked out of the basement at 2810 Tracy and at times had people lined up in the basement and outside down to the street waiting to get their skates sharpened. I charged 25¢ a pair and during Christmas vacation I would sometimes make as much as $600. I did this for several years.

There is one thing about me that a lot of people won't believe, but when I was a boy I was the most shy and timid person you could ever imagine. I wanted to get off to myself and did not want to be with other people.

This worried my mother so much that she would take me to lunch at the Muehlebach Hotel at times just to get me out and around people. She also did lots of other small things to help me overcome this problem.

As a young man, traveling and selling tile, I carried brick samples around with me which weighed about 35 pounds. When I got on an elevator I was too shy to call out the floor I wanted, but would wait for someone else to do it.

Sailing through Life: Ninety-three years of adventure

It is hard to explain to people who did not live through the depression of the 1930s the steps we would take to save a few cents, but one such experience stands out in my mind.

My dad had an office at 12th and Oak and there was a cafeteria where we liked to eat our lunch at 8th and Grand. It was the Forum Cafeteria and the food was good, it was an inexpensive place to eat.

We had quite a little mail to send out each day consisting of bids on jobs, bills to pay and a lot of general correspondence so we would get the mail ready, sort it out and each of us would take a stack to deliver in person thus saving the 2¢ necessary to mail it.

After delivering all the mail we could, we would meet at the cafeteria where we would have saved enough money on postage to pay for our lunch. Our lunch would not cost more than fifteen or twenty cents each unless I decided to have their apricot chiffon pie which I thought was the best I had ever eaten.

My older brothers took me with them on float trips down the James and White Rivers in South Missouri. You could float for many miles as the rivers wound around in the Ozarks, yet at the end of the float you could obtain a team of horses and drive back to where you started, a distance of only 15 or 20 miles. We floated for a whole week, shooting rapids, catching fish and camping on gravel bars. It was quite an adventure.

We could see rafts, some of them a hundred feet long made of fence posts or railroad ties. We learned that they cut the timber, pushed it down to the river bank and then took grape vines to lash the logs together. The rafts were their means of delivering the logs and ties to the nearest railroad. A man on each end used a long pole to guide the raft.

There were lanterns at intervals along the rafts and between the lanterns we could see young boys with a club in their hands, hitting the fish as they jumped up on the raft. By morning, they would have a gunny sack full of fish; in fact, fish sometimes jumped into our boat and this is no fish story either. I really enjoyed these trips and made them for a couple of summers.

During the days when tie timber was in demand, my father bought quite a little acreage in the Ozarks. There were lots of trees which were big enough to be used to hew a railroad tie. As I understood it at the time, the natives did not want their timber cut and I guess some of them were pretty "rough and ready." I have heard Dad tell about going to a little town and getting a team of horses and a buggy from the livery stable to go look over his land. He had to decide when certain trees were ready to be taken out and sold.

He would be met by hillbillies armed with guns, threatening him and telling him to get out. He told us lots of stories of how he finally talked them out of any violence for Dad never did carry a gun.

There was a vacant lot at 29th and Troost, next door to the Campbell Baking Company.

Mr. Campbell had copyrights on the name Holsum and received royalties for the use of this name for bread. The company also made Hostess Cakes. They delivered bread and cakes door to door and when the delivery men came in the late afternoon, they would park along a wall outside the building and leave their trucks while they were checking in with the cashier.

We had dug holes or caves in this vacant lot. We had all kinds of tunnels and even rooms with fireplaces. While the trucks were lined up and the men were inside, we would take the cakes out of the trucks, throw them over the wall and take them into our tunnels or caves.

One day they caught us and called the police. The police tore the tops off our caves and tunnels and completely wrecked our set-up.

When I was a young boy I had a job with Ed Price who, by the way, was a very brilliant man with a wide knowledge of radio. I think he had one of the first broadcasting stations in Kansas City.
At the time I worked for him, he drove a bread route for the Campbell Baking Company. They used electric trucks, steered with a sort of stick, and up in front of the seat were the racks filled with bread.

Around 24th and Troost, there were what could be called first-class boarding houses and as the women came out to buy bread, he would have them spotted. He would pull a loaf of bread from under the counter, put it under the stool or seat, bounce up and down on it a couple of times and when these women would ask him if he had saved them some really fresh bread he would reply. "Sure. Here it is, feel it". They thought he was wonderful. He was quite an interesting person and I made a little spending money shagging bread for him.

I later knew Ed Price at Lake Lotawana. He still had many talents but unfortunately, his health went bad.

One summer, I went to work for Dad in St. Louis. My brother Meredith was building a big tile barn on a farm owned by Mr. Champlin of Champlin Spring Works.

The farm was located next to Lambert Field and while I was there, Charles Lindbergh was flying his SPIRIT OF ST.

LOUIS, tying it down just across the fence from Mr. Champlin's farm.

I would go over and chat with him quite often. He was always very nice and explained things to me about the plane.
The next time I saw him was in Honolulu shortly before he died. I went up and spoke to him about this incident; he remembered it very well.

He was a very interesting person and a fine man.

When I was thirteen years old, Dad gave me the tool bench, which is still in our garage. It is solid, clear maple, which is a very hard wood. The top is a chopping block, such as butchers use. I have used this to build many things: two boats, two miniature automobiles, furniture for the children, the cabinets that are still at the Lake, the door to the closet, drawers, and everything I could possibly build and haul out on a trailer. Considering how much I have used it, the bench is still in good shape today.
I still have some of the tools Dad gave me, although during the years when I was so involved in the business, I didn't use them very much. I know I gave some of them away, but I still have quite a few.

I might also mention that the shovels and a lot of the garden tools I am using today belonged to my father. They are just as good, if not better than when he bought them. At least, they are all slick and shiny with hard use.

I went to school at Valparaiso, Indiana and during all the time I went back and forth between school and home, I never paid a railway fare, I either bummed, hitch-hiked or drove some old automobile I had bought.

Sometimes I shipped out on cattle trains. At that time, the law required somebody to be in attendance when cattle were shipped as they had to be fed and watered every 24 hours. I might be able to get a ride into Chicago and then ship out to Kansas City on one of these cattle trains.

One experience in particular was thrilling to me at the time. I rode the Santa Fe from Chicago to Kansas City. I knew how to read time tables and after checking the schedules, I would decide what train to use. Then I would find out what track the train would leave on, then go down and count the rails until I got to the track for the train I wanted to ride.

One Christmas, I decided to come home and I didn't tell my folks about it. I borrowed a sheep skin lined coat from Walt Bixby, a boy at school. In Chicago, I located the train I wanted, walked around it and crawled up on top of the water tank. I laid back on my back with my arms spread out until the train pulled out. Just ahead of the water tank was the coal car; there was always a difference in height between them of about three feet so I would nestle in back of the coal car to break the wind.

We pulled out of Chicago - the next stop was Joliet then Fort Madison, Iowa, just across the Missouri River. As the train got ready to leave Joliet, a couple of railroad detectives came along, saw me, and asked what I was doing up there. I told them I was riding to Kansas City and they told me to get off. I got off on the opposite side of the train and waited for it to start. Then I grabbed on to the second or third car, crawled up, walked the tops back to the coal car and stayed there.

It got bitterly cold that night so at Fort Madison I went into the station to warm up a bit. It was early in the morning; the air was very cold, and believe it or not, I saw the sun shining double. I took a mail train out of Fort Madison which left about half an hour after the passenger train I had been on. As usual, I rode in back of the coal car on the water tank because this was the safest place to be and it afforded the windbreak I have mentioned. I got so cold I couldn't stand it any longer but I saw a little valve on the stoker and opened it to see what would happen. Out came the steam and I sat in that steam all night and kept warm.

When I arrived in Kansas City, it was four degrees below zero and I was sick as I could be for I had been sitting behind the engine all night long with the smoke in my face. I walked into the Union Station just as if I owned the place not realizing how black and dirty I was. It took me weeks to get the smoke and soot from around my eyes.

When the story on the cable car was written up Walt Bixby wrote to me reminding me of the marks I left on his coat that night.

Another time I bought a Model T Ford in Valparaiso for $7. After fixing it up, I drove it home and sold it for $14. There were no paved highways in those days; I drove most of the way over dirt roads and down farm roads. In some places, there was a little concrete but not much.

Also, I hitch-hiked between Kansas City and Chicago. I had reached St. Louis and was trying to pick up another ride when a chauffeur driven car stopped for me. There were two men in the car and after talking with them, I learned they were Cas Welsh and Welch Sanders, both a part of the Pendergast machine that controlled Kansas City politically at that time.

I rode up in front with the chauffeur and as we went through Fulton, Missouri we passed the reformatory. Cas Welsh said "I have put many a kid in that place." He had been a judge at one time and I thought it was pretty bad for a man of his stature to make the remark he did almost bragging about the number of young boys he had put in the reformatory there in Fulton.

Once we bought another Model T Ford; this one with no top and no fenders. Five of us got together to drive down to see the Kentucky Derby. One of the boys was Jewish and had very kinky hair. Also, he was dark and tanned from riding in the sun and wind. After we were seated in the grandstand, the police came and accused him of being a negro, telling him he would have to leave. But there were five of us who didn't agree and we caused considerable commotion.

There was a fence between the grandstand where we were and the Clubhouse where the elite were enjoying their Mint Juleps. I looked up and on the other side of the fence I recognized Walt Driscoll who was there with his mother and step-father. He had heard the commotion and looked over the fence to see what was going on. They invited all of us to join them and showed us one great time. This was the last time I ever saw Walt.

We took this same car, no top and no fenders, and drove to Watertown, New York to spend our Easter vacation at the home of one of the boys. His parents took us on a ride through the Thousand Islands, one of the most beautiful spots there is. These islands are in the St. Lawrence River on both the American and Canadian side.

On our way back to school, we ran into some roads that had been freshly oiled. Since the car had no fenders, the oil was thrown up in our faces which were already sunburned. They started to blister.

Here is another case of necessity being the mother of invention. We went to a grocery store where we got a supply of paper sacks. We punched out holes so we could see, tied the sacks around our necks to keep off the sun and wind, and wore them back to school.

My father was really a tee-totaler. He thought that anyone who drank or smoked would end in the penitentiary at the very least. He believed this so strongly that with four boys in the family, he promised each of us $1,000 if we didn't drink, smoke or chew tobacco until after we were twenty-one years old.

Our family always had breakfast together and on Bill's birthday when my mother removed his plate, there was a new crisp $1,000 bill. It is the only one I ever saw.

As time went on though, it was obvious that we were going to have to tell Dad that both Florence and Olive smoked cigarettes. They had been sneaking off to hide when they wanted to smoke, but we finally decided it was time to tell him. I think this was at Christmas time. We mustered up our courage and the girls smoked their cigarettes. Strangely, Dad had become so fond of both of them, he didn't say anything and from then on, there were no more conversations about smoking.

On Christmas Day, we decided we would like to have a highball, which Olive fixed. She made one for Dad that tasted like lemonade, but she put some gin in it. Dad got to feeling really high and said he had never tasted such good lemonade. I know he never carved a turkey faster in his life. Later on, we told him what we had done and as time went on, he would sit down occasionally and have a drink with us.

Later on in his life, he moved to Carmel, California and out there he had a couple of heart attacks due to thrombosis. We would go out to visit him and drive him around. He loved to watch the ocean waves and Olive sat with him and talked to him by the hour.

One day about lunch time while we were sitting in his living room, Olive and I decided to have a drink and he had one with us. He was sitting on the divan and said to me, "Son. I am going to tell you something I thought I would never tell you. The doctor tells me if I had had some whiskey every day. I wouldn't be in the trouble I am now."

During the height of the depression an ex-boyfriend of your mother's named Ernest Coffin was employed by the A & P Tea Company in their coffee division. A & P sold three brands of coffee: Red Circle, Eight O'Clock, and Bokar. Ernest asked me to build a display for him which he wanted to use at some sort of trade show or fair over in North Kansas City. We had no place to work, but through A & P we got permission to use a vacant store room on the Plaza right next door to the Plaza Theater. I fixed up a nice display and A & P gave him an award for it.

But there is more to the story than that. I had to hire an artist, Ed Rush, to paint the names Red Circle, Eight O'Clock, and Bokar on the display which was over six feet tall so it was quite a job. Ed had been out of work for some time and was pleased to get the job at the 75¢ an hour I offered him.

When we were all through, Ernest came to me and asked how many hours we had spent and I told him. He later gave me a check from A & P, and when I figured my time, it came out to about 25¢ an hour. I paid Ed Rush 75¢ an hour, so you can see I didn't make much for myself.

Ed said he was going to do something for me because he felt I had been "gypped" and he did. We were working on the little house at the Lake and the four maps over the bunks which are now in our kitchen were drawn by him and given to us. He was a fine artist and if you don't believe it, study these maps carefully some time.
Speaking of the depression, when I drive through the Plaza today, I cannot help but remember how destitute it looked at the time I was building the coffee display. There were not

nearly as many buildings as there are today, of course, but businesses had gone broke and stores were vacant everywhere. Where Swanson's is now located, Chandlers had a greenhouse and a nursery so times have changed, but the beauty of the Plaza is unsurpassed.

When we first started Clipper overseas, it was necessary for us to go to Europe frequently; in fact, I cannot tell you how many times we have crossed the Atlantic both by ship an airplane. The first planes were DC-4 and it took about twenty-two hours to go from New York to London. They flew from New York to Gander, Newfoundland, then to Shannon, Ireland. They did not serve meals on airplanes then, but you could eat at Gander and Shannon. They did, however, have berths and you could go to bed. Actually, it was a long, hard flight. The English government had two ships at certain locations in the Atlantic to serve as weather stations and the planes flew from one weather station to the next. I have sat up with the pilots many times when they were talking to the weather ships and they would fly so close to the water, you could see the waves and the ships that reported weather conditions.

The only means of communication the pilot had was radio contact with these weather ships. Of course, there was a weather navigator on the plane who would "shoot the stars" looking through a plastic dome.

Later on, I happened to see in the paper where a navigator was shooting the stars through the dome when the dome popped off. Of course, the planes were pressurized and this poor fellow was pulled out through the opening and they never did find him. As time went on, planes got much bigger, better and faster. They had better communications and navigation. In fact, I think they did away with the weather ships not long after we began flying the Atlantic so much.

Some of these early flights became very luxurious; they had begun to "wine and dine" the passengers yet they still had berths so you could sleep.

Speaking of sleeping, one time coming back from London, we stopped at Gander. The pilot reversed his propellers and I thought I had had it. The plane just shuddered and the noise was terrific. I woke up and even after I found out what had happened, I never did get back to sleep.

We used to like to fly Air France when they first started flying the Constellation. The service was beautiful and the French food was simply great. Fine food was in abundance on the little carts which were pushed up and down the aisle. The French chef presided with a waiter to help. You could select your meat and the chef would slice it - it was really great. They served anything you wanted to drink: whiskey, wine, champagne. If you weren't careful, you didn't feel so well when you reached your destination.

At that time, I don't think anyone could visualize what the airplane would finally come to and how fast you can go from New York to London today, especially with the degree of accuracy and the number of planes flying with comparatively few accidents.

I just have to tell you another little story about an airplane trip we will always remember. We were going to London on a DC-4 and that time we decided to fly to Chicago then on to Gander, Shannon and London.

In Chicago, the hostess informed us that someone had forgotten to load the liquor kit. There was a liquor store across the street so we proceeded over there and obtained all the supplies we needed. There were only two other passengers on this particular flight: one was a Greek being deported to

Greece, the other man was a butcher from Chicago who was going to Belgium to see his mother.

We had berths on this flight but the Greek sat up all night looking down at the floor. The butcher began to sing; he had a very good voice and by the time we got to Shannon, we were really living it up. By the way, this was around Christmas time.

We were to get breakfast at the Shannon Airport, but first we went into the bar which opened off the big dining room. Lots of planes stopped at Shannon to refuel and allow the passengers time to eat. The butcher was happy and started to sing. People began to flock into the bar, coaxing him to keep singing. He sang mostly Irish songs – I remember "The Irish Eyes Are Smiling" and "Mother Machree" especially. The passengers would not leave the bar so the plane just waited. In those days it was nothing to hold up a scheduled departure.

In fact, I have called the airport myself to tell them I would be fifteen minutes late arriving and they would hold the plane for me—but those days are gone.

The first time mother and I went to Europe on the Queen Mary, Candy and Edith Huston went with us on the Twentieth Century Limited from Chicago to New York. We had suggested they go to Europe with us but Candy said he couldn't get away just then.

We stayed overnight at the Waldorf Astoria and the next day went aboard the Queen Mary. We had a lovely stateroom and were showered with telegrams, flowers. champagne all wishing us bon voyage. When the ship sailed, the most impressive sight was the people standing on the pier singing "Now Is the Hour."

After we returned, Candy came to the office at Clipper one day and told me that he and Rex and Edith were planning to go to Honolulu. He said he had bought tickets for mother and me to join them. I insisted I did not have time to go to Hawaii just then. That night at the dinner table I was telling the family what Candy had done. All of a sudden Carol popped up and said. "Why don't you and mother fly over there and meet them?" We talked it over and finally decided it was a pretty good idea especially since they had gone to New York to see us off on the Queen Mary.

So Mother and I went to Los Angeles and we drove them out to the pier where the S.S. Lurline was to leave. We saw them off with all the fanfare that goes with a sailing. From there, we went to San Francisco and flew to Hawaii.

Of course, we arrived several days ahead of them which gave us time to get our Aloha shirts and all that goes with the atmosphere of Hawaii. Candy had told me they were going to stay at the Royal Hawaiian hotel so I went there and arranged for us to have adjoining rooms.

The morning the Lurline was to arrive we went to the pier and what a sight it was. Here were bands playing; everyone was wearing leis jubilant over the arrival of the Lurline. As the boat came in we saw the passengers throwing money in the water. The little native children were swimming alongside the boat begging and they would dive for the money. This was the first time I had ever seen these youngsters diving for money and it was quite a sight.

We got a place on the pier and while I was taking moving pictures, the boat pulled in to dock. When they had tied up, the cabins were within about three feet from where we were standing. Looking out the window were Candy and Edith. I just said "Hi Candy" and he was speechless. We all went to the Royal Hawaiian and had ten wonderful days.

When your mother and I and the Ellises were in Africa, the pilot took us to the Chobe Inn on the White Nile. The pilot had a friend named Ian who had a camp not far from the Inn. We borrowed a car and drove over there. It was a very interesting place. Around this camp, which was on the river bank, he had all kinds of elephant and rhinoceros skulls which were scientifically tagged for some form of research they were doing. After talking with him for a while, he could see we were very much interested and asked our pilot to fly him over to where his own plane had gone down when he flipped over in a wind storm. We all decided to go. On the way over, we flew right down the Nile and could see hundreds of hippopotamuses in the water; then on out over the brush country where there were so many herds of elephants it was unbelievable. In all my trips to Africa, I never saw a sight like this again.

We learned later that Ian had a contract with the government to thin out the herds of elephants and the hippopotamuses. He got the tusks from the elephants and the ivory from the hippos. In addition, he was paid so much for the kill.

This program to thin down the herds had been started because they were afraid the animals would turn the country into a desert. An elephant could take one paw and push over a good sized tree just to get to the leaves. Also, they peeled and ate the bark off the trees. The hippos would come out of the river and go over to a sort of plateau where they ate the grass so short it was being killed off so it was felt that some measures had to be taken to preserve the land.

When they planned to make a kill, they notified the traders who would come in with big trucks loaded with men and poles. After the kill, the natives tied the poles into a rack of sorts where they could lay the meat out to dry.

There was always more fresh meat than they could dispose of. There was some kind of arrangement whereby they sold the meat and paid the government so much.

They always killed the hippos at night by going out with very bright lights, which caused the animals to freeze, then they shot them one after another. Ian had two boys with him who helped do the shooting and he also had natives to maintain his camp.

After we had been acquainted for a while and he saw how interested we had become in what he was doing, he told me he would get his boys together that night and kill a hippo. He came by with two jeeps; one for us, the other loaded with his men.

We went to a very pretty spot; it was a sort of cove in the river and we could see a lot of hippos swimming around. Ian and the fellows who were to do the shooting were running around with the powerful rifles yet dressed only in sandals and a pair of shorts. They started to shoot and got a hippo. The big problem was getting him out of the water. They used poles about twelve feet long to sound the bottom and this way they could tell when they had found him. All the time, while they were jabbing around with their poles, there were other hippos and alligators swimming around to see what was going on. They had their mouths open and were making a lot of noise, but these fellows would just try to run them off using the poles with which they were trying to locate the hippo they had shot. They kept swimming around among the hippos and alligators - it was quite a sight. When the hippo they had shot went down, he had become lodged between two rocks so it was very hard to get him out of the water. They used chains to put around his neck then dragged him out using a winch on the jeep. I had never realized that men had as much endurance as these men had diving down, working with the chains, swimming to chase off the alligators and so on, but they finally brought him to shore.

They laid him out and started to work on him. It is impossible to describe how they handled the knives they used which were big, somewhat like a corn knife. When they cut off a leg and thigh, it took four or five men to lift it into the truck.

Before they did any cutting though, they measured his length, height, and the size of the ivory. They opened his stomach and took samples to send to the laboratory and wrote down all other kinds of data.

After it was all over, I became very upset when I found that the flash on my camera was not working so I did not get all the pictures I wanted, although I did get some.

It was dark by this time and I don't know how they ever found the road back to the Inn. They wanted us to go with them the next morning to see them make a kill right across from the hotel, but we were all too tired to go; however, I woke up and saw all the bright lights and heard the trucks running back and forth. Later, when we flew to the next camp, we could look down and see them still working on the hippos they had killed.

The elephant kills were handled differently. They would set a time and place, then drive in several very large trucks along with the jeeps. They took a jeep and drove right into the herd, then the men would start to walk around in a circle. The elephants would also start to circle while all the time they were closing in on them. There were just three men doing this.

When they got the elephants closely packed together, one man gave a signal and all three of them started to shoot until there was just a big pile of elephant bodies. Then the traders came in and got to work loading their trucks. They sold the elephant meat. Ian got the ivory and so much money for the kill.

I might add that Ian took a liking to us due to our curiosity and showed us a lot of things. Along the river bank he showed us where beautifully colored birds built their nests in the sand on the river bank.

Again, the Ellises were with us when we went to Tahiti. We had made arrangements to get a car and a driver from a Tourist Bureau in the hotel, but when I went there, they informed me that although they had two cars. They had only one man who could speak English and he was not available to us. I went across the hall to a taxicab window and told them what I wanted. They furnished us one of the finest drivers and guides we have ever had.

After showing us around, he told us there was going to be a wedding in his village and asked us if we would like to see the wedding ceremonies. Of course we told him we would, so he picked us up the next morning.

The bride-to-be was in a little sort of hut with some lattice work around it - really sort of like a chicken coop. The people came bringing her gifts and food wrapped in tea leaves. As I understand it, she had to stay there for a week before the wedding and time went on and on. Finally we were told that the priest who was to perform the ceremony had arrived.

By this time, they had the groom lying on a table. He was covered with blankets even though the temperature was very high. The priest filed a little off his front teeth as he laid on this table. It made chills go up and down our backs to hear that file grinding those teeth but after that ritual, they were married.

It so happened that later we saw an issue of the National Geographic which described this teeth filing ritual just as we had seen it performed in Tahiti.

The original Missouri Yacht Club was located in Kansas City at the foot of Main Street on the Missouri River. Over the years, many of the members had dropped out but a few of us were still interested, and when we built homes at Lake Lotawana we decided to reorganize the Club at the Lake.

We first rented a vacant farm house which we cleaned up and repaired somewhat. We hired Mr. and Mrs. Queen to act as caretakers and prepare food. They served mostly fried chicken and all meals were country style. She was a good cook and it was a treat to go out there.

One Saturday night, three couples of us went out to have dinner and a little party. It started to rain and the roof leaked badly; we could not mop up the water fast enough. We drilled holes in the floor so it could run on through.

The old farm house was beyond further repair and it was obvious that if we wanted to continue the club, we would have to do something about different quarters.

Candy Huston and I were driving out to the Lake together one afternoon and got to talking about what we could do in the way of a new building. We soon had our plans drawn up which we presented to the membership. At first there was a storm of protest that the plans were too elaborate, but after a long evening of debate, the members agreed to go along and appropriated $50.000. We spent about $46,000.

When completed, we had some 5,000 square feet of space on two floors. On the main floor we had a large dining room, a lounge, a screened porch, a card room where private lockers were available and a glazed tile kitchen with a walk-in refrigerator. In addition, there were living quarters for the manager.

Below the main floor, there was an open veranda and a playroom for the children. Outside was a nice grass terrace where people could sit and watch the sailboat races.

After the Queens retired, we were fortunate to be able to hire Alice and Fred Stephenson. Fred was not only an excellent cook, but he was very versatile and an excellent manager. The club made money as long as the Stephensons were there, but they finally felt they had to leave. The Yacht Club is still a fine building and has been a source of pleasure to many people over the years.

My father always believed that owning farmland was a good investment and in the early 1940s after Clipper had made a good start, he told me the first thing I should do was to go buy a good 160 acre farm. I told him I did not know anything about farms, nor did I have time to look, but if he wanted to come to Kansas City, I would have someone drive him around to see if he could find something suitable.

We were living at Lake Lotawana at that time and one night he came in to tell us a "For Sale" sign had just gone up on a 400 acre farm right in back of our lake property. He said he could not imagine a better location.

We bought it and named it Lakeridge Farm. It was in poor condition as far as buildings and fences were concerned, but since it was so close, we went up and worked at every opportunity trying to get it cleaned up.

We first remodeled the old farm house which was made of solid walnut. It had been built before the Civil War and had bullet holes in it from a battle that had been fought on the farm itself.

After that, we built a barn, a chicken house, a machinery shed and what we called a "pig patio" where we fed the pigs. All the time we owned the farm, we were either building something or accumulating farm machinery.

We made a beautiful winding lane up to the farm house and on each side we planted a row of pin oaks, about a hundred of them. At the time they were planted, they were tiny and Olive and I watered them, pruned them and watched over them as if they were babies. I saw the farm recently and these trees are now about 14 inches in diameter and look like a picture.

We built the farm up to a sort of show place and then decided we had better sell it because, contrary to what my dad thought, you could not make enough money on a 400 acre farm to support it. We were surrounded by the lake and other large farms so there was no way we could acquire more land.

We had a big auction when the farm was sold. I felt I had put so much into it, I could not bear to see things sold, but I went after all and had a very good time.

Howard Adams is the man who bought it and he wanted it primarily because of its historical value and the fact that it had been a battle ground in the Civil War. He made arrangements to move the old original farm house to Missouri Town where it is nearing complete restoration. I understand that present plans are to convert the farm to a golf course and to sell some of the land as lots for the construction of quality homes.

Neligh Coates Sr.'s Patents

Concrete Saw Patent

1939: Tile Cutting Machine
Heretofore it has been the common practice to definitely set the cutting blade and secure it in position to produce a kerf in the stone at a given depth, and after said kerf is cut, then readjusting the cutter to a further depth and repeating the operation. It is the purpose of this invention to overcome this extremely slow operation due to the foot or hand control of the cutter at all times during the cutting operation. By means of W the present machine, it is possible to cut a surface which is at an angle to the direction of travel of the tile being cut.

1944: US2338318
A Mounting and Guard for Rotary Cutters
The principal object of this invention is the provision of a cutting machine wherein the rotary cutting blade is provided with a streamlined guard which ensures greater safety and efficiency. Another object is the provision of a mounting and guard for oscillating rotary cutters wherein the guard is provided with an adjustable front extension. Other objects are simplicity and sturdiness of construction, efficiency of operation and adjustability of the guard to proper function when the cutting blade is positioned at various heights relative to the operator.

1948: 2455113 Masonry Saw

This invention relates to improvements in masonry saws and refers more particularly to a power saw employing a disk cutter mounted upon an adjustable head held rigid during the cutting operation.

1949: 2464117 Conveyer Cart for Masonry Saws

This invention relates to the art of cutting material such as masonry or the like and has for its primary aim the provision of improvements to the conveyor or cart forming a part of equipment which has heretofore been perfected and that is shown for example in my previously issued U. S. One of the important objects of the invention is the provision of a conveyor cart for masonry saws having structure for releasably clamping the material in place for engagement by the cutting disk of the saw, which structure is capable of maintaining the material being cut at an angle to the plane of the cutting disk.

1956: Track MountedCutter for Concrete Slabs

This invention relates to masonry equipment and particularly to cutting structure for use with relatively heavy, bulky slabs not easily moved about, the primary object being therefore, to provide cutting apparatus adapted to be easily positioned in cutting relationship to the rock-like cementitious slab, thereby avoiding the necessity of handling or otherwise manipulating the latter.

Sailing through Life: Ninety-three years of adventure

PERSONAL LIFE

Playground

Aerial view of house and little house Lake Lotawana

Three days a week Hercules and I attend adult education classes at ALIR (Adult Learning in Retirement). Marian, the instructor of one of our favorite classes, Memoir Writing, assigns a prompt as a subject for the next week's essay. Sometimes these prompts are difficult for me but Playground, the prompt assignment for this week, was dead easy. I immediately thought of Lake Lotawana, the man-made, 365 acre body of water where I grew up, located just 30 miles east of Kansas City.

As I reflect on my time growing up there, I realize how miraculous our lake house was! For starters, my parents bought the land in 1929, when the country was in full depression. My father was self-employed selling construction supplies and business was slow but somehow my parents managed to buy lot H-12 which, at that time, was literally miles from any water. A dam had just been built over a local stream and the lake was just starting to take shape.

The second miracle was the house itself. Dad had designed a combination of a house and boathouse, which was built on dry land before the lake was formed. The house had to be at the perfect level in order for a boat to fit properly in the boathouse section; if the house was too low, there wouldn't be enough headroom for the boat, if the house was too high there wouldn't be enough water to float a boat. The dam that determined the level of the lake was five miles away, but when the Lake finally filled, dad had figured everything perfectly, the water covered the foundation and the boat slipped perfectly into its space—a remarkable feat! There were a couple heavy rains that raised the level of the lake too quickly for the spillway therefore causing the house to flood, but those were few and far between.

The next miracle was that they were able to build a house at all! They didn't have funds to hire a contractor so they built the house without spending a single dollar on outside labor. They did everything themselves, including the plumbing and electrical work. My dad even heated and bent railway ties to make beautiful andirons for the fireplace. The final touch was a beautiful stained-glass sailboat that graced the window in the entrance door.

As kids we were always around the water and the rule was that no kid left the house without his kapok life vest on. One Saturday the whole family was on the dock so we were allowed to take our life vests off. Mine accidentally got kicked in the water and to everyone's amazement, it sank. I had been swimming around keeping both myself and my waterlogged life vest afloat. By age five I had learned to drive the outboard and even ride a surfboard. This was long before the invention of waterskiing.

I enjoyed wonderful summers at the lake through my high school and college days. When I was fourteen I got a job working in the parts department of an automobile dealer in Kansas City but still commuted to the lake with my friends every night. Waterskiing came along and we made six-person pyramids for the holiday shows. The water ski jump we built was pretty crude because we couldn't afford plywood for the surface so we used boards instead; they were never perfectly even so it was like jumping off a washboard.

And, of course, sailing there was fantastic! The time I spent playing on that lake no doubt led to the time I spent as an adult teaching kids to sail, racing competitively, and exploring the world on a sailboat with my wife, Betty. I looked at the world as my playground, thanks to those early years on Lake Lotawana.

The Little House

The little house at Lake Lotawana with the big house in the background

My backyard "playhouse" had a "trap door." To reach it you went through the bathroom at the very back of the house, up three steps to the bathtub. Beyond the tub was a trapdoor that opened up so you could drop down into the boat that was stored below.

This wasn't any ordinary playhouse. When I was about ten years old, I ended up living in the Little House to make a separate bedroom available for guests in the big house. Since there were four bunk beds it was easy to have a couple of friends over to spend the night. I enjoyed the independence and having a place where I could keep my treasures — especially the snakes I liked to collect.

My father was very organized. He was a list man. He was continually making lists. Every morning before he went to work, he would post a list of chores for me to do on the refrigerator in the big house where I had breakfast. The rule was "Complete the list before any play time." The list included keeping the Little House neat and clean, cutting the grass, weeding certain areas, washing the boat, and of course, watering the petunias.

There are a number of miracles surrounding the Little House but the biggest one is that it was built at all. Lake Lotawana, where the property is located, was named for an Indian princess who was murdered on her wedding night by a jealous lover. The name means sparkling water. An auspicious start! The dam to form the lake was built in 1928, but, because of the drought, the lake did not fill until the spring of 1935.

In 1930 my parents bought a lot in what was to become Union Cove. The lot was designated as H 12 and was fairly steep and heavily wooded. Their idea was to have a combination workshop/boathouse built over the planned lake in front of their property, then later build a house on the hill.

These plans were destroyed when the depression hit, their bank folded, and they ended up with six cents on the dollar. Thus, in 1931, with a new baby and very limited funds, they decided to turn the workshop plans into a home they would build themselves. They started construction of what turned out to be a totally unique house on the lake. It was unique in so many ways. The first being the house was not built on the lot itself, but rather over the water in front of the lot.

And, amazingly they completed the house without spending one dollar on outside labor. Even the plumbing and electrical work was theirs. When the project was started the lake water was still more than a mile away so they poured the foundation where the lake would eventually be and started work. Their plans had to be exact because, if the house was too low it would flood when the lake filled and, if it was too high, there wouldn't be enough water for the boat storage they planned underneath.

My grandfather was a distributor of structural glazed tile, which was usually used in gymnasiums and public bathrooms, so they were able to buy this product at a very good price. This house may be the only one in the world with outside walls of glazed tile.

The workshop turned home was primarily one big room with four bunk beds[5] on the east wall. There were drawers under the lower bunks —the upper bunks were reached by ladder. Each bunk had a reading light. These were 12-volt lights taken from the interior of cars my parents found in the junkyard. Because there was no electricity near the lot at that time, my father rigged up a 12-volt generator from a junkyard car and originally all the lights in the house were 12-volts.

The floor was a beautiful random oak planking. They bought the knotty pine boards for the interior walls from a lumberyard near the railroad tracks for practically nothing because they had been damaged by sparks from the steam engines. Countless hours were spent planing and sanding these boards and, when finished, the wood grain and luster of the boards were beautiful.

The magnificent stone fireplace was built from rock quarried right on the site and the mantle was hand hewn from one of their oak trees.

Dad made the beautifully curved andirons from old railroad ties. There was a hammered iron bar that hung over the fire and also swung out into the room with a cauldron hung from it so you could cook by the heat of the fire yet easily swing the cauldron out into the room to check the food.

The window at the end of the room was made with exquisite art glass as were the hanging light fixtures. The window that graced the front door was my father's beautiful stained-glass sailboat.

The closet was unique because from the room it looked like a dressing table with a mirror, but it swung open to reveal a spacious hanging area. There was a fairly conventional bathroom except that the tub was three steps up to another level and beyond the tub they installed a trapdoor that opened up so you could drop down into the boat that was stored below. This boat slip was accessed from the outside by paneled wood garage doors. The lake side of the house had a catwalk with bumpers for tying at least two boats.

The roof was one large, flat deck with a stunning railing around it. There was a stone pedestal with a flat top every 12 feet. This is where my parents would put pots of petunias and my job was to haul watering buckets from the lake every day to water the flowers. I carried the buckets of water up 20 feet of stairway and each watering took six trips. I grew to hate petunias!

Because the land sloped, they built a yard that was flat and retained the uphill side of the yard by building a dry-stone wall. By this I mean they did not use any mortar and every stone had to be hand fit. The wall was a work of beauty and craftsmanship.

We all spent summer weekends in the little house until my father became successful enough to build another house on the hillside. When they moved into that house the little house became my room.

The Big House

The Big House on Lotawana

Memory has always been a mystery to me; how much do we actually remember from our childhood and how much do we think we remember but actually just heard our parents talk about?

My time growing up at Lake Lotawana brings back precious memories. Some of those are recalled in my essay "The Little House." When my father became more successful, he decided to build a house up on the hill that we always called "The Big House." Unlike the little house he did not build it himself, but he was essentially the architect and he incorporated some unusual Neligh Coates features.

The heating system was supplemented by creating an airspace around the flue for the fireplace. When a fire was burning this airspace would heat up and a fan could be turned on to blow this warm air into the bedrooms to heat them.

The bedrooms were up three steps, which left a vacant space under them. This space contained a king-size bed hidden behind paneled doors which you could open and pull out the bed to provide extra sleeping space.

The road that serviced the property was at the top of a rather steep hill. Getting tired of hauling luggage and groceries up and down the hill, Dad decided to install a cable car. Most people would just build a box to move things but not Neligh Coates. Dad took a trip to San Francisco to study the real thing and not only came back with ideas but a real cable car bell. The Coates cable car was an authentic replica of the real thing: a pleasure to ride and featured in several magazines.

From Troublemaker to Stand-Up Citizen

Nick Coates

Early School Days: Mischief

I have never let my schooling interfere with my education.
– Mark Twain

I can truly say that I was educated in a one-room schoolhouse, à la Abe Lincoln. When I was five years old, I attended a one-room schoolhouse that was just off the lake—about three miles away. I understand that on good days I walked the three miles to and from school, but I don't really remember kindergarten.

The first school I remember attending was J.C. Nichols School where each desk had an ink well in the upper left corner. Can you believe that the teacher got upset with me when I dipped a girl's pigtail into my inkwell?

After we moved, I went to Hale Cook for the rest of my elementary school career. The next school was the Bryant School on the south side of Kansas City. I was able to stay out of trouble there until one day I was called to the principal's office. It seemed that someone had written my name in rather bold black letters on one of the risers of the steps at the second entrance to the school. I would have been in serious trouble if I had not pointed out to the principal that it could not have been my work since whoever had painted the name had spelled my name wrong. The culprit had spelled it C-O-A-T-S. Logic prevailed and I was exonerated.

In those days in Kansas City you went from the 7th grade right into high school whereas the rest of the world had an 8th grade. We started practicing for our 7th grade graduation ceremony before Christmas so that by the time graduation came along in June, we had perfected the songs we were going to sing for our parents. I will never forget the night of graduation. We were all dressed up, ready to go on stage for the big performance, when the teacher came up to me and said, "don't sing, just move your mouth, you might spoil it!" I was deeply hurt, but I sang anyway. That was the end of my musical ambitions.

While most of my contemporaries around the country were going into eighth grade, I was only thirteen when I enrolled in Southwest High, along with 1500+ other students. Southwest was a big, impersonal high school with large classes. I'm sure it was good scholastically, but you had to be highly motivated to get a good education. It was easy to get lost in the shuffle, which happened to me. It didn't help that I was more interested in sports and girls than I was in education.

Louie House was the Southwest High football coach, who I got to know the following summer when my parents sent me to camp So So (Sosawagaming) located on the banks of Lake Superior, in the upper Peninsula of Michigan. Coach House was a camp counselor and seemed to take an interest in me as I remember him giving me stern lectures on the evils of smoking (which I never did). Besides coach House, my memories are of frigid plunges into the icy waters of Lake Superior that all camp goers were required to take every morning and standing between two cabins at night trying to hit the bats that whistled by with tennis rackets.

Some of us Missouri boys had talked our parents into buying us motor scooters. Technically, you need a driver's license to drive a motor scooter, although at first the police were lax. Then they started to crack down. In Missouri you had to be 16 to drive, but in Kansas you could drive at 14 if you were "going to and from school or on errands for your parents." All my Kansas friends drove; they were always on 'errands' for their parents.

One night a group of us were touring on our scooters when police stopped us, determined that we were underage drivers, and told us to follow them to the station. I wasn't supposed to be out that night and I was afraid of the consequences from my parents, so as we were driving down the street I made a sharp right-hand turn down a side street and reached under the seat to turn the scooter lights off. The police left one officer to guard my buddies and took off after me. I had enough of a head start that I was able to duck up a dark driveway and the police went by without seeing me.

I'll never forget how I agonized that weekend. My parents had taken me to their boat on the Lake of the Ozark and since this was long before the days of cellphones, there was no way for me to find out what had happened to my buddies. No phones, no communication of any kind and we returned too late on Sunday for me to call any of my friends. On Monday, the room phone rang, the teacher looked at me and said I was needed in the principal's office. The jig was up – my friends had ratted on me. I was in trouble with the police, and in a lot more trouble with my parents. That was the end of my motor scooter days for some time.

I hate to admit it, but my friend Richard Miller and I were always in trouble. There was a streetcar line not far from our home. It electrically propelled cars by an overhead line connected to the streetcar by a long, spring-loaded pole. We made great sport of waiting for a streetcar to stop, running behind it, and pulling on the wire that ran to the pole, disconnecting it from its electrical source. All the lights would go out and the conductor would have to reconnect the pole and restore power. If we were really brave, we'd do it a second time before the driver got started again—it drove 'em nuts.

We also were known to throw rocks at an occasional streetlight and sometimes were accurate enough to hit and break one. I'm chagrined to say that we also "borrowed" a few cars when friends' parents left the keys in the ignition. I don't know why we were constantly looking for trouble. Maybe we had too much energy. We definitely had too much free time on our hands.

The classes at Southwest were big enough that I could generally get a C with little or no studying, and that's what I did. The first semester of my sophomore year I brought home a D and the shit hit the fan. My parents decided I was in a bad environment and that I needed to go away to school. Strangely enough, I realized that myself and didn't fight the idea at all.

They selected the Peddie School in Hightstown, New Jersey, because a friend of theirs by the name of Art Weidman (See the characters section for more on Art) had gone there. That's when things started to turn around for me.

Boarding School

My parents were afraid I might become a juvenile delinquent if I continued going to Kansas City public schools. I could not seem to focus on anything but sports, girls and mischief, so they decided to send me to Peddie, a private boys school in Hightstown, New Jersey. They picked Peddie because that is where their close friend, Art Wideman, had gone to school. Even though he had graduated in 1925, I am sure my parents hoped Peddie would turn me into a gentleman like Art. (See my essay on Art in the Characters section.)

To get me off to a good start, they asked Art to accompany me on the long train ride East. We had a lot of time to talk on that trip. He explained that I had a unique opportunity as I was going to a school where no one knew me and or my reputation, so I had the unique chance to make anything I wanted of myself. Since I didn't know a single person at Peddie, I took Arts advice and concentrated on school work and sports. I was proud to make the honors list while playing varsity football, basketball and track, and later. During my sophomore year I earned a fully paid scholarship to study for a year abroad in England. (See my essay on my year abroad.)

Many people and moments have changed my life, but none more than Art Weidman and the advice he gave me on that train.

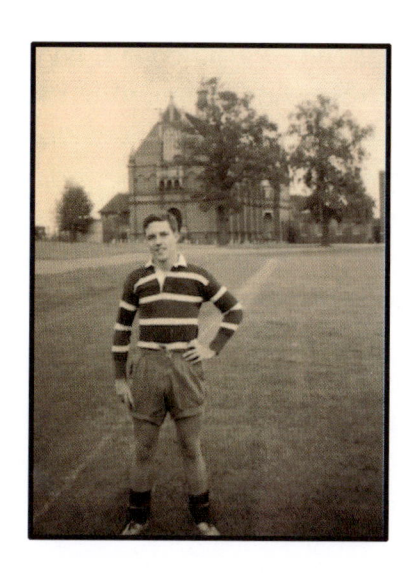

Although school in England was a great experience, I received no scholastic credit for it. I returned to Peddie for my junior year, which was a good year with lots of studying, sports, and a limited social life. Six of us lived on the edge of campus in a house called Wycoff, where Don Rich was the housemaster. He was a good guy, a fun teacher who got us all interested in politics and current events, and we students had a certain amount of freedom.

While at Peddie, my only home vacation was for Christmas in Kansas City. The other vacations I spent with friends. One time I went with Jerry Snavely who lived deep in the Amish part of Pennsylvania (at that time, I didn't know that people still lived like that—no one had a phone, they dressed all in black, and used horses and buggies instead of cars). Weekends I frequently had dinner at my roommate, Ace Barkley's house, who lived only 15 minutes away in Cranberry, New Jersey. His parents, Marian and Shag, were great characters and we had fun times together.

Like most high school seniors, I was very interested in applying to college. I applied to two, Yale and Northwestern, and was accepted to both. I took a weekend to go to New Haven to see what Yale was like and was given a wonderful reception. For some reason, Herman Hickman, who was their famous football coach at the time, thought I had potential as a player (he was wrong), so I got the royal treatment.

I was tempted to go to Yale. There was a wonderful new athletic facility but it was still an all-male school, and as I was just finishing four years of all male schools, I figured I needed a change. In the end, my decision was influenced by the fact that the current love of my life, Robbie Gibbon, was going to Northwestern. I have often wondered how my life would have been different had I chosen Yale.

My Year in England

Nick and Neligh Sr.

Of all the books in the world, the best stories are found between the pages of a passport.— Unknown

"Europe somehow."

During my junior year, my parents encouraged me to apply for an English-Speaking Union Scholarship to go to school in England. Although I won the scholarship, I was never sure why I was selected by the English-Speaking Union as one of the 22 students from American private schools to attend an English public school (in England what they call public schools are actually private schools). I had good grades but was not at the top of my class. I played varsity sports but was anything but outstanding. All I can figure is that they were looking for a typical American student; I guess I was typical.

There was good news and bad news about the scholarship. The year was free including transportation, meals, etc., however, exchange students received no academic credit, therefore, extending our high school education by a year. No matter.

In September of 1947, I found myself aboard the Queen Mary with 21 other ESU scholarship students headed for England. At that time, the Queen Mary was a three-class ship and we, of course, were assigned to the lowest part of the ship: the tourist class. Fortunately, there were only limited physical barriers separating the classes, and we quickly learned how to explore the whole ship. First class was a little snooty, so we spent a lot of time in cabin class, which had great food and a very comfortable movie theater.

We landed at Southampton, and I was dazzled by how intensely green the countryside looked. A stark difference from the Kansas prairies. At that time Haileybury was called "Haileybury and Imperial Service College." It was a combination of two schools and was known as a place where officers and diplomats serving in India and the Far East sent their sons back to study. Lawrence of Arabia was a former student.

You wouldn't know World War II was over from the way things were in England. Everything was still rationed—food, fuel, clothing. English Public School was anything but luxurious.

The main entrance to the school was opposite Lawrence House where I was assigned.[6] I was in a dorm with 43 other boys as young as 10. The younger kids were called "fags," and part of their school life was to do errands (like make tea and shine shoes) for the older boys, called prefects.

We slept in one large room with a partition about three feet high between each cubicle. The cubicles had only a bed and dresser.

A communal bathroom held two big tubs and what they called foot baths around the edge. Foot baths were a three-foot square and about six inches deep; you squatted in them and sort of splashed yourself to get clean—no showers. Fuel was rationed so hot water was short. Younger kids were restricted to the foot baths, while the older kids would use the tub, which was filled almost to overflowing. A boy would get in each end, soap up, and rinse off. They didn't change the water between baths; instead, they "cleaned it" by using a paddle to remove the soap scum and then dumped it on the floor.

Anyone who says it doesn't get cold in England in the wintertime hasn't spent a winter there. While it seldom snows, it can get really cold, especially since there wasn't any heat, and the dorm windows were always open. There was a little heat in the studies and common room where the older kids gathered in the evening and debated things like whether it made more sense to drive on the left as the Brits did or the right as Americans did.

My first days of class were really tough. The British were miles ahead of us in education. There were twelve-year-olds studying Latin and Greek and even putting on plays in those languages. Fortunately, they put me with the slower kids who were destined for one of the state universities rather than Oxford or Cambridge.

The amazing thing was the language barrier. There's English, and then there's American. I can honestly say that for the first couple of days I was not sure if I was in the right class—I couldn't understand a word. The classes were small and the instruction intense, and there was plenty of homework. I adapted fairly well and in a few days was in the swing of things.

Each house had its own rugby, track, and cricket teams; the competition between houses was intense. I made the rugby team and loved the sport, but I had to unlearn one of the fundamentals of American football. When you're tackled in rugby you must immediately release the ball, or you are subject to a penalty. In football, you hang on to the ball for dear life so as to avoid a fumble. The idea in rugby is to roll between the ball and the opposing team, so that when the two scrums (think: the line of men in football) attack, your scrum can move the ball back to the running backs whereas the other team would have to kick through you to get it to their running backs! No helmets, no pads, no substitutions, no time-outs, and, interestingly enough, very few injuries. Once I got the hang of it, I loved rugby and got to be pretty good at it.

I also tried to learn cricket. Although rugby bears a great deal of similarity to U.S. football, cricket bears almost no similarity to baseball, and I found I couldn't master it. So instead, I joined the track team during the spring and did some competitive sailing on the rivers that weren't far from the school.

We took our meals at long tables in one huge dining room. Food was still rationed in England, so we only got one pat of butter per day and lots of potatoes and Brussels sprouts. Overall, there was plenty of food and no one went hungry.

My first holiday was a brief trip to Ireland with a group of other ESU students. Rationing had ended there, and my main memory is of gorging myself on things I had been missing at Haileybury.

One food item I had the pleasure of introducing to my classmates was popcorn. My parents sent me a bag of kernels and, very importantly, a can of popping oil, as oil was strictly rationed. I got a big pan and started the process on the burner outside our study. We take popcorn for granted. Imagine if you had never experienced the bursting of the kernels. It was quite a sight, and I was a hero for introducing the dish.

The English have a much better system for organizing their school year than we have in the U.S. They have a one-month vacation for Christmas and another month for spring vacation then just over a month for summer. The long summer break students have in the U.S. goes back to the days when most people were farmers and kids would help work on the farm during the summer.
Once I learned the "language," school went quickly and before long it was time for Christmas break. On the ship over, a group of us ESU students had decided we would get together for a skiing vacation over Christmas. We went as a group to the Swiss resort of Lauterbrunnen, which had been picked because of budget restraints. The food was plentiful and wonderful, especially compared to England, and the family we stayed with was extremely hospitable. They issued us skis and we trekked up the hill, doing the herringbone[7] and then skiing down. It was hard work.

On the third day, one of our group twisted his ankle and decided to stay home. When we returned from skiing that afternoon, he greeted us with exciting news. He'd wandered down to the train station where he'd seen people getting on a train with skis, so he decided to follow. Just up the mountain from Lauterbrunnen, which basically was a summer resort and therefore empty in the winter, was Wengen, one of the great Swiss ski resorts. He told us that there were lots of people up there, ski lifts and ski trains, and best of all: girls!

The next day, we said goodbye to our Swiss hosts and headed up the hill to Wengen in search of the perfect ski technique and female companionship. While there, I met a Swiss girl with whom I tried hard to develop a holiday romance. Even though she seemed willing, her parents kept a very, very close eye on their daughter and "the American." No luck.

Later on that vacation, I met my father at the famous Palace Hotel in St. Moritz. That was living! My father was a good sport and he agreed to go skiing with me so I could show him what I'd learned. Showing off, I went too fast, hit some soft snow, and broke both my wooden skis. I was lucky I didn't break both legs.

From St. Moritz, Dad and I went to Nice, France, where I had been envisioning sunshine, sandy beaches, and girls in bikinis. Alas, it can be cold in Nice in January. We found empty, rocky beaches and cold, cloudy weather. The only picture I have of that trip is the two of us riding bicycles wearing our overcoats.

The best part of this trip was when my father discovered the French-built, motorized bicycle called a VéloSoleX. It was a typical bicycle you could propel by pedaling, and it had a small gasoline engine that you could lower, and it would engage the front tire and propel you forward. On a flat surface, it would go about 15 miles an hour and, on a hill, it would aid you in peddling. My father got the right to import them to the U.S. and they would have been a huge success except the police consider them a motorized vehicle and you had to have a driver's license to operate one. That restriction killed the market.

For spring vacation, I somehow ended up in Madrid in the company of Sue Newcomer, a girl from Kansas City. This wasn't a romantic liaison; she was a bit older and just a friend who happened to be going to Madrid at the same time. I'd been reading books on bullfighting and was very interested to see some good ones, which we did.

Easter was approaching and we heard that Seville was the place to be. We talked to a travel agent who told us there were no accommodations in Seville and even he, being Spanish, wouldn't try to go there over the Easter holiday. We ignored him and decided to go anyway.

We somehow got on a small, twin-engine plane and arrived in Seville without hotel reservations. We managed to find two rather dingy rooms. It didn't matter because we were hardly ever in them, there was so much going on.
Processions started from almost every church. There were 50 brotherhoods called "cofradias" that organized the processions, some with over 2,000 men. The highlight of each was a single float or "paso," or a series of them. These were huge, heavy affairs depicting Jesus or the Virgin Mary, carried on the shoulders of up to 60 men. Each procession started at a church and took a different route, with some processions lasting more than ten hours.

Sue and I saw our first two bullfights in the Maestranza, one of the most beautiful bullrings in Spain. I thought I knew what to expect at a bullfight, but I could not have imagined the thrill of hearing the majestic bugle fanfare and the ebullience of energy and passion from the cheering crowd. Of course, a bullfight is not a fight at all as the bull is not going to leave the arena alive. It is a beautiful spectacle and an emotional life and death drama that demonstrates the courage of both the matador and the bull. The Seville audience was very knowledgeable and demanding, adding to the excellence of the whole performance.

Later that same Spring break, I met a buddy from Peddie, Ace Barkley, for a week in Paris. Ace was studying at a different English school. It was the end of our vacation, and we were both poor as church mice. We paid 50 cents a night for a tiny room with a double bed and a bath down the hall. We skipped breakfast and at about eleven in the morning we'd buy a napoleon which served as breakfast and lunch. For dinner, we went to eateries where you could get a small steak, fries, and dessert for a dollar or two. We took the Metro and saw the sights of Paris the way broke and hungry kids our age ought to see them.

July came and all my friends in America were sailing and having fun while I was looking at another three weeks of school. On the 4th of July, I decided to do something to celebrate; I took a pillow slip; some felt tip pens; and made an American flag and raised it on the flagpole at the entrance to the school. There it was. Bright and early on the 4th of July. Of course, no one could guess who did it (I was the only American in the school).

I knew I was in trouble and was not surprised when I was summoned to the headmaster's office. He was not as upset about the flag as he was about the fact that I had broken curfew and made a dangerous crawl across rooftops to get to the flagpole. The normal punishment would have been six of the best with a cane on my backside, which I was prepared for, except my punishment was even worse: he made me write a 1,000-word essay on the futility of the American Revolution. The headmaster was even good enough to send the flag to my mother, who later had it framed. I still have it.

When school was finally out, our group returned home on the Queen Elizabeth. Gone for almost a year, I had acquired a fairly strong English accent. All my friends thought I was being phony. The accent quickly disappeared once I was back among my American friends.

Although England was a great experience, I received no scholastic credit for it, and I returned to Peddie for my junior year. My junior year was a good year, with lots of studying, sports, and a limited social life. About six of us lived on the edge of campus in a house called Wycoff, where Don Rich was the housemaster. He was a good guy, a fun teacher, and we students had a certain amount of freedom.

School in England

Flag that Nick made at Haileybury

Learning is a treasure that will follow its owner everywhere.
– Chinese Proverb

A typical student?

As I approach my 90th birthday, I reflect on the fond memories of the year I spent at Haileybury and Imperial Service College in Hertford, England. Somewhere down the line, the school dropped Imperial Service College from the name, and they didn't even consult me! It was 1947 and I had been selected as one member of a group of 22 U.S. private school students who were awarded a full scholarship to attend an English Public School. No one could explain why these elite English private schools were called Public Schools. And no one could explain to me why I was chosen to join this select group. I had a good scholastic record but was not in the top five percent of my class. I was on the varsity football, basketball and track teams but there were far better athletes. I was active in student government but not a class officer. The only thing I could figure out was that I had been selected because I was a "typical" student.

New York City was a long way from my home in Kansas City, still I found my way and joined 21 other English-Speaking Union students boarding the Queen Mary for our trip to England. In those days, the Queen Mary was a three-class ship and we students were relegated to the lowly tourist class with cabins at the bottom, just above the hull. Of course, that did not prevent a group of curious teenagers from exploring the entire ship.

Monet must have painted the grass in South Hampton. I had never seen grass that lush and green. When they showed me my cubicle in Lawrence House, the Haileybury school term had started two weeks earlier. They obviously did not expect too much of me academically for I was assigned courses with the boys who were destined for state colleges, not Oxford or Cambridge. And it was just as well because I found the academic level was far higher than it was in the U.S. Also, there was a language problem. For the first few days, I was not always sure which class I was attending as the accent was so strong, I wasn't sure they were speaking English. Of course, they were speaking English and I was speaking American.

At my U.S. school, I had shared a room with two others, but now I was sharing with 43 others. Each student had a cubicle separated from its neighbor by a short, three-foot wall. A cubicle contained a bed, a chest of drawers and a footlocker. The youngest students' cubicles were at one end of this large room and the more senior students at the other. I was shocked to learn that the ten-year-olds at the far end served as "fags" and were required to shine shoes and do other errands for the more senior students housed at the other end of the room. I was quite proud that I had a picture of my U.S. girlfriend for my dresser. To the best of my knowledge, I was the only one in the dorm that had a girlfriend. The British may have been miles ahead of us scholastically, but they were way behind socially. It seemed that the opposite sex was seldom discussed.

There was a strong sense of community, team play and sportsmanship at Haileybury. I was eager to join the house rugby team and I felt welcomed right from the start. Rugby football is a distant relative of American football. Since players played without all the American padding, I assumed it was not as rough, but I was very wrong. There were no substitutions and no timeouts. I had to unlearn hanging on to the ball after being tackled. If you did not immediately release the ball you would be penalized. So, when tackled you release the ball, but keep your body between the ball and the opposite team, because once you are down, a scrum would form and the biggest guys on both sides would try to kick the ball back to the smaller runners. Once I got the hang of it, I fell in love with rugby, and I was pretty good.

I was on the track team. But I never had a chance at cricket, which to play properly, a player must start in grade school. But I did learn that cricket was not a game for sissies and the ball was harder than a baseball, and no one wore gloves. It takes nerve to be standing less than 10 feet from a batter who could hit the ball as hard as any baseball, yet you had to handle it barehanded.

My housemates and I had many cordial debates about the merits of our countries. The craziest debate was over which country drives on the correct side of the road!

What I hadn't thought about until I arrived in England was how much they had suffered during the war. Although the war had been over for two years, the rationing in England was far worse than in the U.S. at the height of the war. Meat, shoes, butter, everything was rationed, and no one complained about it. I never liked Brussels sprouts but we sure ate a lot of them. There was the usual casual griping about the food, but it was good-natured. Serving that limited diet in the U.S. would cause rioting in the streets.

If any of my schoolmates remember me, they probably remember me for introducing popcorn into their diet. My parents had sent me a bag of popcorn and a bottle of popping oil. There was a stove near our study for making tea. I found a pan, put in the oil to heat, and added the popcorn. Think about it. If you have never seen popcorn pop, it is truly unbelievable.

The British school year makes far more sense than ours does. Our school year was designed when they needed the kids to work on the farm, so we have long summer vacations, so long that kids get out of the routine of school. The British have a more enlightened system of a month vacation at Christmas, a month in the spring, and about six weeks in summer. This meant that when July 4 came along, all my U.S. buddies were sailing and swimming, and I was still in the classroom. Being the only American in the school I felt I had to make a statement. I took a pillow slip and felt tip markers and made an American flag. That was the easy part. The hard part was sneaking out a window and climbing across the rooftops to reach the flagpole that graced the school entrance. There it was waving proudly the next morning. Of course, no one could guess who the culprit was.

I was not surprised when I had a summons from the Head of school that morning. I figured that he would not be as upset with me for raising the flag as he would be for my breaking curfew and risking my neck climbing across the roofs. The traditional punishment was caning where you were bent over a desk and received as many as 10 lashes with a cane. I wasn't looking forward to that but was prepared. Instead he gave me a far worse punishment. I was required to write a 1,000-word essay on the futility of the American Revolution. The Head was a good sport and sent the flag back to my mother who had it framed.

In those days international phone calls were prohibitively expensive, and, to my knowledge, we did not even have a phone accessible to students in the school. I hadn't talked to my mother for almost a year so when I called her from New York she recognized my voice but thought I was putting her on because I had a strong English accent. That was gone within a week.

Unlike U.S. schools I did not hear anything from Haileybury for at least 10 years. There were no fund-raising letters, no alumni publications, and I don't believe there was an alumni organization. I tried to contact my classmates, but this was long before the days of the internet. I wrote a couple of letters to the school requesting contact information but had no success. To this day I think about my classmates and wonder what they did with their lives. They were a brilliant group, and I am sure they accomplished great things.

High School

Nick Coates High School

While at Peddie, my only home vacation was Christmas in Kansas City. The other vacations I spent with friends. One time I went with Jerry Snavely who lived in the Amish part of Pennsylvania (at that time, I didn't know that people still lived like that—no one had phones, they used horses and buggies, and dressed in solid black). Weekends I frequently had dinner at my roommate Ace Barkley's house, who lived only 15 minutes away in Cranberry, New Jersey. His parents were great people and great characters and we had fun times together.

Like most high school seniors, I was very interested in applying to college. I applied to two, Yale and Northwestern, and was accepted to both. I took a weekend to go to New Haven to see what Yale was like and was given a wonderful reception. For some reason, Herman Hickman, who was their famous football coach at the time, thought I had potential as a player (he was wrong), so I got the royal treatment.

There was a wonderful new athletic facility at Yale, and I was tempted. Yale was still an all-male school, and since I was just finishing four years of all male schools, I needed a change. I thought it would be good to go to a top ranked school somewhere in the Midwest. In the end, my decision was influenced by the fact that the current love of my life, Robbie Gibbon, was going to Northwestern.

I had met Robbie during the summer of 1946, when I was 15 (see my story, Love at First Sight). A group of sailors from Lake Lotawana had decided to take their sailboats north to try them out against the sailors from Lake Okoboji, a beautiful blue water Lake in Northern Iowa, near the Minnesota border. I went along as one of the crew. We were unloading our boats from the farm trailers we had used to transport them when a beautiful wood-paneled Chrysler convertible pulled up and two gorgeous young ladies got out to watch the entertainment. The most gorgeous was Robbie Gibbon and she took my breath away.

Although Robbie lived in Sioux City, her parents rented a summer home at Okoboji. The following summer I had my driver's license and went with a friend, Joe Birmingham, to visit the Gibbons. This led to an on-and-off romance that somehow survived even when I went to England for a year of school after my junior year of high school. More on Robbie later (See Love at First Sight: Robbie Gibbon). Now, onto college.

Sailing through Life: Ninety-three years of adventure

My College Years

Nick and Robbie in their teens

Filled with anticipation about college life, I arrived in Evanston, Illinois, in the fall of 1950 to enroll in the Northwestern business school. In those days fraternities and sororities were a big deal at Northwestern, and rush started as soon as you arrived. I was torn between the Sigma Chis, the Phi Delts, and the SAE's. SAEs had the inside track because a good friend from Kansas City and Lake Lotawana, Joe Jack Merriman, had been an SAE at Northwestern and encouraged me to join. I pledged, moved into the fraternity house, and went through "Hell Week."

Hell Week for our group was a little unusual and quite challenging. There was the usual paddling, but it wasn't bad. The thing that was unique was the treasure hunt we were sent on. We had only one night to complete our list. One task was to get the autograph of a famous opera star and after we tracked her down, she graciously accommodated us. The symbol of SAE is the lion and one of our more challenging tasks was to return with fresh lion poop. Not easy at night when the zoo was closed. A guard caught us as we were sneaking in. It turned out he was a good sport, and we were successful. Hell Week accomplished its intended purpose as it bonded us into a tight group that continues some 70 years later.

I was still very much in love with Robbie who joined Kappa Kappa Gamma and we had a ball our freshman year. Both of us had such strong high school educations that the academic work was not difficult. We still studied hard and made good grades. Our dates were often library dates since we found it hard to study in the chaos of the fraternity/sorority houses. We frequently double dated with Bertie Buffett. We did not know that Bertie's brother, Warren, would later become one of America's wealthiest magnates. Bertie later donated $100 million to Northwestern. Maybe I was dating the wrong girl!

As a going-away-to-college present, my father had given me a beat-up Plymouth that had been used as a demonstration vehicle to sell construction equipment. There was just a front seat and a huge empty space in the back where they had carried a masonry saw. Although it was a weird vehicle and definitely not what I would have chosen, it was wheels and that was more than a lot of my friends had. The huge area that should have been a backseat was very uncomfortable sitting up but very comfortable lying down and stretched out. There was a line to double date with Robbie and me.

Those years at Northwestern were great ones. The fraternity had wonderful parties—always off campus, as there was no drinking in Evanston. It was one of the last places in the country to be "dry" as it was the home of the WCTU (Women's

Christian Temperance Union). At first a "dry Evanston" seemed like a big drawback, however, we had wonderful fraternity parties at downtown Chicago hotels and the house never suffered the damage of wild parties.

Although I liked my business courses, I really enjoyed taking some elective liberal arts courses taught by famous instructors. One I particularly remember was taught by Dr. McGowan and was on far Eastern religions. He lectured on the Shinto religion where they were so fanatic about not killing animals, they swept ahead of themselves as they walked to prevent stepping on stray bugs.

I joined the NROTC program and won several scholarship awards. I remember all of us NROTC cadets being assembled on the huge lawn in front of the Dearing Library, and I had to march up to receive my award. We had had no instruction in marching, and I was embarrassed by how sloppy my movements were.

My sophomore year I was elected treasurer of the fraternity, which meant I roomed with the current president, Howie Benedict. Howie was in journalism school and had just returned from Korea where he was a correspondent for Stars & Stripes. He probably could have taught the course. Being older, he loved to hit the bars. While we did not have much in common, we became good friends. After graduation, Howie became the AP correspondent covering the space program and had an apartment in Cape Canaveral overlooking the launching pad. I was honored when he invited me down to stay with him and watch a space launch from his balcony.

I got involved in school politics. The SAE's appointed me as their representative to the Interfraternity Council (IFC) and I was eventually elected president. Another honor was being elected president of DERU, the business school equivalent of Phi Beta Kappa.

My romance with Robbie had continued, and in my junior year, we discovered that she was pregnant. It was a long drive to Sioux City to announce this to her parents, but they took it remarkably well. Robbie's father, being a doctor, told us he could arrange for us to terminate the pregnancy, but we immediately rejected the idea.

Everything about school changed on December 12, 1953, when Candy was born.

That fall, Robbie and I had found an affordable apartment on the north side of Chicago not far from Evanston. We had to walk up three flights of stairs to arrive home. That was the good news. The bad news was that the bedroom was located no more than 40 feet from the elevated track, and every time a train went by (they ran 24 hours a day) the whole building shook. Eventually, we didn't even hear the trains, yet friends would come over and

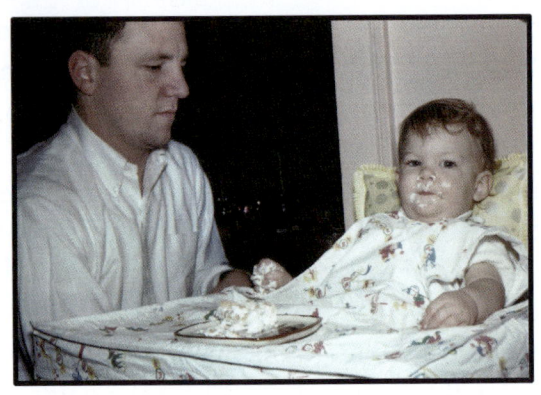

Nick feeding Candy

look at us in alarm when a train went rumbling by during dinner, practically shaking the dishes off the dinner table.

Robbie dropped out of school; I continued. During my senior year, we rented a house on Ridge Avenue just on the edge of the Northwestern campus. Since it was a big home, we became a boarding house and rented rooms to some of my fraternity brothers: Roger Dickinson, Tom Woodward, and Chuck Hollinshead. We didn't serve them meals; everybody shared the kitchen. In the spring of 1954, we had great sessions watching the Cubs play on TV while we drank Hamm's beer and Roger popped popcorn. Even Candy participated from her crib. The games were a great opportunity for Robbie to go shopping. I kept my grades up, however, school and the fraternity became less important with a wife and a baby to think about. Robbie and I weren't interested in the graduation ceremony, so we didn't attend. Since I was working for my father selling construction equipment, I received my diploma by mail.

Love at First Sight: Robbie Gibbon

Nick and Robbie at Luau

There will be a time when you are forced to follow your heart away from someone you love.—Ashly Lorenzana

When I was 15, before I had my own sailboat, I went as crew with a group of Lake Lotawana sailors to their first out of town Regatta at Lake Okoboji in northern Iowa. This trip would change my life.

This was the first-time sailors from our lake had traveled to an out-of-town Regatta and no one had a proper boat trailer. Instead, we had brought the boats north on a mix of farm trailers. I am sure the Okoboji sailors wanted to laugh at our ragtag group, but they couldn't have been more hospitable and pitched right in to help us get our boats into the water. While this unloading was taking place two of the most gorgeous girls I had ever seen drove up in a beautiful wood-sided Chrysler convertible. They were Robbie Gibbon and Tigar Beacons. I was instantly in love!

Robbie attended the yacht club parties that weekend and we hit it off as well as two 15-year-olds can. I was in love although I wasn't so sure about Robbie. I knew she had many suitors at the lake. The Lotawana sailors were completely outclassed on the race course but the hospitality was outstanding, and I got to spend a lot of time with Robbie and was able to slip in one quick kiss.

Like every young teenager I had my share of high school romances. I was crazy about Dolores Anderson for a few weeks and thought Ann Mackey was the one, however they were both nothing serious.

Robbie and I exchanged letters, a few phone calls and a minor romance flourished. The next summer I had my driver's license, and I convinced my folks that I should take a family car and a friend, Joe Birmingham, to Okoboji for a five-day visit to the Gibbons as house guests, an invitation I had finagled. Even though I was still well aware, that Robbie had many other suitors
at the lake, our romance continued.

That fall I left for my year of school in England, and I took a framed picture of Robbie to put on my nightstand. The British may have been miles ahead of us scholastically but were far behind socially and I think I was the only guy in my house that had a "girlfriend."

During my year abroad we wrote to each other since it was virtually impossible to make international phone calls. I'm not even sure there was a telephone available to students at Haileybury College.

When I returned to school at Peddie, Robbie had enrolled at Abbott Academy in Andover, Massachusetts, where I knew she had a series of boyfriends, but we still stayed in touch by mail and an occasional phone call. In my senior year, I was able to convince her to come to my Peddie Senior prom where we spent more time necking in a professor's car than we spent on the dance floor. I was seriously in love.

I had been accepted at Yale and Robbie chose Northwestern. At this time, Yale was all male so when Robbie selected Northwestern, I decided that seven years of all male schools was
enough and enrolled at Northwestern, too. Over the years I have pondered many times how my life would have been different had I chosen Yale. Would the distance have been too much to continue our romance? Would I have met a nice Vassar girl? We will never know. Robbie and I arrived at Northwestern in the fall of 1950. At that time fraternities and sororities were very strong on campus and Robbie joined Kappa Kappa Gamma and I pledged Sigma Alpha Epsilon. As is usual with romances at that age, we had our occasional ups and downs, and both dated other people, but by our sophomore year, we were going steady. In our junior year things got serious and we discovered that Robbie was pregnant.

The 480-mile drive from Evanston to Sioux City to inform her parents seemed like it was 10,000 miles long.

With great trepidation, we announced the news, and the Gibbons were unbelievably supportive. Robbie's father, a doctor, told us that he could arrange the termination of the pregnancy if that is what we wanted. We rejected the idea immediately, Robbie dropped out of school, and we rented a one-bedroom on the near north side of Chicago. It was on the third floor with no elevator and the bedroom window was only 20 feet from the elevated tracks. Every 20 minutes a train would go by, and the entire building would shake. We got used to it, but you can imagine the expressions on the faces of occasional dinner guests when a train went by, and it looked like the dishes were going to shake off the table. A good thing about being on the 3rd floor with no elevator—carrying groceries up three flights of stairs kept us in shape!

Being married changed my school life. I had to resign from president of the fraternity and president of the inter-fraternity Council as well as the NORTC program, avoiding two years in the Navy upon graduation.

Candy was born in December 1953, and we started a new life. We moved into a large house on Ridge Ave. in Evanston which we could afford by renting rooms to some of my fraternity brothers. Tom Woodward, Chuck Hollinshead and Roger Dickinson were easy to have around, and in the spring of 1954, we had great sessions watching Cubs games on TV while Roger, the popcorn master, cooked up a hot batch and we guzzled Hamm's beer. Sometimes Candy joined us in her crib, if Robbie went shopping.

We skipped my graduation and moved to a small rental home in Glenview, Illinois, where I started selling masonry saws for Clipper. We felt right at home. The noise from airplanes taking off from the nearby Glenview Naval Air Station reminded us of our Chicago apartment.

We had a good life in Glenview. I worked hard and liked my job, and we had pleasant weekends exploring the Chicago area in the little MG convertible that we bought as a second car.

In 1955, Kim was brought into the world with the help of the same doctor that had delivered Candy. The wonderful care Robbie and Kim received was worth the long drive from Glenview to the hospital on the far south side of Chicago.

In 1957, I got the big promotion at Clipper—as the man says it is easier to climb the ladder of success if your daddy owns the ladder—and we moved to Kansas City. My father guaranteed the mortgage on a nice house on Falmouth Street and our life in Kansas City began. And it was a good life. My job involved some travel but not too much and we had the use of my parents' Lake Lotawana home for most weekends. Robbie was my regular crew for the sailboat races, and we were regular winners.

In 1958, Jeff was born, and the family was complete.

Robbie was great fun to be with, loved parties and was a wonderful wife and mother until we moved to Aspen in 1967, when she developed a serious drinking habit. I don't know what caused her alcohol problem. It may have been my fault for being so involved in my work or it may have been the party environment of Aspen. Either way, it was for real. Robbie went to three of the best alcohol rehabilitation facilities in the country, however, she would only be back more than a week or two before I would find a bottle of vodka in the back of the toilet tank, and she would spiral out of control. I finally decided that it had to end and filed for divorce. We were divorced in 1972 and Robbie moved back to Kansas City where she managed to recover and marry another reformed alcoholic, an old friend from Lake Lotawana. I found myself a single parent with three kids to raise.

Unfortunately, Robbie's years of abusing her body caught up with her and she died of a heart attack in 1992 at far too early an age.

A Love like Friendship: Betty Byers

Nick and Betty

A friendship that like love is warm;
A love like friendship, steady.—Thomas Moore

From Kansas City to Aspen, Puerto Vallarta, North and South America, Europe, Asia, Australia, Africa, and last stop San Antonio, we were explorers.

When Robbie and I lived in Kansas City on Cherokee Drive there was a park in back of our home. Kitty-cornered across the park lived, unbeknownst to us, Betty and George Byers. A few years after we moved, Betty and George bought the house next to us at Lake Lotawana. (The former owners of the house had been excellent friends with my parents and had built a common dock.) We quickly became great friends.

Betty and two of her relatives were all interior designers and had opened a store in the Westport area of Kansas City called Byers Three Interiors. Robbie and I hired Betty to help with the interiors of our Kansas City home, and after moving to Aspen, hired her to do the interiors of all 48 units in the Château Chaumont and Château Dumont.

After Buddy Wallen and I split up, I went into partnership with George and Betty to build the Château Eau Claire, and, again, Betty did the interiors. George was a fabulous individual and we had become best friends. George, Betty, Robbie and I went on multiple trips to Europe together.

George developed leukemia and died in 1972 at the MD Anderson Hospital in Houston. Before his death, we had bought property in Aspen to build another condominium. Betty did not want to go ahead with this project, and we sold it. Probably a big mistake since that is where the Clarendon townhomes are today. Robbie and I divorced in 1975.

Betty had developed an Aspen clientele and opened an interior design studio on Main Street. She helped me with the interiors of a duplex I had developed in the Oklahoma Flats area.

By this time, our relationship had turned romantic, and Betty moved into the duplex with me. In 1977, we were married at John Gardner's tennis ranch in Scottsdale and began 34 years of traveling adventures.

Betty was a creative interior designer with an artistic eye for beauty. She taught me about beauty, lines, colors, textures, balance, and how to choose artwork. She was a talented floral designer and worked with the Getty's professional flower arranger when we were in San Francisco.

We had great fun decorating our homes and properties. During our travels, we were always looking for that perfect piece. Some of Betty's most creative projects were homes in Mexico, featured in both Veranda and Architectural Digest.

Cassoulet! Betty liked to try new things. She loved finding an undiscovered restaurant. When we were traveling in France, she wanted to try all of the Michelin Guides Red R Restaurants. These are the restaurants that are typical of the region yet reasonable. That is how we discovered cassoulet. We tried many Red R eateries, and they were wonderful, but we never quite got to eat at all of them.

Betty's only sailing experience had been as a crew at Lake Lotawana, but she took readily to the cruising life and, for 12 years, we would spend as much as eight months at a time cruising Mexico and the Caribbean. She was equally crazy about traveling by RV and we went through a whole series of motorhomes starting with a VW Pop-Top and eventually traveling in a 36-foot Class A motorhome. Betty was just as happy, maybe more so, camping in a motorhome as she was living in our 20,000 square-foot home in Puerto Vallarta with a staff of 10.

We were living in Aspen at 8000 feet and Betty was going to have to be on oxygen full-time if we stayed so we moved to San Antonio near her son, George, and to be at a much lower altitude. She was a smoker and caught pneumonia and was told that if she did not stop smoking it would kill her. Remember, I have been trying to get her to stop for 20 years. A week after she quit, I asked her, "Was it very hard stopping?" "No, if I had known it would be this easy, I would have stopped years ago!" Our wonderful 34 years of marriage ended sadly when Betty developed leukemia and passed away on July 5, 2014.

When the Lights Went Out

Nick and Hercules at the Alamo

I was in Aspen waiting for a flight to Denver and then connecting on to San Antonio when suddenly, my vision changed radically, and not for the better. For some time, I had suffered with limited vision in my left eye but now, in an instant, I was having trouble seeing anything out of my right eye.

As soon as I landed in San Antonio, I went to an ophthalmologist, who determined it was a retina problem and referred me to Dr. Jeremiah Brown, the doctor he thought was the leading retina specialist in San Antonio. Fortunately, I was able to get an appointment immediately with Dr. Brown. He examined my eye, said that my retina was badly swollen and gave me a shot in my eyeball. Sounds painful, but it was not at all. I was impressed with Dr. Brown and thought he had a wonderful manner and voice. In fact, I commented to him that I bet he was a killer with the girls in the office. What I did not realize at the time, because I could hardly see, was that Dr. Brown was black and all the girls in the office were white. Probably not too appropriate.

The shot returned some of my vision, however, at that time, I had absolutely no vision in my left eye—I could not even see light—and the vision in my right eye was so poor that I was legally blind. I had a lot of adjustments to make, but fortunately I had Betty to help me. What I quickly realized is that a good memory is essential for a blind person. You have to remember where you left your toothpaste, which drawer has your razor, and where your favorite cheese is in the refrigerator.

Betty and I decided to move into a retirement home to make things easier and chose Franklin Park where we had a nice one-bedroom apartment with a kitchen and a meal plan, so we did not have to worry about meal preparation. This worked out very well until Betty developed leukemia and passed away in 2014.

At that time, I moved into a one-bedroom unit in an independent apartment.

I decided that life would be much easier if I had a guide dog to lead the way and applied to Guide Dogs of Texas. They said it would be at least a year before I could have a dog but, once the idea had formed, I was impatient. Someone recommended Southeastern Guide Dogs and I applied.

It was an impressive experience from the start. They were friendly and helpful over the phone and soon sent a representative from Florida to evaluate me and my situation. I must've passed the evaluation, because shortly thereafter they invited me to come to their Florida campus to receive a dog. I arrived in Florida at the same time as eight other students and we were each assigned our own room—basically a nice single room with a bath and a small refrigerator. The next day I was introduced to Hercules, and we hit it off from the beginning. For 28 days I was trained on how to work with Hercules.

We students were each assigned a seat in the dining room, and I was fortunate to be seated next to Barbara Reeves and her guide dog, Atlas. Hercules and Atlas were the only two Black Labs in the class while all the others were Yellow Labs. Barbara and I became best of friends.

The apartment Hercules and I were living in was fine, but the other residents were young with families, and we had little in common. When we returned from Aspen in 2016, Kim and George decided I was better off in an independent living facility and they chose Adante, where, as I write this, we are still living quite happily.

MY WORLD OF BUSINESS

Clipper Manufacturing Company: A Tale of Invention and Innovation

Clipper Saw

It all began with a chipped tile.

My grandfather, William Coates, was in the business of selling building materials as a manufacturer's agent. His primary products were brick, concrete block and a new product called structural glazed tile. Structural glazed tile was a clay product the size of a concrete block. It was intended to be used in the walls of public bathrooms, gymnasiums and other places where sanitation and cleanliness were important. Instead of building the wall with concrete block and then facing the wall with ceramic tile, a structural tile wall would provide the structural support and, at the same time, present a smooth, colorful surface that was simple to maintain and clean.

The problem was that any interruption in the wall or irregular dimension meant that the final tile to be set, had to be cut to fit and, when the tile was cut, the glaze would frequently chip and the tile would have to be discarded. This waste made architects reluctant to specify glazed tile. At that time there were machines that would cut the tile cleanly, but they were large industrial machines unsuited for construction jobs.

My father and his two brothers, Gordon and Bill, went to work for my grandfather selling building materials and the most profitable product they could sell was structural glazed tile. The product had to be sold by convincing architects to specify it on projects they were designing, and the chipping problem was making this difficult. Dad, who was an inventor all his life, came up with the idea of a portable machine that would use a 1/8-inch-wide silken carbide blade to cut the tile. His machine would work because, instead of forcing the cutting blade through the material to be cut like you would a wood saw, he used a cart to hold the material so it could be moved back-and-forth under the blade making small cuts on each pass until the material was severed. He called this the multiple-cutting principle and patented the idea.

When Dad decided to form a company to sell his invention, his father insisted that, in the spirit of family, he would make his two brothers partners. Many years later, when the company had been successful and was paying nice dividends, a dispute arose with his brothers who wanted to continue large dividends while my father wanted to invest most of the profits back into the business. A nasty lawsuit ensued but my father finally prevailed because he had foreseen problems and put his brothers' stock in a voting trust that he controlled. Thus, he was able to buy his brothers out and maintain complete control. Interestingly this lawsuit went all the way to the Supreme Court before being decided in my father's favor.

Dad called the company the Clipper Manufacturing Company because the men who cut the tile by hand were called clippers.

Originally the saws were made of wood and produced in my parents' garage by my father and an assistant with my mother doing the mailings, bookkeeping, etc. My mother and father were a team at this as they were in everything in their lives. Usually, this type of product would have been sold by equipment dealers selling wheelbarrows, trowels and other construction equipment. Dad decided to take a different route and sell Clipper Saws by direct mail, offering something completely unique – a five-day free trial. The company struggled at first, however my parents persevered, and the business grew. They knew the product was unique and they worked with a patent attorney and patented the multiple-cutting principle. Good idea except they later found that there always seems to be a way around a patent and eventually they had competition producing essentially the same product.

Later, Dad became aware of a segment of the market that wanted to buy through equipment dealers, consequently he started a second company to sell an almost identical product, painted a different color, through the dealer network. He named the new company Eveready Brick Saw.

Hindsight is always 20/20 and in retrospect one of the biggest mistakes that Dad made was to promote people into executive positions without getting them to sign a noncompete agreement. One of these individuals was Bob Evans, who was his sales manager. When Bob saw what a good business Clipper was, he left and started a competitive company called Target. Evans sold through dealers.

My father always equated the masonry saw business to the razor blade business. As he explained, Gillette could afford to give away the razors as the real money was in the blades that continually had to be replaced. He bought his blades from the Norton Company, a large New York Stock Exchange company, whose principal business was making grinding wheels for the automotive and other manufacturing companies. The original blades were made of silken carbide and were 1/8-inch wide. The cutting process created a great deal of dust which was objectionable and today would probably be considered toxic and prohibited. He overcame this by converting the base of his saw to a water reservoir and installing a circulating pump that introduced water to the cutting blade, thus eliminating the dust.

Clipper introduced a diamond blade that was a metal disk with a rim impregnated with tiny industrial diamonds. This not only eliminated the dust but maintained a constant diameter whereas the silken carbide blades wore down with each cut and eventually were too small to cut all the way through the material. Diamond blades became extremely popular and eventually Clipper was one of the world's largest consumers of industrial diamonds. Dad became friends with the Oppenheimer's who, at that time, had a virtual monopoly on diamond mining as they controlled the mines in South Africa.

Dad later recognized the potential of the concrete saw that was originally used to create a smooth cutting-edge when breaking into concrete highways or concrete plant floors. A new use had developed for cutting contraction joints in concrete highway and airport construction. The process was to continually pour the slab and then as the concrete hardened, go back and cut the contraction joints because they were narrow and that eliminated the driving thump, thump of the wider hand tooled joints. Later Clipper came out with a large machine for melting and installing the tar that was used to seal joints in concrete pavement.

Dad later recognized the potential of the concrete saw that was originally used to create a smooth cutting-edge when breaking into concrete highways or concrete plant floors. A new use had developed for cutting contraction joints in concrete highway and airport construction. The process was to continually pour the slab and then as the concrete hardened, go back and cut the contraction joints because they were narrow and that eliminated the driving thump, thump of the wider hand tooled joints. Later Clipper came out with a large machine for melting and installing the tar that was used to seal joints in concrete pavement.

Clipper Key Club

As the business grew, Dad opened sales offices in principal cities throughout the U. S. to promote and sell the products. A Clipper Manufacturing salesforce worked out of each office calling on construction jobs and industrial plants. He also appreciated that there was a large foreign market and began opening Clipper offices in major foreign countries. Because of Clipper's close relationship with the Norton Company he usually solicited the manager of the local Norton plant as a partner. The first foreign plant was in Leicester, England, followed by offices in six other foreign countries.

The foreign operations required frequent overseas travel at a time when that type of travel was a real adventure. The airplanes did not have the range for long flights so a flight from Kansas City to England would require stops in Chicago, New York and Gander, Newfoundland. Originally the flights were made in DC3's but later we flew on Constellations where beds were provided. Slow but quite luxurious.

Dad quickly saw that wooden machines should be replaced by metal and subcontracted their manufacture to a local metalworking plant while he concentrated on the sales aspect of the business. This went on successfully for a number of years but eventually he decided to take over this aspect of the business, too. Clipper was very profitable and with the introduction of concrete saws and later core drilling machines Dad made what was, in my opinion, his first serious error. He went from modest offices and a rather simple manufacturing operation to new and very grand offices and factory which he built in Grandview, Missouri, a suburb of Kansas City. The offices would have been a credit to a large New York Stock Exchange company or a major Wall Street brokerage house. My father took great pride in the fact that he had built this amazing business without ever having to borrow money, but the new Grandview operation changed that, and he was uncomfortable with the change. He decided it was time to sell the company and retire. The most logical buyer was the Norton Company because, by now, Clipper was their largest customer. Dad made the sale and retired.

In 1954, when I graduated from Northwestern, I went to work for Clipper as a salesman in the Chicago area. Like all Clipper salesmen I was provided with a Plymouth automobile with a masonry saw mounted in the huge trunk. I worked hard and did a good job but obviously got my promotion to general sales manager on my lineage rather than my sales results.

Nick in Clipper Office

There I was only a few years out of university, running a nationwide sales force, but I don't think I did a bad job of it. When Dad sold the company to Norton and retired, they brought in Jacque Martinoni, the French manager, as general manager. Norton did not really understand our business and I think Jaquez resented me and it was not surprising that I was fired. As it turned out it was the best thing that ever happened to me. I became a developer in Aspen and made enough money that, just a few years after being fired, I was making more than the president of Norton Company. But that's another essay.

My Development and Real Estate Career (Aspen and Beyond)

The Château Eau Claire Aspen

When one door closes, buy another one and open it yourself.
—Anonymous

After being fired from my job at Clipper Manufacturing Company (see the "Invention and Innovation" essay), I purchased Gasket Engineering Company.

While the Gasket business was profitable, I hated it. Sales were made by calling on purchasing agents of small companies, taking them to lunch and giving them a bottle of whiskey at Christmas and on their birthdays. It was dull and unchallenging. Then the phone rang about six months later. It was a Northwestern College friend who proposed that I partner with him on the development of a condominium project in Aspen.

Condominiums? In Aspen? I had never been to Aspen and the concept of condominiums was new. I knew nothing about it, but Buddy Wallen had already built two successful condominiums and was looking for someone who would put up half the money and do the on-site work. He planned to concentrate on his very successful insurance business in Chicago. I walked through that door of opportunity.

Bud and I met in Aspen to look for property for our project. He told me that we should buy something close to the base of Little Nell which, in the middle of summer, looked like a barren wasteland. The first property we tried to buy was where the North of Nell Condominiums are today, but Buddy managed to upset the foreign owner to the point where we were told that he would not sell us his property at any price.

We finally were able to make a deal with Mrs. Paepcke to buy her property, which was also close to the base of Little Nell. We hired Jim Otis as the architect and my life changed forever.[4]

Robbie and I rented our house in Kansas City and moved to Aspen with three young kids, a cat and a huge Newfoundland dog. For the first year we lived in a small three-bedroom apartment in the Château Aspen.

As we were laying out the Château Chaumont and Dumont, Sandy Lunow, our neighbor, who owned the Glory Hole Lodge across the street, told us he thought the building was being laid out incorrectly. Sandy was known to be a little crazy, so we ignored him. A couple of months later when the excavation for the garage was complete and we had started on the first floor, Sandy came back with a surveyor and proved he was right. He wanted us to tear down everything and move the building back 10 feet.

The cost and time delay might have bankrupted the project, so we went before the Board of Adjustment to seek a variance. The variance was granted with the logic that we would never have done this intentionally because it was in our interest to move the buildings as far back from the Glory Hole as possible to give the apartments better views of Aspen Mountain.

Those were remarkable days in the Aspen real estate market. We sold all 48 apartments ourselves without a realtor and with an investment of less than $500 for black and white price lists and floor plans. 100% of our buyers were investing in second homes and wanted things simple. We hired designer Betty Byers to put together a furniture package to go with each of the three colors of shag carpet we were offering. It was touch and go, but we were able to deliver the apartments completely furnished before Christmas of 1967.

By this time I was hooked on the development business. We sold our house in Kansas City and moved into a three-bedroom ground floor apartment in the Château Chaumont. With the addition of a spiral staircase, we converted the basement storage space below the unit into the kids' bedrooms and playrooms.

Land at the base of the mountain had gotten expensive and scarce so I proposed building on a site that fronted the Roaring Fork River three full blocks from the base of the mountain— the boonies in those days. Again, a survey mistake meant the Riverfront Apartments had balconies that were literally hanging over the river when we had envisioned them being separated by a grassy area. I solved the distance from the ski lift by inventing the Château Mobile, a very decorative trailer pulled by a Jeep that held 10 people and their skis.

Around this time, I went to Chicago to meet with Bud Wallen. However, the first night I was there, Buddy had hockey tickets, so I stayed in the office to work with Stan, our accountant. As soon as Buddy was out the door, Stan started showing me all the ways that I was being cheated. I was paying for downtown Chicago parking for Bud's insurance business, his hockey tickets and a host of other things (see my essay "Trust and Betrayal").

This led to the breakup of our business and gave me the freedom to go on my own and build the Château Eau Claire with a new and honest partner, George Byers. George and his wife, Betty, had been close friends in Kansas City and I had hired Betty to do the interiors of the first Château. We had a wonderful partnership. Shortly after completing the Château Eau Claire George developed a fatal case of leukemia. We had already purchased the land for a future condominium project, but Betty was uncomfortable moving forward without George, so we sold that land. That was unfortunate because the land we sold is where the Deerbrook Condominiums are today.

During this period, Robbie had succumbed to alcoholism that she could not overcome in spite of stays at three of the best alcohol rehabilitation facilities in the US. It finally got to the point where I had to file for divorce and ended up with custody of all three kids as Robbie moved back to Kansas City. (She married an old mutual friend who was also a recovering alcoholic, but her disease had taken its toll and she died at an early age.)

Realty Business: Coates, Reid & Waldron

I had realized that I was missing a real opportunity by not being in the real estate business. In Colorado you can sell your own property without being licensed, elsewhere you had to have a real estate license. In 1968, I passed the test for a broker's license and started Aspen Château Realty. Later, I took on Brent Waldron as a partner, bought Reid Realty and changed the name to Coates, Reid & Waldron. It was not long before we were the largest real estate firm in the Aspen/Snowmass area.

Christmas 1986 Coates, Reid and Waldron

My personal life also took a major turn as Betty Byers and I became very close through working together. We were married in 1977 (see "A Love Like Friendship: Betty Byers" for the full story.)

The success of these early projects inspired me to continue in the development business and I was fortunate in creating a number of successful projects. I partnered with Fritz and Fabi Benedict (see my essay on Fritz and Fabi Benedict) to build the Snowmass Center and the Ridge Condominiums in Snowmass. On my own, I developed the Aspen Athletic Club building, the Racquet Club Condominiums and several single-family homes and duplexes.

When Betty and I were visiting Puerto Vallarta, Mexico, we discovered a unique piece of beachfront property and built four large, luxury villas that were sold as soon as we finished them, except for the one we kept.

There were challenges to building in Mexico, but we found the lack of regulation and the creativity of the workers made the building experience remarkably challenging and creative. For example, the villa we were building for ourselves was right on the ocean with a wonderful view of the Bay but no view down the coast. We asked the contractor if it would be possible to extend the pool out about six feet so we would have a view down the coast when sitting in the pool. He said no problem and proceeded to build this extension even though it was 25 feet in the air.

One day we realized that the window of the third bedroom was essentially looking into a landscaped wall and suggested that it should be located on another wall to have a better view. We went to lunch with the contractor and by the time we returned the old opening was closed and the new window installed!

Later, we built a 20,000 square-foot beachfront home that had two elevators and was featured in Veranda magazine. We also restored a colonial home in San Miguel de Allende that was featured in Architectural Digest.

Mexico: It All Began at the Oceana Bar

It all began at the Oceana Bar in downtown Puerto Vallarta.

Jean Ingham and I were having a few margaritas and discussing our Colorado development projects. After the third—maybe it was the fourth—margarita we decided it would be fun to join forces and build a development in Puerto Vallarta.

The next day, now that we were sober, we still thought it was a good idea and started to look for land. Jean found a beautiful piece of land high on a hill with a view of the entire crystal-blue bay. I was impressed but insisted that we should look for something on the water because I felt the romance of being right on the water with the mesmeric sound of the surf was what most buyers were looking for in a vacation home.

Our search finally took us to an abandoned project right on the ocean just south of the Camino Real Hotel. The architect for the hotel had started a condo project, but he had run out of money and the land was for sale. We suspected he was stealing his materials from the hotel project and was caught. Jean and I did not like his design, so we decided to tear out his work and build four luxury villas. We were each going to keep one and sell the other two.

Although we hired a local architect/builder, we did most of the design work ourselves. In those days, building in Puerto Vallarta was nearly unregulated. There seemed to be no zoning and getting a building permit just required paying the fee. We hired Tony Santivania as our architect/builder and were underway.

The construction crew proved to be very hard-working and very creative. They took real pride in their work. One day Betty and I went into a bedroom that was almost finished and decided that we had put the window on the wrong wall. In the U. S. this would have meant preparing a change order and a lot of other red tape, but we simply told Tony what we wanted, went to lunch together, and when we came back the crew had bricked up the original window and cut out the opening for the new one.

I was intrigued by the crew's approach to light switches and outlets. They simply finished all the walls in a room then came back and marked exactly where you wanted the electricity to go. Then they would channel out the grooves for the wiring. It made a lot of sense when your walls were brick and sometimes electrical ideas change when you see the completed room.

The patio of our villa was only 20 feet back from the ocean and about 25 feet above the shoreline. We had an idyllic view straight out at the bay except our view up and down the coast was limited. We remarked how nice it would be if the swimming pool, which stopped at the edge of the patio, could be extended out over the shore to give a view up and down the coast. It sounded impossible as this would mean extending the pool out in space 25 feet above the rocks. The answer we got was the same answer we always got – no problem!

The next day the crew had cut trees to support the steel framework for the pool extension 25 feet above the beach and only a few days later we had our spectacular extended pool that seemed to be floating in air.

Paying the workers was also unique. Every Saturday afternoon a Briggs-type armored truck would roll into the driveway and the crew would line up and receive their pay in cash from a window in the truck.

While the house was being built, Betty and I traveled all over Mexico buying antiques and folk art and commissioning custom-made furniture. We rented a small warehouse near the airport to store the purchases until the house was completed.

The only hiccup on the project came when Tony, our architect/builder, was thrown in jail, apparently for a fight with his wife. That's when we learned that you never want to be in a Mexican jail. The food is so bad and so scarce that everyone in the jail had a friend bring their meals. We only had to feed Tony for four days. We surmise that he was able to get his wife to drop the charges.
Betty and I had villa one and our partners, Jean and Carol Ingham, had villa number two. That left villas number three, a three-bedroom three bath home and villa number four a five-bedroom, five-bath villa available for sale.

Shortly after we moved in, we invited Lee and Joanne Lyon down from Aspen and they fell in love with villa number three and bought it. Almost 30 years later their kids still own it. Villa number four was sold to Debbi and Randy Fields and, although they later divorced, they still own it.

Jean Ingham was a man easily bored and he sold his villa after a year and went back to work in Colorado. Betty and I loved the creativity of the business, so we went on to buy, remodel, furnish and sell a number of villas in both Puerto Vallarta and San Miguel de Allende.

Trust and Betrayal

It is a terrible thing to say but I believe my biggest failing in life and business was being far too trusting of people, especially business associates.

My first disappointment was Buddy Wallen, who was my partner on the first Châteaux we built in Aspen. One night in Chicago, I declined his invitation to a hockey game and stayed behind with our accountant, Stan. As soon as the door closed behind Buddy, Stan took a deep breath and began "spilling the beans" about how Buddy was cooking the books and I was being cheated. This led to the dissolution of our partnership. While I was disappointed to find out that Buddy was less than honest, I have been forever grateful for him because he introduced me to Aspen and the development business.

My next disappointment was José Montes, the man Dale Eubank and I hired to manage a large development in Puerto Vallarta. At first, we were impressed with José's enthusiasm and ability, then we decided to sell the project. The crooked things that were revealed could fill a juicy crime novel.

José had reported one of our dump trucks stolen but later we found that he had sold it. When we found a cement mixer missing from the inventory, he claimed it had been damaged and scrapped. We could not prove this was not true, however we knew the Mexican mentality was to fix things, not junk them.
When we hired José, he proposed that instead of paying him a salary we should hire him as an independent contractor since that would give him certain tax advantages. We did this and

paid him his contractor fee until the day we sold the project. José went to the labor board and claimed he was due vacation pay for the entire time he had worked for us and several months termination pay. He even claimed he was due a commission on the sale although he had had nothing to do with it. We had to make a substantial payment to complete the sale, and he still made claims against us in the labor court.

The real blow came when José produced a forged note claiming that I owed him the equivalent of $500,000 USD. In the U.S. this would have been easy to resolve as he would have had to show the court the bank records where the money had changed hands. Under Mexican law you cannot use the lack of an exchange as evidence – the signed note stands on its own. A forgery claim is settled by each party appointing an expert witness and the court appointing an independent expert witness. This was done and the court appointed experts to testify that it was a forgery. José appealed and lost, appealed again and lost, but at the final appeal the court ruled in his favor. I will never know if my attorney was bought off or the court was bribed because their decision against me made no sense. They ruled in favor of José because the expert appointed by the court had testified from a photocopy of the note and not the real note. Of course, the obvious ruling would be to have that expert, or another court-appointed expert, examine the real document. Instead they ruled against me and, because there was no further appeal, I had to pay José the $500,000.

And even this did not stop him as, to this day, he is trying to place liens on my Mexican properties claiming compensation awarded by the Mexican labor court. I have had to engage an attorney to fight this, and it appears that the statute of limitation may have run out.

My next and probably greatest disappointment was with my San Miguel partner, Jim Dolan. When Jim returned to San

Miguel from overseas services in the Army, I hired him to oversee the construction of our San Miguel home since Betty and I were busy with other projects and could not be there on a day-to-day basis. Although we went over budget, he did a good job, so we started looking for other business opportunities. A large, 119-hectare ranch outside of San Miguel became available and we purchased it in Jim's wife's name as I understood she was the only one with the right immigration papers to own farmland in Mexico. Since I had put up all the money, I drafted a brief document outlining the ownership and management of the property that we all signed. I was too trusting to hire a lawyer.

Jim and I went on to buy adjacent properties using my money without being titled in my name. Then we purchased a large tract of land on the outskirts of San Miguel to do a large residential subdivision. We spent money on the planning of the subdivision, a wall around it, etc. before we had actually closed on the property. When it came time to close, we did not have the funds, still we were optimistic about the project as sales were strong. Jim arranged the loan through a mutual friend, and we would have had no trouble paying it off had sales continued at even close to their present pace. Unfortunately, our timing was terrible. 2008 came along, and sales stopped. The 2008 Great Recession, the worst crisis in nearly eight decades engulfed the global financial system, bringing Wall Street's giants to their knees. While the Great Recession officially ended in 2009, many people felt its effects for years to come as the job market and home prices remained depressed.

Our lenders wanted their money and rightly so and I suggested we sell the ranch property, which had appreciated, pay off a big portion of the note and buy some time for the economy to recover. That never happened; since Jim didn't want to sell, he made no real effort. In the meantime, I had loaned Jim and

Ann the funds to build a large home without securing a formal note, much less a mortgage.

As my daddy always said about partnerships—it is much easier to divide up the profits than to share the losses.

CHARACTERS

Art Weidman

He made a difference in my life.

In Kansas City, Mr. Weidman was one of my parents' closest friends and a frequent guest at our dinner table. I don't know if Art was gay or not (I'm not even sure if that was a term back in the early 40s), but Art was one of those individuals who was always meticulously dressed and unusually polite and courteous. He hated manual labor and exercise; I don't believe I ever saw him exercise or even break a sweat.

So, imagine everyone's surprise when Art was drafted into the Army in World War II and ended up in the infantry, of all places. He absolutely hated it and wrote my parents long letters about the horrors of marching and basic training. But there was a war to fight.

Eventually, Art was shipped overseas to Africa and then Europe. Everyone was shocked to learn that he was in the hospital after stepping on a landmine. A month later a small box arrived from Italy. In the box was a vial and a poem. The vial contained Art's toe. The poem read:

Louisiana, Africa, Italy, Atoll.
  I'm resting at last in alcohol!

Art recovered and returned to Kansas City wearing a special buildup shoe on his right foot.

This was around the time that my parents were afraid I might become a juvenile delinquent if I continued going to Kansas City public schools. I could not seem to focus on anything but sports, girls and mischief, so they decided to send me to Peddie, a private school in Hightstown, New Jersey. They picked Peddie because that is where Art had gone to school. Even though he had graduated in 1925, I am sure my parents hoped Peddie would turn me into a gentleman like Art.

To get me off to a good start, they asked Art to accompany me on the long train ride east. We had a lot of time to talk on that trip. Art explained that I was going to a school where no one knew me and no one knew my reputation, so I had the unique opportunity to make anything I wanted of myself. It was sound advice. I went from being a mediocre student to making the honors list, playing varsity football and basketball and running track. I even earned a fully paid scholarship to study for a year abroad in England.

Many people and moments have changed my life, but none more than Art Weidman and the advice he gave me on that train.

Buddy Melges: My Sailing Hero

Nick Coates, Dick Stearns, Buddy Melges

The blonde wood hull was magnificent, and the deck was a beautiful shade of pink. I saw Buddy Melges sail the most beautiful "C" boat I had ever seen to victory in the ILYA (Inland Lake Yachting Association) regatta in Wisconsin in the summer of 1948.

That summer I persuaded my parents to buy one just like it for me. When my father saw the boat, he could only describe the deck color as "Titty Pink."

While Buddy was building boats and perfecting his spectacular world class sailing skills, I, too, was learning, racing, and becoming even more involved in sailing.

Up until this time everyone at Lake Lotawana where I grew up, sailed Johnson boats built by the Johnson Boat Works of White

Bear Lake, Minnesota. All the boats were wooden, and the wood dried out when the boats were out of the water for any extended period of time, the seams opened up, and the boats leaked like sieves until the planks swelled shut again.

For that reason, we kept our boats in the water on buoys near our homes until 1946 when five boats from the local Lotawana fleet traveled north to Lake Okoboji for our first try at sailing against the big boys.

The Okoboji boats were kept on lifts suspended above the water when they were not racing and, as a result, the bottom seams were always tight, so they were much closer to the minimum 450-pound weight limit. Despite our carefully planned strategies, we were dead last. The light Okoboji fleet cleaned our clocks as they were excellent sailors with superior equipment.

After that trip, we put lifts in front of our homes and started sailing our boats "dry." By this time, I was a dedicated sailor practicing hard and reading all the books on sailboat racing.

When I started racing my first Melges boat, Creeper, the boat I had obtained after the 1948 ILYA, I was a genuine factor in the Lotawana fleet and a real favorite at the Melges Boat Works as the Lotawana fleet started converting to Melges boats.

In the early spring of 1953, I took my then girlfriend, later wife, Robbie Gibbon, to Lake Geneva to try out a new Melges "C" boat. Melges boats were still rare enough to arouse curiosity. It was a beautiful Saturday afternoon, and the wind was light, so we were hardly moving when Robbie decided to sunbathe topless on the forward deck. I was dozing off at the helm and did not notice the approaching speedboat with our Lotawana neighbors, the Athas aboard. The Athas were a super straight-laced group and strict Christian Scientists, so I am sure they saw a lot more than they had bargained for. They did end up buying a Melges boat.

In 1953 Buddy Melges was off serving in Korea and I occasionally escorted his girlfriend, Gloria, who we always called Susie, to yachting functions in the Chicago area. They later married and are still married these many years.

After graduating from Northwestern and working a year in the Chicago area, Robbie and I moved back to Kansas City and mostly took over my parents' Lotawana summer home on weekends. Our Lotawana fleet had become competitive, and we would occasionally run into Buddy and Susie at regattas in the Midwest. I may have even beaten Buddy on rare occasions.

In 1957, the Lotawana fleet started hosting a fall regatta in early October while our weather was still good, and the northern lakes were getting cold. Buddy attended many of these Lotawana regattas and would usually stay at our home. The sailing was excellent and some of the parties were legendary. One year, Buddy introduced a new drink to the group—the Starboard Light—crème de menthe and vodka. It was deadly!

Buddy never brought a boat to these regattas, instead he served as a goodwill ambassador for the Melges Boat Works. One time he offered to crew for me, and I had a taste of what made him great. Not only was he always aware of everything that was going on in the fleet, but he was all over that boat, adjusting things, shifting his weight and making suggestions to me. It was easy to see why he was in a class by himself when it came to sailing.

The impressive thing was that on these visits to our regatta he was just as generous with tips and suggestions to the Johnson owners as he was to the ones owning Melges boats.

My contacts with Buddy and Susie were mostly Christmas cards and the occasional phone call after we moved to Colorado and quit competitive sailing, but we followed his illustrious career and were continually amazed that he could step into any kind of sailboat and compete at an international level.

In 1993, Betty and I were traveling in Corsica in our Volkswagen Pop-Top and knew the final race of the America's Cup was coming up. We had no TV, so we arranged to watch the final race on a small, hotel-lobby TV. The race was still in doubt when a group of French tourists arrived and two fancifully dressed French women stepped in front of the TV and switched it to their favorite soap opera. Fortunately, we were able to negotiate a return to the race coverage without bloodshed and watch America3 approach the finish line with a clear lead. It was with characteristic sportsmanship that Buddy turned the wheel over to Bill Koch, giving Bill the honor of being at the helm when America3 crossed the finish line to win the America's Cup. The French thought the two Anglos were crazy —shouting with joy at their TV. This was the last successful American defense of the America's Cup.

We followed Buddy's career, but unfortunately, we were unable to witness Buddy's numerous other sailing victories including Olympic medals in two different classes, world championships in numerous classes and even seven International Skeeter Ice Boat Championships.

Our last personal contact with Buddy was when we all attended an ILYA regatta at Lake Okoboji and gathered for more than a few drinks at the home of my good friend, Jerry Huse. In addition to Buddy, another good friend was there, Dick Stearns, Olympic gold medalist in the Star class, and my skipper in that class when we sailed out of Wilmette Harbor back in 1955. How I wished I could have recorded the banter going back and forth between us and the belly laughs we all had. It was one of those magical nights of camaraderie you never forget.

Now my contacts with the Melges are limited to the occasional phone call or Christmas greeting but when I hang up, I am always amazed that they seem delighted with my call knowing they undoubtedly receive calls from famous people all over the world.

Sailing through Life: Ninety-three years of adventure

David McCullough

David McCullough

It all started with a phone call from my good friend, Rod McPhee.

Rod was the president of Punahou School. As the head of most private secondary schools, he would've been called headmaster but Punahou was the largest private secondary school in the US, with an enrollment of almost 3000 students, so the man in charge was called the President. I first met Rod and his wife, Sharon, when Rod's brother, Mike, and his wife bought a condominium from me. Then, in 1971, Rod and Sharon purchased unit number one in the Château Eau Claire and we became good friends. As an aside, although Rod passed away, forty-seven years later Sharon still owns the apartment.

Trusted friend connections lead to good introductions. I'm not sure how Rod knew David McCullough (probably through some educational conference), but when Rod found out David was coming to Aspen, he gave me David's contact information.

Sailing through Life: Ninety-three years of adventure

I was honored and thrilled to meet David, historian and best-selling author of 1776, John Adams, and Mornings on Horseback to mention a few because I was a great admirer of his writing. I think I had read most of his books, but my fondest memory was reading The Path Between the Seas about the building of the Panama Canal while Betty and I were transiting the Canal in Expectation, our 44-foot cutter.

I called David and he was delighted with the idea of going for a hike. Not being sure of his hiking abilities and his adjustment to the 8,000-foot altitude, I decided to take him up Snowmass Creek as it has spectacular views of the mountains along the Continental Divide but is not too steep. It was a beautiful day and I was struck by how observant and enthusiastic David was on our drive to the trailhead. He was pointing out and asking questions about things I had hardly noticed in the many times I had made the same drive. He even noted that hay bales are a different shape back East.

And, totally by coincidence, I had been listening to his book, Truman, on cd in my car. I played it and David remarked that this was one of his favorite parts of the book and told me about his research.

Our hike was a big success and we decided to continue our conversation over dinner at Poppies restaurant that evening. It was one of my most memorable dinners as David was not only interested in everything but told wonderful stories about his adventures. The owners of the restaurant sent brandy to our table and later joined us as we partied on for at least another hour after the restaurant closed.

That was the last time I saw David in person, but we have kept in contact via phone.

Debbi Fields: One Positive Cookie

Debbi Fields

A negative person sees the glass as half empty, a positive person sees the glass as half-full, Debbi sees the glass as overflowing! Debbi is without doubt the most positive person I have ever met.

There was a tap on our bedroom door. Fresh baked cookies, still warm from the oven, were being delivered to our bed! In fact they were Mrs. Fields Cookies made and delivered by Mrs. Fields herself.

I had taken our Puerto Vallarta guests, Debbi Fields and her daughters, on a predawn whale watching adventure in our powerboat. By the time we returned to the Villa, Betty and I were so exhausted that we decided to take a nap. Debbi had another idea. She went to the store, bought the ingredients and baked her wonderful chocolate chip cookies, and delivered them to us in our bed.

In the early 1980s, I had just completed the Cuatro Villas project in Puerto Vallarta. Debbi and her husband, Randy, were in Vallarta on business, had fallen in love with the area, and decided to purchase a villa. They were a family of seven with five beautiful young girls so Villa Ventura with six bedrooms was perfect for them.

Debbi told me the story of how Mrs. Fields Cookies, a multimillion-dollar company, started. Randy, an investment advisor. did much of his consulting from their home in California. When clients would come to the house Debbi would make chocolate chip cookies for them and her cookies became extremely popular.

"Randy, I am going to start a cookie business."
Randy thought it was the craziest idea he had ever heard. But Debbi, being Debbi, decided to go for it and opened a shop in a local mall. Business was slow at first so Debbi would take a tray of cookie samples throughout the mall to entice people to her shop. One thing led to another, and a national chain was born.

Debbi and Randy divorced and Debbi later married Michael Rose who was also a divorced father of five kids. Their first Christmas card was unforgettable – a picture of the whole group with the caption "From a Dozen Roses."

Michael was one of the founders of Harrah's and The Promise Company, the parent company of several major hotel chains. He built a beautiful home in Wildcat, a very exclusive area near Aspen. Soon Michael and Debbi built a second home on the property large enough to accommodate all the kids! Michael died in 2017. Debbi, who has always loved Aspen, continues to maintain a home there. She is a great friend of my daughter, Kim, and happily, I get to enjoy her company and her cookies when I am in Aspen during the summer.

And her enthusiasm? Just listen to her message on her answering machine, "Oh my God I'm so glad you called! I will call you back as soon as possible…in the meantime, the only thing I want is for you to have the most phenomenal, happy and sensational day. Talk to you soon."

Sailing through Life: Ninety-three years of adventure

Fritz and Fabi Benedict: The Ultimate Partners

Fritz and Fabi Benedict

Collaboration begins with mutual understanding and respect.
– Astronaut Ron Garan

Fritz and Fabi Benedict were among the best-known characters in Aspen when I moved there in 1967. Everyone knew them.

Fritz was raised in Wisconsin and studied architecture under Frank Lloyd Wright who suggested he might consider practicing in Aspen. After being drafted and serving in the 10th Mountain Division as a ski trooper in the mountains of northern Italy, he moved to Aspen where he set up one of the earliest architectural firms. He successfully designed a number of homes in Aspen's West End.

Fritz met Fabi when she came to Aspen from France to visit her sister. Romance bloomed and they were married.

Sailing through Life: Ninety-three years of adventure

Having a shrewd eye for land, Fritz purchased Red Mountain Ranch and subdivided it into homesites. Almost every lot faced south and had a magnificent view of Aspen and the ski slopes on Aspen Mountain. Many years later Fritz confided that when it was all said and done, he had made a very small profit on the sale of the lots and was in a lawsuit with the famous author, Leon Uris, over water rights.

Fritz and Fabi moved into the only existing house on their new purchase even though it was more than a mile from town, on a road that was unpaved and, in winter, unplowed. That first winter they raised hogs, which Fritz had accidentally purchased by raising his hand at the wrong time at an auction in Grand Junction. To feed their hogs Fritz collected slop from the only two restaurants in town, the Red Onion and the Jerome Hotel. He hauled the slop up the mountain on snowshoes until he was stopped by the health department and had to sell his meal ticket.

I got to know Fritz much better when I was asked to join the board of directors of the very prestigious Aspen Music Festival. Fritz was chairman of the board, and I knew I was chosen for my business skills rather than my meager knowledge of classical music.

Our relationship became more than casual when Fritz contacted me in 1975 about the possibility of working together to develop a shopping center at Snowmass Village. Fritz had owned land at the bottom of the ski mountain for many years, and when he was selected to design the original base village, thought it should be placed along Brush Creek, using the creek itself as an amenity. However, he was overruled and instructed to design the original base village halfway up the mountain.

At that time Snowmass was an unincorporated town but growing fast and there was a real need for many essential services including a post office. Our deal was that Fritz's firm would design the building and I would be in charge of the construction and the rentals. I made a good choice by hiring Greer Construction to build the building.

Our timing was perfect. I already had the building, which I named the Snowmass Center, totally rented by the time we opened. I knew a post office was essential with no mail delivery in the village, everyone would have to go to the post office every day to get their mail. This would bring traffic to help the other businesses. At that time, the locals had to drive ten miles to Aspen to get their mail.

A grocery store might have a hard time initially with such a small village population, therefore, I selected John Buxman for the grocery because he had experience with a store in tiny Vail. We had multiple applications for a liquor store. I made one of my better business decisions by insisting that whoever signed a liquor store lease would have to also install a pharmacy with an on-site pharmacist. Steve and Barbara Wicks were perfect and are still operating the pharmacy/liquor store almost 50 years later.

Fritz and I purchased the land across the creek from our shopping center and built phase one of the Ridge Condominiums, another successful project. We owned the property adjacent to the ski run and had plans to build a hotel, but we were concerned about the distance from base village, so, when we received a good offer from another developer, we sold this land. Probably a mistake as he built the Deerbrook Condominiums instead of a hotel and was successful. You can't win them all!

Sailing through Life: Ninety-three years of adventure

Pat Maddalone, Fritz and Fabi's assistant, was extremely protective of their interests. Pat worked so closely with the Benedicts for so many years that she was like a member of the family. Pat saw the benefits of our partnership—Fritz was the creative partner, and I made the business work.

Fritz and Fabi were wonderful parents and I think that story can best be told in the words of their daughter, Jesse Gordon.

> *I was the first to be adopted. I was born in Denver and went through three foster homes by the time I was three-and-a-half years old. Fritz and Fabi picked me up in Denver. When we drove back to Aspen, we stopped in Glenwood Springs to buy clothes, The adoption agency didn't allow me to take any of my belongings so as not to remind me of previous homes.*
>
> *Fabi said I was so excited that I would tell people "I got a mommy and a daddy...I ben adopted"!*
>
> *Nicolas came next. He was just about 8 months old and from Grand Junction.*
>
> *Charlotte and Emilie were from an Aspen family. They were living in the trailer park (below where the Eagles are now) with their alcoholic father and their grandmother. Their mother had abandoned them. The girls (ages 10 and 13) would run around town unsupervised and Fabi petitioned the local social services for custody and somehow got it. There were actually 3 sisters but the third one, Patti, wanted to be adopted by Nate Finesinger's family.*
>
> *I think my parents would have adopted as many kids as the authorities would have let them. Fabi really should have opened a children's orphanage! She just loved kids so much!* —*Jesse Gordon*

Fritz and Fabi Benedict were incredibly generous and gave a significant amount of very valuable land to charities. They will be remembered forever for their wonderful contributions to the Aspen area. And I will always remember them for our wonderful times together. In many ways I felt that Fritz was like a second father to me.

Fritz died in 1995. In 1997, I was leaving on a trip to Europe and called Fabi to say goodbye. I was shocked to have John Gordon answer her phone and give me the sad message, "I'm sorry Fabi has taken her pills." I knew that John was telling me that Fabi had passed away.

Sailing through Life: Ninety-three years of adventure

Hal Russell: One-of-a-Kind

Betty Coates and Hal Russell

Two men look out the same prison bars, one sees mud and the other sees stars.– Frederick Langbridge

I first met Hal when he came to Aspen to build Château Snow, which upset me because I had already built three condominiums with the Château name. Hal explained to me that imitation was the sincerest form of flattery, and then asked that I manage the building.

At the same time, Hal opened his first Aspen restaurant, The Starboard Tack. He had partners and their goal was to open Starboard Tacks across the country. One day, his partners came to me and expressed how upset they were that Hal was terrible at details and the paperwork. I tried to explain to them that Hal would never be good at details and that they should hire a detail man to follow him around; Hal could make them big money by selling and being creative, not by focusing on details.

Sailing through Life: Ninety-three years of adventure

Hal was also known as The Ripper from his days playing halfback for Michigan State. His best story about his football days was the Michigan State versus Notre Dame game at South Bend. The forecast was for rain, so Hal purchased a thousand surplus army ponchos at a dollar apiece and got classmates to drive them to South Bend to sell. Saturday dawned bright and clear, and it looked like a bad investment, but just before game time a thunderstorm rolled in, and they sold the ponchos for $10 apiece. Hal was on the Michigan State varsity squad for all four years. They won a national championship and the Rose Bowl, but The Ripper never played a single down. The coach kept him on the squad because he liked him, and he was entertaining.

As his first business venture, Hal developed the concept of a high-end Mexican restaurant and opened his first Guadalaharry's in Scottsdale, Arizona. It was an instant success and when Betty and I were married in Scottsdale, Hal threw our bridal dinner on the patio of his restaurant. With 35 guests on the patio, all went quiet when Carson Bell announced that Hal's margaritas were like "love in a canoe." Hal bit, and asked what Carson meant. Carson answered, "they are fuckin near water." That brought the house down and was one of the few times I ever heard anyone get the last word on Hal.

The first Guadalaharry's was followed by restaurants in Minneapolis, Chicago, Boston, and Detroit. At this point, he sold the business and the concept to General Foods and went to work with them to open restaurants all over the country.

Hal was living high and flying around in the corporate jet when he got a little greedy and was indicted and convicted for taking kickbacks. Hal and Jerry, his attorney, were sure he would be sent to a white-collar prison. Just before Hal had to report, while at a family goodbye party, his attorney called and asked if he was sitting down. The family could only hear Hal's side of the conversation, so he greeted Jerry cheerfully and said how great it was to hear from him.

Jerry said he had called Hal to tell him that he had not gotten a white-collar prison but instead one of the toughest federal penitentiaries in the country, to which Hal replied,
"Great news, Jerry!" so the family never had an inkling of what was going on.

Hal took a cab to the New Mexico prison dressed in a suit and carrying a briefcase. The cab driver asked if he should wait for him, and Hal replied, "I don't think so."

We didn't hear from Hal during his prison years. Then one Sunday morning, when Betty and I were still in bed in our Ridge apartment in Snowmass, Hal appeared at our front door. He came in and sat on our bed and entertained us for two hours with tales of his prison life. I think it was the funniest two hours we ever had. The funny part was all about his year or so in the federal pen before he was transferred to a white-collar prison where he could play tennis and jog around the track.

During our days in Aspen, Hal would arrive on weekends with a different voluptuous woman every time. But once he got out of prison, he started looking at property in Corona Del Mar. Deborah saw him from her house next door and called her widowed mother to tell her that an older man driving a Mercedes was looking at the house next to hers and he must be rich, so she should rush over to meet him. Well, her mom lost out, because Deborah ended up marrying Hal.

Deborah was divorced with two young daughters. Hal told Deborah that these girls were not going to be mall rats and he started them on tennis, supporting them through the youth program in California, attending all their tournaments, and encouraging them in every way. They ended up becoming great tennis players and were good enough to compete on a level with the Williams girls. They both got full college scholarships; one to SMU, and the other to Notre Dame. The one who went to Notre Dame did exceptionally well; she won the Newt Rockne trophy twice and was voted the top athlete, male or female, her senior year.

Hal continued in the restaurant business, opening one in Scottsdale, Arizona, called Champs. He gave famous athletes a 2% free interest in the restaurant if they would allow their trophies to be put on display. He had the Heisman Trophy, the British Open Trophy, MVP awards, the Cy Young Award, Wimbledon, and many others. Now in his 80s, Hal has finally slowed down a bit and is in an institution suffering from dementia.

Sailing through Life: Ninety-three years of adventure

The Hefner Brothers and Friends

Hugh and Keith Hefner

Hugh Hefner dead? In 2017 it was announced that Hugh Hefner, age 91, had died. What a flood of memories! Reopening this long-closed chapter—so jarring, and so thick with nostalgia.

Hefner founded the Playboy Magazine in 1953 and later opened the Playboy Mansion, a splendid old house, in Chicago featuring attractive women wearing a costume modeled after the Playboy Magazine trademark called a "bunny suit:" a strapless bodysuit paired with a bow tie, rabbit ears and a fluffy tail. As poor Northwestern students, Robbie and I would stop at the Playboy Mansion on a night out in Chicago because the place was pleasant, the drinks reasonable and the hors d'oeuvres so generous we could make it our dinner.

When I moved to Aspen, I became acquainted with Hugh's brother, Keith, a songwriter, actor, Playboy executive and director of recruiting and training bunnies. I went to several parties at Keith's unusual home (which has a mirrored ceiling in the master bedroom) on Shadow Mountain overlooking Aspen. However, Robbie and I never had the courage to attend one of the famous New Year's Eve parties where everyone left their clothes in the entry.

One day Keith Hefner called to tell me that Hugh and Barbi Benton were coming to town and asked if I could get them a really nice apartment. It was 1970 and I had just finished the Château Roaring Fork, so I arranged for them to stay in the Bartlett's apartment, right on the river at the corner of the building. I had the housekeepers make sure the apartment was extra clean and even put in fresh flowers. To my surprise when they moved in Keith called saying the apartment was unsatisfactory. I had forgotten that the Bartlett's were an older Kansas City couple and had twin beds in the master bedroom, so I quickly had the maintenance staff push the beds together and install a king mattress and the problem was solved.

Nothing more was heard from the happy couple and three days later a bottle of wine and a thank you note from Keith showed up at my office. I took the wine home and put it in the wine rack on our kitchen counter. A few days later, Keith's secretary called to be sure the wine had been received because it was Lafite Rothschild, 1952, one of the finest and rarest wines in the world. I rushed home fearing that Robbie may have used that exquisite wine to flavor our stew and was greatly relieved to find it was still in the rack. For several years that bottle was moved carefully from place to place but always kept cool and horizontal. We finally opened it on a special occasion, and it did not disappoint, it truly was a superb wine.

Barbi, who was a Playboy centerfold at the ripe old age of 50, married George Gradow, an eccentric mobile home park developer, in 1979. They built an incredible 25,000 square foot home in Starwood, the only gated community in Aspen. They have matching lap pools because they like the water at different temperatures and they are both shoe freaks with each having a room to store shoes larger than most bedrooms. They also have a balcony off the master bedroom where the bed can be automatically moved so they can sleep outside, under the stars, in nice weather.

George is noted for his flashy, outlandish attire and colorful shoes. He might be wearing gold sandals, a Tux, and a striped T-shirt. He was always weirdly dressed, including bizarre biking outfits and colorful, rhinestone-studded running shoes. He was a bicycle fanatic and frequently passed me on the highway going half again faster than I could and I was not in bad shape.

Barbie and George still live in Starwood in the same house, I have not seen them since I have gone blind.

Jim Briggs: Larger than Life

Now, bring me that horizon.—Jack Sparrow

There were literally acres of boats, from small canoes and windsurfers to huge, 105-foot ocean going motor yachts. There were pontoon boats and kayaks. There were at least 100 RVs. Robbie and I met Jim Briggs for the first time at the Chicago Boat, RV and Sail Show. We were not in the market for a boat, but we heard about the show and wanted to see what it was all about. This was a bright beginning for a friendship with Jim and the many adventures to come.

Jim lived in Lake Forest, known for its natural beauty, located along the shore of Lake Michigan just outside of Chicago, and he also had a second home on the beach at East Hampton, New York, once named the most beautiful American town by National Geographic. He was an executive at Outboard Marine, the major manufacturer of outboard motors at that time. His employment might have had something to do with the fact that his father had founded Outboard Marine. In fact, Jim's father was the only man at that time, and maybe still is, who had founded two companies on the New York Stock Exchange: Briggs & Stratton and Outboard Marine.

Jim took us to see his parents' home, a mansion right on the white sand beach in Naples, Florida. In those days, most people felt lucky to have a second telephone in their master bedroom. The Briggs' house had a telephone in almost every room and a switchboard to control them.

Robbie and I were doing very well competing in our C boat on Lake Lotawana, a man-made lake east of Kansas City. Our boat was named Fin do Mundo after a bar we had discovered in the suburbs of Lisbon, Portugal. We had a series of wild nights in this bar; met some fascinating people including the future King of Spain; and a local character who insisted on taking us up in his private plane.

For some reason, Jim got an inflated opinion of my sailing ability and invited me to be part of his crew on his 46-foot racing yacht that he entered in races around the world. The premier ocean racing series at that time was the SORC (Southern Ocean Racing Circuit) and Jim invited me to join his seven-man crew on the race from Miami to West End, Grand Bahamas. We started in a fresh wind off Miami and Jim asked me to take the helm at the start. Having never sailed a yacht anywhere near this size, my heart was in my mouth. But I managed a decent, if not spectacular, start. Soon it became obvious that while a start could be very significant in small boat racing it is not in the world of ocean racing because being 10 seconds behind at the start is not significant in races that last anywhere from 18 hours to more than three days.

I never took to ocean racing for several reasons. For one, the outcome is largely dependent on the weather because certain yachts perform best in high winds and rough seas but don't have a chance if the wind is light. My second justification was that an hour after the start you seldom see any of your competitors, so you have no idea how you are moving in comparison. To me, ocean racing is best summarized in the saying "Ocean racing is just like standing in a cold saltwater shower tearing up $100 bills!"

The most exciting part of this race was when we finished the race at 3 a.m. and entered the tricky West End harbor in complete darkness and pouring rain. That was the end of my days as an ocean racer.

A couple of years after our ocean racing adventure, Jim invited Robbie and me to meet him and his crew at the finish of the Miami to Isla Mujeres race and sail with him on the return voyage to Miami. Several of his crew had obligations and flew home leaving just six of us on board and we weren't in any particular hurry. The weather was beautiful. We were all sitting in the cockpit enjoying sea stories when someone looked up and saw that we were close enough to Havana to see the buildings. In those days, the Cubans were confiscating yachts that entered their territorial waters without permission; we were obviously way too close. We immediately tacked and headed north just in time to see a Cuban gunboat approach. He circled us, terrified us, but let us sail on our way. You can imagine our relief.

That summer, Outboard Marine was considering going into the inboard/outboard boat business. Jim sent us a 16-foot experimental boat to try; it was a neat little boat, but they decided not to go into production. Robbie and I offered to return it to the factory, but Jim told us just to keep it -- a rather nice gift. We ended up towing this boat over unpaved Independence Pass on CO-82 when we moved to Aspen, Colorado, and later Betty and I towed it all the way to Baja, California, but that's another adventure.

The America's Cup was to be sailed on Long Island Sound, and Jim invited us to be his guests at his home in East Hampton. Our good friends, Tom and Connie Cooper offered to join us and fly us from Kansas City in their twin engine plane. That was a double adventure because we watched the races from the air which, before the days of TV coverage, was really the only way you could get a true perspective on what was happening on the racecourse. Later, Tom was cited for flying too low in restricted airspace, but we saw those races like no one else.

Another highlight was joining Jim on his friend's beautifully restored classic powerboat. We hit a perfect day on Long Island Sound and were introduced to 12-pound lobsters. My parents had always told me that any lobster over a pound and a half would be tough, but how wrong they were. We sliced the tails of these gargantuan lobsters like a piece of prime beef; it was both tender and delicious. We bought two of the monsters and took them back in Tom's plane to impress our Kansas City friends.

Regrettably, we had very little contact with Jim once we moved to Aspen, but I always remember him as one of the most larger-than-life characters I ever knew.

Sailing through Life: Ninety-three years of adventure

Joe Ross: The Unconventional Half Cherokee

I have been fortunate to know a number of fascinating and interesting characters in my life and Joe stands out as one of the most unusual. Joe was half Cherokee Indian and was raised on a reservation in Oklahoma. When I first met Joe, he had moved to Aspen and purchased a Pomegranate condominium.

A few years later, Joe bought a large property in Owl Creek and began building a significant house. But Joe never did anything conventionally. Instead of hiring an excavation contractor to build the driveway Joe bought a bulldozer and proceeded to bulldoze the mile-long entrance from Owl Creek Road to the home site.

Then, instead of hiring a contractor Joe flew his twin-engine plane to Mexico, recruited local workers, and ferried them back to his property. He set up a tent city with everything needed for sleeping and eating, provided food, and told them they were prohibited from leaving the grounds. Only once did a worker disobey and slip into Aspen. He was caught and the next day he was back in Mexico.

One of Joe's businesses was training helicopter pilots for the U.S. government and his training facilities were the largest in the country. Strangely, although an experienced fixed-wing pilot, Joe was terrified of helicopters.

Even Joe's marriage was unconventional. He placed an ad in the Denver Post to find a housekeeper. As many people do, he checked the paper that Sunday to see how his ad looked and happened to see another ad for a lady looking for work with the title "fabulous flyer." Intrigued, Joe called her, chatted on the phone, and invited her to come see him in Aspen.

Romance ensued. Joe wanted to take Pam on a trip but felt he needed her parents' permission—they were approximately his age—so he asked them if it was all right to take Pam to Rome. Pam's father thought it was fine as she had never been to Georgia, but, of course, Joe meant Italy. They had a fabulous trip!'

Betty decorated Joe's and Pam's new house. That is a story in itself of the many trips around the country to buy antiques, etc. Joe was very impatient at times and started giving Betty grief about slow deliveries. Betty got upset and told Joe they had to talk, but Joe sensed the problem and when Betty arrived at the house Joe preempted her by saying "I guess you are here for a 'do better' talk," and he apologized.

One of the great features of the Ross home was an incredible wine cellar. Joe accumulated an unbelievable collection of first-growth wines from Bordeaux. I will never forget the party he had for about 25 close friends where all he served were first-growth wines which, at the time, were $150 a bottle (today they would be more than twice that). I thought it was crazy because after four glasses who knew what they were drinking.

Joe had a way of getting what he wanted. One night, we were all having dinner at the Lyon's home near Aspen and Joe admired a very large Pletka painting that was hanging in the stairway. He offered to buy it from Lee but was told it was not for sale. Joe contacted Lee several times after that about buying the painting without success. Then one day, Joe arrived at the Lyon home and presented Lee with a signed blank check and told him to fill in the amount. I never asked the amount of the check, but the painting was soon in Joe's home.

Betty and I had some great sailing adventures with Joe and Pam, both on our boat in Mexico and on their boat cruising the coast of Turkey. Pam was a great cook and I have fond memories of the incredible spaghetti carbonara she served us in Turkey. We and another couple joined them on the 46-foot sailboat they kept in Greece. We spent a delightful 10 days cruising the coast of Turkey; however, we were lucky to avoid disaster on the overnight sail from Turkey back to Rhodes. As daylight broke it was obvious, we had missed our intended landfall by more than 5 miles. We realized that JoAnne Lyon, the other lady guest, who had been at the helm for the 3 to 5 a.m. shift, had put her binoculars next to the compass and the magnetism had changed the compass reading by over 10 degrees. Luckily, it took us off course to the right. If the binoculars had been on the other side of the compass, we would have been off course to the left and that would have run us onto the rocks in the dark.

One year, Joe and Pam sent out very formal invitations for a New Year's Eve party. But, about five days before the event, we received a phone call canceling the party. Joe had previously had a round of cancer treatments, and everyone assumed he had suffered a recurrence. Later we learned that the sheriff in Grand Junction had called Joe to ask if he would be home the next Wednesday because he had to serve Joe with some papers. The next day Joe and Pam were in the airplane on their way out of the country and no one knew where they had gone.

Two years later they turned up unexpectedly at our home in Puerto Vallarta. We suspected they were living in South America but really did not want to know because if we were ever asked to testify, we could honestly say we did not know where they were.
A few years later, Canadian friends who knew them read in the Toronto paper that Joe had been arrested on a U.S. warrant in

Vancouver where they were living openly under the name Picon. Pam was even the Council for Belize. Bail was set at $40,000, was paid, and they were gone again.

They turned up in Belize, where there is no extradition treaty with the U.S. for civil crimes. They bought a small resort that they ran openly and successfully until Joe died several years later. Originally, Pam continued her missionary work in Belize, but last I heard, she was living in Guatemala and exploring the country via motorcycle. I had email contact with Pam for a while but have had no response for several months. Pam's parents have long been gone so I have no way of verifying that she is okay, but I have a great sense of foreboding about a 70-year-old woman traveling around Guatemala on a motorcycle.

Sailing through Life: Ninety-three years of adventure

Lee Lyon: Friend and Fellow Adventurer

Lee Lyon

A man is lucky if he has three good friends in his life.
— Neligh Coates Sr.

I was lucky because one of my good friends, in fact, my best friend, was Lee Lyon. Lee had graduated from Harvard, joined the Army, became a pilot and flew the deadly Burmese Hump during World War II (there was no Air Force yet).

I met Lee in 1957 when his family arrived at Lake Lotawana. My family had been spending summers at Lake Lotawana since 1931 when we built one of the first houses on the lake. By this time, I had been competitive sailboat racing for more than ten years and I was glad to mentor the newcomer and novice sailor. Lee absorbed everything. He was highly competitive and ready for our sailing adventures. We quickly developed a friendship that was to last for over 50 years.

I soon learned that my new friend was not only a nice guy but a very innovative and successful businessman. The company he ran, M. Lyon and Company, had been founded by his great-grandfather in 1870 and was originally a fur trading company dealing with the Indians. Later the company became wool traders. M Lyon and company is the oldest family-owned business in Kansas City and the first business to open an account at the First National Bank of Kansas City. Now they are in the business of processing cowhides.

What I did not realize, or had never thought about, was that no one ever killed a cow for its hide. The hide was strictly a byproduct of the slaughterhouse. Lee's company collected the fresh hides from the slaughterhouse, running the hides through a fleshing machine to remove dirt and the fat that remained on the hide, soaking the hides in a saltwater prime to preserve them, sorting and grading them, and then shipping them to the tanneries to be turned into leather. It was a business that processed thousands of hides to make a dollar or so on each one—high-volume, low-margin. The process was virtually unchanged from the time of the Egyptians.

But, my friend, Lee, changed all that. Lee realized that the fat next to the skin was different from normal fat as it did not harden when cold like normal animal fat. This is why cattle do not get stiff in cold weather. Lee developed a centrifuge to turn the special fat into a high-quality oil that could be used in cosmetics and other expensive products. He changed the business that had been unchanged for hundreds of years.

I'll never forget inspecting his boat to find that it was weighed down by all kinds of extra stuff in a class where every ounce over the 450-pound minimum weight was crucial. Lee asked how he could get the weight down and I gave him my smart answer "just like you would eat an elephant—one bite at a time."

Being a fast learner, Lee quickly became a highly competitive sailor, but more importantly, he was the kind of friend who was always game for anything. When I suggested we should compete for a place on the Olympic team in the Finn class, Lee was all in. We chartered two Finns and started practicing on Lake Lotawana. The Finn is a one-man boat and requires not only skill but strength. We went to our first regatta on a lake in Illinois and did fairly well. Because of our success with that regatta. we decided to compete in the semifinal eliminations for the Olympics in Atlanta, Georgia. We were entering the big time.

One of the secrets to sailing a Finn in high winds is to put on as many as four or five sweatshirts, dip your body in the water to get them wet, and use that additional weight to keep the boat upright. Fortunately, class rules required that you also wear a life vest. We were doing fairly well in Atlanta until a huge thunderstorm came up, the race was postponed, and we spent two miserable hours standing in chest-deep water holding the bow of our boats, shivering in spite of the sweatshirts. We both finished in the top half of the fleet but did not make the final Olympic trials.

I talked Lee into chartering a Laser so we could compete in the Laser National Championship that was going to be sailed on Coronado Island near San Diego. Lee and JoAnn met Betty and me at the famous Del Coronado Hotel. The races were held in a huge lagoon about five miles south of the hotel. Since we only had one car and did not want to leave the ladies stranded, every morning, looking like down-and-out bums, wearing multiple sweatshirts, sloppy sailing hats, and with our sail bags and centerboards over our shoulders, Lee and I would hitchhike to the racecourse. We were amazed that hardly a car passed without picking us up. We figured they wanted to know what these strange guys could be doing.

The sailing on these lagoons was magnificent. They were only separated from the Pacific by a flat stretch of sandy beach, consequently, the wind was constant and steady. It would come in fairly light for the morning races then, as the sand heated up, increase during the day. There were about fifty boats competing and these were some of the best sailors in the country.

I could hold my own on the first weather (upwind) leg but when we rounded the mark for the reaching leg it was a different world. The hotshot sailors could get their boats up on a plane instantly and I would go from second or third down to ninth or tenth in no time at all. It was great sailing and we both learned a lot but found out we still had a lot to learn.
After that, our sailing adventures were mostly on cruising boats in Mexico, the Caribbean, and one memorable voyage with our friends, Joe and Pam Ross, in Turkey.

When I moved to Aspen, Lee came out with a group from Kansas City on an early-season ski trip. We had a large enough group to reserve the entire Crystal Palace for a pre-opening night performance. Lee and Joanne fell in love with Aspen and purchased a two-bedroom apartment from me in a building I had just completed, the Château Eau Claire. After spending more time in Aspen, they purchased land just outside of town and built a wonderful home. Later they purchased a villa in a project I developed in Puerto Vallarta, Casa McFuego. The family still owns the villa.

Lee kept their Aspen home after Joanne passed away but finally decided to sell it and move to Kansas City to be close to his kids. It was a sad day in 2016 when Lee died from a fall at the age of 93. We had wonderful years together and I miss him.

Sailing through Life: Ninety-three years of adventure

Lynn Bolkan: A Unique, Brilliant Individual

This is how a friendship that would last for almost 50 years began.

We were told that Lynn was an excellent mechanic, so we contacted him by radio only to be told that it was his birthday, and he did not work on his birthday. However, since we were behind schedule getting back to the U.S., Lynn agreed that if we would sail the boat back to the harbor, he would look at it. Betty and I first met Lynn and his wife, Deloris, in 1983 when we were cruising Expectation in the Sea of Cortez and developed engine problems. We were in the islands north of La Paz and within VHF radio range of the fleet there.

In 1966, Lynn had been a logger in Oregon, when his house burned down. He and his wife, Deloris, decided they wanted a better life and contemplated moving to Australia. They visited Australia, stopping on the way in Hawaii, Tahiti and New Zealand where they observed cruising boats and a life that had great appeal.

Australia was expensive, and it was tough to find employment. They returned to Oregon and began building a sailboat to explore the world with their family. No problem that neither one of them knew how to sail or even the first thing about sailboats, there were books on the subject after all. So in 1971 Deloris took a hospital job and Lynn continued logging as they started construction of a 65-foot ferro-cement yacht which they named Endless Summer. Deloris headed South to cruise the

Sea of Cortez. A pattern developed whereby we would sail Expectation from late October until May, and Lynn would come to the boat wherever we had left it each fall, complete a list of repairs and improvements, and get the boat ready for our arrival.

It was all pretty routine until the first summer we left the boat in Panama. Knowing how damp their summers were, I had gone to the Panama Canal free zone to buy a dehumidifier to keep the boat dry while it was at the dock in Colon. Dehumidifiers were out of stock, so I made a deal with another sailor to buy one when they were back in stock and install it. The sailor misunderstood and bought and installed a humidifier so by the time Lynn arrived at the boat it was so damp inside that there was green mold everywhere, the doors and drawers were swollen shut and Expectation was uninhabitable. Remarkably Lynn had everything in perfect shape by the time Betty and I arrived in Panama.

At that time, Colon, Panama, was one of the most dangerous cities in the Western Hemisphere and the only safe place was the heavily fenced and guarded area around the Panama Canal Yacht Club. On our third day there, the four of us went to a nearby restaurant for dinner. As we were walking down the road to the yacht club gates, two men with knives started chasing us. Providentially, a guard at a container yard saw our predicament and fired his pistol into the air and scared off our attackers. They had gotten close enough to me, since I was bringing up the rear, that the guard asked if I had been cut!

After that, Betty and I would call a cab to the yacht club if we had an errand to do and the driver insisted Betty stay in the car with the windows closed while I went into a shop. One day the yacht club phone was out so I decided the only way to get a cab was to get out on the main street, which I did after taking off my watch and turning the pockets of my shorts inside out to prove I had no valuables and was not worth robbing.

One day, we were sailing across the Sea of Cortez next to Endless Summer and, being an old racing sailor, I realized that Lynn's sails were as beautifully cut as fine racing sails. Knowing his budget was limited I called in on the radio and asked him where he had gotten them. Lynn said he had made them himself. When I asked him how he could do this without a sail loft or any experience his reply was "I read a book." Lynn was so smart that I'm sure he could build a computer if he had a book and a few crude parts.

Lynn and Deloris continued their annual fall overhaul and upgrade for all twelve years Betty and I had the boat and, in addition, we had some wonderful shoreside adventures including a visit to the ruins of Tikal in Guatemala, traveling together to explore St. Lucia, and many other exotic places.

Our final adventure was Carnival in Trinidad after which they sailed Expectation on its final voyage (under our ownership) back to Fort Lauderdale to be donated to a charitable sailing organization for student training. Lynn and Deloris extended our cruising enjoyment by several years.

Paul Koontz: Over 70 Years of Friendship

I first met Paul in 1945 when we were both attending Southwest High School in Kansas City. After a year at Southwest, I went away to school at Peddie in Hightstown, New Jersey and Paul went to Penday in Kansas City, but we always kept in contact. Paul went on to Princeton while I attended Northwestern.

At that time, I was very active in sailboat racing, and I asked Paul to crew for me. Paul did not have any knowledge of sailing or sailboats, but he was a good athlete, dependable and I knew I could teach him to sail. And he quickly became a skilled and faithful crew, driving out to Lake Lotawana every Saturday and Sunday. We were consistently near the top of the fleet.

In the summer of 1952, I decided that we should challenge the big boys up north. And so, we were off to a Regatta on Lake Geneva, in southern Wisconsin, driving the family station wagon, sailboat in tow. We did not win and in fact I was quite embarrassed because we were beaten by Jane Pagel, a girl!

To save a hotel bill on the return trip, we stayed at the SAE fraternity house in Evanston. That night I took Paul to Calumet City to see some of the seamier side of the Chicago area nightlife. I had forewarned him that some of the topless performers could be relentless, so imagine my surprise to return to our table from the men's room and find Paul with a topless performer on his lap. She already had five drinks on the table. Paul said he was trying to convince her that she was too nice to be in this line of work. There are some things they don't teach you at Princeton.

Paul went on to medical school and I visited him in New York where he was taking his surgical residency. He invited me to watch him remove a ruptured appendix. I was impressed with how clean the operating room was and how the nurses respected and admired Paul. Paul returned to Kansas City and became one of the top surgeons in the area, specializing in breast cancer. As he neared retirement, he was honored by having the breast cancer section of St. Luke's Hospital named after him.

Over the years Paul would occasionally join me as crew on some of my sailing adventures aboard Expectation. On our almost disastrous 1983 voyage from San Diego to Puerto Vallarta, I managed to rip our mainsail from luff to leach in an accidental jibe. Paul, being the only one in the crew who could sew, was assigned the job of making the repair. His stitching was beautiful, but it soon became apparent that, at the rate he was progressing, we were going to be stuck on this island all winter. We took the damaged sail to the local village and Paul got to watch a native woman look in disdain at $10,000 worth of stitches, Paul's surgical rate, and then rip them out.

Paul and I had a wonderful mutual friend, Jerry McCann. I had invited them to join me in Panama to transit the canal and explore the Pacific islands. I had not seen Jerry for some time and did not realize how weak he was from a heart condition. Paul was attentive and caring in tending Jerry and I still have a picture of Paul helping Jerry up a steep ramp after we had beached the dinghy. Jerry died far too early and his wonderful wife, Suzie, married and buried one more man.

In 1959 I had attended Paul's wedding to Xanie in New York but that did not last. Later he married Susan but again, the marriage failed.

In 2015 Paul and Suzie were married, which to me is a match made in heaven.

What are the ingredients of Paul's and my seventy plus years of friendship? Maybe it's the kindnesses. Perhaps it's trust. Possibly, it's the wicked dry humor. Likely a love of sailing has a lot to do with it. And the adventures. And mutual respect. Yes, we have all of that.

Pierre Baruzy: The Crazy French Man

Has your host ever escorted you to your hotel room doing handstands?

I met Pierre in 1953 when I was accompanying my father on his trip to France. As soon after the war as was practical, my father had started establishing foreign companies to produce and sell Clipper saws and blades locally since it was extremely hard and expensive to import them from Kansas City. Pierre had been selected as the head of Clipper France not only because he was a good man but, most importantly, the president of Norton France who would be our supplier of blades for cutting brick, concrete block, etc.

Norton was a leading manufacturer of grinding wheels all over the world. Their primary customers were companies like Ford Motor and General Motors where Norton supplied grinding wheels for machining automotive parts. Becoming a supplier to Clipper, they had entered an entirely new market: supplying blades under the Clipper label for cutting structural glazed tile, brick and concrete block. Clipper had become Norton's single largest customer in the U.S., so it was natural to look to them as a supplier in other countries. This led to my father making the president of Norton in each country a partner in that country's local Clipper operation.

At the time I met him, Pierre was in his 60s and in remarkable shape. On the first night of our visit, while taking us down the hall to our Paris hotel room, he expressed exuberance for the evening by doing handstands as we proceeded down the hall. At a fraction of his age, I would not have attempted that.

Pierre and his wife, Simone, were a fascinating couple. As head of Norton during the Second World War, Pierre had secretly been part of the French underground. He was also a member of the very select group of French gourmets who rated Paris restaurants.

His wife, Simone, was a quintessential French lady, petite and always beautifully dressed.

Going to a Paris restaurant with Pierre and Simone was like opening up a whole new world where people of refined tastes were enjoying fine food and drink. Everyone knew who he was, and we were always given a prime table and received impeccable service.

Although I got to know a number of the Clipper foreign managers, Pierre was always my favorite. It was a sad day when Pierre passed away.

Ron Miller and Diane Disney: Silent Partners

Ron Miller and Diane Disney: Silent Partners

Drive 20 minutes to Aspen for a loaf of bread?

In 1977, before Snowmass Village became an incorporated town, Fritz Benedict and I decided to build a shopping center on his land at the base of the Village. We needed a financial partner, and Fritz suggested Ron and Diane Miller. After hearing our plans, the Millers agreed to become our partners. We sent them quarterly reports but, in all the years we were partners, we never received a question or comment from them.

The Snowmass Center, the name I gave our shopping center, was a success from the start. Need groceries? The Snowmass Center has a grocery store. Need something from the drugstore? Stop by the Snowmass Center. The Miller's home was only a couple of miles away and they regularly shopped at the Snowmass Center, but they never had a complaint or a suggestion.

Diane was the daughter of Walt Disney and Ron was the president of Disney (he was later removed in a coup led by Walt's brother, Roy, who was the subject of the best-selling book Storming the Magic Kingdom.)

When I told them that Betty and I were going to take a vacation to Disney World in Orlando, Diane orchestrated our visit. She set up a private tour for us. The Managing Director spent almost a full day showing us the underground city, the yet unopened wildlife island, and the soon to be opened, Epcot. It was a tour few people have had of the facility and a magical experience.

Ron and Diane did wonderful things in their lives including the building of the Disney Center for the Performing Arts in Los Angeles and the development of Silverado Vineyards on their property in Napa.

After Diane and then Betty had passed away, Ron and I kept in touch by phone every few weeks. We talked about the adjustments we had to make after losing Diane and Betty. Ron liked to discuss activities at his vineyard and the challenges and joys of the wine business. In our last conversation, he was very excited about turning over his huge Colorado ranch to the Nature Conservancy.

I was shocked and saddened when I heard of Ron's untimely death at age 85 on February 19, 2019. I miss our phone calls.

And more memories from my son, Jeff...
When I broke my leg as a kid, I spent the night in the Aspen Valley hospital with Walt Disney's grandson "Walter." Later on, while attending Colorado Rocky Mountain School, Tamara

Miller was in my class. She must have been Diane and Ron Miller's daughter. When I asked Tamara if she had a brother named Walter, she was very surprised and said, "How would you know that?"

George Waring

Kansas City Club

In the 1970's I was living in Kansas City and working for my father's firm, Clipper Manufacturing Company. One of the luxuries I thought that I could afford was a junior membership in the Kansas City Club. At that time the Kansas City Club was a combination eating club, athletic facility, with rooms for out of town guests.

As a junior member I had access to the athletic facilities which included a small gym and two regulation handball courts. The man in charge of this facility was George Waring. And since George also gave massages we called him an "Ass Rubber". It is strange that more than fifty years later I think of George and things he preached to all of us clients. One thing I always remember when I step into a shower is that George told us not to worry about washing our backs, just rinse them off. We could not afford regular massages but if we were feeling particularly rich we would hire George and he was outstanding.

My most frequent handball opponent was Dave Smart who was making much more money than me but was too cheap to pay for a club membership. Another frequent handball rival was Hank Stram who was coach of the Kansa City Chiefs football team. Hank was a fireplug of a man, but I found that he was so competitive that he tended to cheat.

I understand that the Kansas City Club has changed completely, but those were great days.

ADVENTURES

Baja Adventures

In 1967, when we moved from Kansas City to Aspen, we towed our old 16-foot inboard/outboard motorboat along with us. That trip was an adventure in itself. I decided to take the shortcut over 12,095-foot Independence Pass. At that time, some spots of the pass were extremely narrow, unpaved, and without guardrails to protect from 500-foot drop offs. Of course, the boat was useless during ski season and the nearest lake where we could use it was 45 miles away and ice cold, even in summer.

In 1976, Betty and I decided to have one last hurrah with the boat and were contemplating a trip to Baja, California, but were worried about the terrible Mexican roads. One day, as we were discussing this on the phone, it just so happened that Bernardo Quintana, one of our condominium rental guests from Mexico was walking by my office. I asked him if he had any knowledge of the Baja highway. To my complete surprise he told me he had quite a lot as his company had built it! According to Bernardo the two-lane road was fine, although it did not have shoulders. We decided to give it a try and were on the road the day the ski season ended.

Our first stop was San Diego for camping supplies and trailer repairs, then we headed south through Ensenada and down the narrow Baja Road. Our guidebook had told us about a fishing camp in the north part of the Sea of Cortez called Papa Diaz, so we took off east on an even cruder road to try it out.

Papa Diaz was primarily a fly in resort with an airstrip right next to the cabins. The cabins themselves were pretty basic with a single bare light bulb that went off when the generator stopped at 10 p.m. We had water, but the only time it was hot enough to bathe was late in the day when the sun had heated the water pipes that ran just a few inches under the sand.

But there was nothing wrong with the food, which was served family style at long tables and almost always featured huge piles of delicious turtle meat (this was before anyone knew about the turtles being endangered), refried beans, lots of salsa, and homemade tortillas.

On our second day we met a group of young people from Chicago who had chartered a sailboat for a four-day exploration of the islands offshore. One of the girls had left her sunglasses behind, so we decided to have an adventure and take them to her (at dinner, she had told us about the bay they were headed to).
The bay was at the end of an island, about 10 miles offshore. At our speed it was only three hours away. The sea was calm, and we found the sailboat just before dusk. We beached the boat to set up camp, intending to rejoin our friends for cocktails. What we hadn't counted on was a huge tide which went out so fast that by the time we realized what was happening there was not enough water to launch the boat. We were a bit panicked, but the captain of the sailboat told us there would be another tide at about three in the morning and, of course, the one we came in on would return the next afternoon. No worries!

Before going to bed we dug a trench around the boat to make it easier to float and took turns staying awake so we would not miss the next tide. We were very disappointed when that tide came in and did not even get the boat wet.

Our friends were gone at dawn, so we tried to relax while waiting for the afternoon tide. When it finally came in, we were able to easily relaunch the boat, but it was too late to try to return to camp so we moved to the next bay, anchored in plenty of water and swam ashore to spend a quiet night.

By morning, our cooler was almost empty and our water supply low, but we knew it was only about a three-hour trip back to camp, and we were in a beautiful spot teeming with sea life. What we didn't realize in our protected place was that the wind had come up strong from the south. As soon as we poked our nose out from behind the shelter of the island we were greeted by huge whitecaps, far too rough for our little vessel.
The rest of the morning and early afternoon was spent observing the sea life. Every hour or so we would stick our nose out to see if the wind had died, no such luck. At one point a whale sounded right next to us and when the air from his blowhole reached us, we discovered, for the first time, that whales have bad breath.

Late in the afternoon, I realized we were using up our gas making these exploratory surges so decided we had better go for it no matter what. Every wave was breaking over our bow and I knew that if the engine swamped, we would be swept onto the 150-foot cliffs off the island that rose right out of the water.

A bone rattling three hours later we made it back to Papa Diaz with only fumes in the gas tank, we were soaking wet and almost frozen. One of the campers saw the shape we were in, helped us get the boat out of the water and gave me a big slog of wonderful bourbon. Can't describe how good the turtle tasted that night.

The rest of our trip was pretty routine. We drove to La Paz, took the ferry across to the mainland and made it home to Aspen without incident.

Barking Dog

Nick and Hercules

If your dog doesn't like someone, you probably shouldn't either.—Unknown

I am blind and Hercules is my Black Labrador guide dog. When I received Hercules in June 2015, he was fully trained. However, in addition to training him to guide a blind person, stop for curbs, stairways and obstacles, they had also taught him to pee like a girl and not to bark.

Hercules had not lost his barker, it was just that, unlike most dogs, he did not bark when a stranger came to the door or when he met another dog. About once every couple of months he will let out a single "wolf" but that is it.

Hercules sleeps locked in a wire kennel at the foot of my bed so I could hardly believe my ears when, in the summer of 2016, he started barking like a real dog. It was 3 o'clock in the morning so I staggered out of bed, unlocked his kennel and he streaked into the living room. I staggered after him and my eyesight was good enough that I could see that both the refrigerator and freezer doors were open on our side-by-side unit. Immediately I realized the problem. We had been invaded by an Aspen black bear and my hero, Hercules, had scared him off. I let Herc sleep on my bed the rest of the night.

In the morning, my daughter came by to assess the damage. Other than muddy bear prints on the floor and the shelves of the refrigerator there was none. I had left the sliding glass door to our patio open but closed the screen for fresh air and to hear the sound of the river. The bear had politely opened the screen for entry and all that was stolen was one carton of cottage cheese. I considered us lucky and Hercules a hero because many of our friends, including my daughter, had suffered substantial damage from bear invasions.

The next summer there was a repeat incident at 1:30 in the morning. I realize that I had been crazy to let Hercules loose on the bear because, if he had been cornered, the bear could easily have killed the dog. So, instead of releasing Herc, I stormed into the living room shouting to scare the bear away. Imagine my surprise when a male voice answers, "What's the problem?"

I thought I had a burglar, but it was just a visitor who, while not obviously intoxicated, must have been high on something. We had a semi-civilized conversation for a few minutes, and he left quietly when I said I was going to call the police. I did and it is interesting that when the policeman arrived 15 minutes later Hercules did not make a sound. He can apparently tell the difference between the good guys and uninvited guests. I wonder if they taught him that at guide dog school.

Bullfighting

I have a philosophy on bullfighting – there is nothing better than a great one and there is nothing worse than a bad one.

My interest in bullfighting began in 1947. I was 17 and a student at Haileybury College in Hertfordshire, England. We had been assigned to read Ernest Hemingway's book Death in the Afternoon. I was fascinated by the subject and read every book I could find on the art of bullfighting.

While I was on spring break in Spain, I ran into a friend from Lake Lotawana. Sue Newcomer was also interested in bullfights and had read that the best ones were in Seville. We went to a travel agency to find out more and were told by the agent that Seville was impossible over Easter and, although he was Spanish, he would not even attempt to go.

Sue, not to be denied, chartered a small plane, and we were off to Seville. We were lucky and were able to book two dingy hotel rooms knowing we would seldom use them with all the Easter excitement, pageantry, processions, and revelry every day, 24 hours a day.

For a time, we joined the jostling crowd standing three deep along the street for the daily Holy Week procession of over 100 huge wooden floats, creeping toward us, each preceded by dirge music. Every church mounts their image of Christ on a float, carried by as many as 40 men. Even with 40 men, they must continually change bearers due to the weight of the platform. Then off to our first bullfight.

I thought I knew what to expect at a bullfight, but I could not have imagined the thrill of hearing the majestic bugle fanfare and the ebullience of energy and passion from the cheering crowd.

Sue and I saw our first two bullfights in the Maestranza, one of the most beautiful bullrings in Spain. Of course, a bullfight is not a fight at all as the bull is not going to leave the arena alive. It is a beautiful spectacle and an emotional life and death drama that demonstrates the courage of both the matador and the bull. The Seville audience was very knowledgeable and demanding, adding to the excellence of the whole performance.

Later Robbie and I saw some excellent bullfights in Mexico City, which has the largest bullring in the world, seating 55,000. One Sunday we were in Mexico City and read that the renowned Spanish bullfighter, El Cortabez, was to fight that afternoon. We paid a scalper an exorbitant amount of money for our tickets only to be terribly disappointed at El Cotabez's mediocre performance. The next day we read in the paper that he had apologized to his fans and would come back the following Sunday to vindicate himself. He even offered to buy the bulls.

A brave bull that charges straight is an essential part of a great bullfight. If the bull is erratic and hooks his head instead of charging straight and true even the most skillful matador can do little with him.

We were back in the stands the following Sunday to watch El Cortabez execute his graceful cape work and daring. The excitement of the crowd grew with each pass of the bull. Adrenalin was high. The atmosphere intoxicating. We had seen a number of bullfights and occasionally a matador had been awarded an ear for an unusually good performance and once we had seen one awarded two ears but that was very unusual The judges awarded El Cortabez two ears for his performance with the first bull and an unprecedented two ears and the tail for his second bull. There is nothing quite like the sound of 55,000 people shouting Olé! at once.

There were times during that fight that I thought Robbie might have an orgasm right there in the stands.

As the crowd was exiting the Plaza a black limousine with El Cortabez in the backseat came through the crowd and I found my wife pounding on the backseat window trying to get his attention. El Cortabez was truly magnificent.

I have had the good fortune to see a number of bullfights in Mexico City, San Miguel, Tijuana, and even in the little bullring at Puerto Vallarta, but I have never seen anything to compare with that afternoon in Mexico City.

Cuba

I love making new friends and I respect people for a lot of different reasons.—Taylor Swift

I had heard of the civil rights abuses by the Batista government, and it was definitely an autocratic regime, yet the streets were filled with lively restaurants and there was jazz and Cuban salsa music everywhere. Although there were rumors of rebels in the mountains, it seemed that the general public was not concerned about nor particularly interested in what was happening in the countryside. People in brightly colored clothes were dancing in the street. These people could not have been more carefree or fun-loving.

The death of Fidel Castro in 2016 brought back vivid memories of my friend, Billy Goventes. I first met Billy in Havana, Cuba, in 1957 when I was there to sell construction equipment to companies that were doing road and airport construction work for the Batista government. At that time Cuba was engaged in a multitude of highway and airport projects sponsored by their dictatorial government. Billy, who spoke perfect English, was the assistant manager on a highway project, and after a couple of lunches and dinners together we became good friends.

When I returned to Cuba in 1960, Batista had been ousted, the Castro government was in charge and things had changed radically, although not as much as they eventually would. Billy was desperate to get out of the country and asked for my help. There was really nothing I could do but lend him a small amount of money. I learned later that Billy escaped by buying passage on a small powerboat fleeing the islands for Florida. They waited for a calm night and the overcrowded boat made the 90-mile crossing to Florida without losing a passenger.

A couple of years later I was living in Kansas City when Billy came to visit, and we caught up. After that, I was busy with my job and my family and lost contact with Billy. I have no idea what happened to him, but he was a smart guy and a good engineer so I'm sure he was successful, as were many of his countrymen.

I have always had strong feelings that our government made a huge mistake by banning all trade and travel with Cuba after the rise of Castro. Since Cuba could still trade with Canada and the major European countries, our trade ban was not that effective nor were our policies consistent. We have never gone to war with Cuba (although Kennedy tried to invade them unsuccessfully.) Yet not long after the war with communist Vietnam ended, we began trading and sending tourists to that country. I have always found the Cubans to be industrious, fun-loving people and I felt that if they had had more exposure to our culture Castro might have been ousted years earlier.

Note: the above was written before we resumed relations with Cuba. I would love to go back, but I am not sure they would accept my guide dog, nor, without my sight, how much I would get out of it.

And that's how I see it.

Diving: A Family Passion

"Spit in my face mask and rub the saliva around to keep my mask from fogging up?" An alternative to attending a Los Angeles business meeting with my dad?

Marvin Warner, one of the employees at the Los Angeles company, had offered to teach me how to scuba dive!

At age seven, I had learned to snorkel in Lake Lotawana, a man-made lake outside of Kansas City, where we spent our summers. It was fun, but visibility was barely two feet and I saw some tadpoles. Now, I was going scuba diving in the ocean.

The next morning, Marvin and I were in his 20-foot aluminum boat, equipped with diving gear, and anchored in the bay in 30 feet of calm water. Marvin explained each piece of equipment and the fundamentals of diving.
"Never panic and shoot to the surface. If your air fails, swim to the surface without holding your breath, and at the same speed your bubbles rise. Most importantly never panic — do things slowly!"

Yes, Marvin taught me to spit in my face mask and rub the saliva around. We strapped on the tank and regulator, weight belt, and swim fins. Then he showed me the proper way to enter the water—sit on the side of the boat facing in and roll backwards into the water while tightly holding your mask, to keep it from falling off. My heart racing, I rolled backward into the water. We dove together so I could get the feel of it.

Weightless! This must be how an astronaut feels in space. I could move effortlessly. My breathing was noisy. The water magnifies everything!

Marvin gave me a tire iron to gather abalone. Abalone produce a suction to attach themselves to the bottom, but they must raise part of the shell to feed. The purists take abalone with their bare hands by reaching under the raised part and flipping the abalone loose. If you are not quick enough the abalone can clamp down on your hand and drown you. Thus, the tire iron.

We each got two nice 8 to 10-inch abalone. This is when the work begins. We had to dig the meat out of the ear-shaped abalone shell. Not an easy task. Then we pounded the meat until it was tender being careful not to overdo it and destroy the meal. Done properly and sautéed in butter there is nothing more delicious.

I wanted to dive again and was eager to go back to California. On my next trip, Marvin proposed that we go to an area below Ensenada in Baja California, Mexico, an area famous for large lobster. (They are called lobster but are actually crayfish as they do not have the great claws of the Maine lobster.) After a three-hour drive, we came to a stop on large cliffs overlooking a rocky beach. Too late to turn back, we managed to find a Mexican fisherman who owned a shack on the beach and a boat we could rent. We lugged our equipment down the steep hill.

The next morning, we set out and soon we were over a rocky bottom in about 40 feet of water. Again, the purist takes lobster by hand, but you really have to be skilled to do that, so we took our spear guns. We had each gotten a decent-sized lobster when I spotted a monster. I got a good shot and hit him solidly, but my monster wouldn't give up and backed into a hole. Even though I could brace my feet against the rocks I could not pull him out. It was getting close to lunchtime, so I left my spear gun on the bottom, returned to the boat, and had lunch figuring that in 20 minutes some of the fight would be out of him. Returning after lunch I braced my feet against the rocks again and started pulling. Eventually he came out and I was able to get him to the boat where Marvin pulled him in. We didn't have a scale, but we estimated he weighed over 15 pounds. I took a picture of the monster that I'm still carrying in my wallet more than 60 years later.

When Betty and I started our 12 years of cruising, we equipped Expectation with scuba equipment and an air compressor. This came in extremely handy to free a fouled anchor and for the occasional spearfishing expedition. By this time, I had a lot of experience with scuba diving, but diving is always an adventure into a different world, and I had the occasional scare.

On one dive Betty and I went through an opening into a cave and realized that the opening that had been so apparent from the outside was impossible to find in the darkness on the inside. No one knew we were there! My heart was in my throat by the time we finally found that opening.

In St. Lucia, I went on a dive with commercial divers who took us through a tunnel. I will admit to real panic even though I knew that if I kept following the guy ahead of me, we would get out. There is something about not being able to tell where the surface is that scares the hell out of me.

I wanted to dive on the famous Palancar Reef with a guide when we had Expectation in the waters off Cozumel. I learned that I had to be certified. In spite of all the diving I had done I had never been certified, so I took a quick certification course.

Crystal clear water, with visibility up to 200 feet, perfect to mingle with Hawksbill Turtles, Splendid Toadfish, and kaleidoscopic schools of tropical fish. Spectacular, and the boat made it super easy. Although there was a fairly strong current, I did not have to fight it because the dive boat drifted with the current, and when it was time to surface, the dive boat was right there.

No spearfishing is allowed so the fish are super friendly. I had taken a plastic bag full of bread to feed the fish and they loved it. However, one huge, 100-pound grouper managed to sneak up on me and grab my bag. Carlos, my diving partner, saw it happen and the two of us chased the grouper, trying to get the bag back before he choked on it. The giant imp, with the bag still in his mouth, would keep just out of our reach. We told the dive master about it, and he assured us the bag would not be a problem for the grouper—apparently it happens frequently.

My last diving adventure was National Geographic worthy! My friend, Stan Starn, invited me on his powerboat, POSH, to dive with the hammerheads. We powered for almost 24 hours from the harbor in Costa Rica to the Cocoas Islands, known as a gathering place for the huge hammerhead sharks. Arriving at the cove where the sharks were reported to gather, we discovered them in about 50 feet of crystal-clear water. The area was thick with the mammoths, and we were able to dive right among them—close enough to touch—without incident. We knew we were in a celebrated place when we were joined by the National Geographic vessel that had come from the U.S. just to photograph our sharks.

Postscript form my son, Jeff:

Pops,

When I was 5 our family and the Lyon's family drove from Kansas City to Acapulco in the family station wagons, nearly a 2,000-mile drive. I remember when you saw a gas station a mile

or so away you would make all the kids walk to get some exercise.
You and Lee had rented a villa and I remember our houseman, Belo, made the best bolillos in the world. Bolillos are a crusty, oval-shaped roll that everyone loved.

We were in some sort of an enclosed mini bay near Acapulco but still in the ocean. You and Lee strapped a Pony scuba tank on my back. I went straight to the bottom and was having a great time not knowing I might run out of air. Apparently, it was so deep that you and Lee could not reach my depth to tell me to surface. Well hell. I was only five years old. Finally, Lee got deep enough to tell me to surface, and I did. That was my first diving experience.

When I was about 16 years old, I was certified at Fountain Valley School in Colorado Springs. We did our first open water dive in Ensenada and I remember our dive Master Sid Stovall took a bunch of high school kids on a 300-foot dive. Dangerous and a terrible idea. Years later, I had lost my certification card and I located Sid in Corpus Christi. He said, "How can I know I certified you in 1974?" I reminded him of the 300-foot dive, and I had my dive card within the week.

Since then, I have had the opportunity to dive all over the world. On our boat, the Office, I had a compressor and tanks. I dove with sharks, rode giant Mantas, and in one dive alone I would harvest 12 big lobsters. None as big as yours but they were big. After diving Papua New Guinea, Thailand, Malaysia, Curacao, Cozumel and many more I feel very fortunate that you put a tank on my back when I was 5 years old.

Sailing through Life: Ninety-three years of adventure

Dolphin Delight, Tehuantepec, and Sea Turtles

... a dream hangs over the whole region.
—The Log from the Sea of Cortez by John Steinbeck

Betty and I were anchored on a remote bay in the Sea of Cortez enjoying a cocktail when we spotted hundreds of sleek-bodied, glistening, dark gray and cream-colored dolphins surfacing, vaulting, piercing the sparkling water as far as the eye could see. In our 12 years of cruising, we had countless encounters with dolphins. It was not uncommon to have a pod of six to eight playing in our bow wake. On this occasion and it was an occasion, frolicking dolphins by the hundreds were gliding and leaping clear of the water in perfect arcs. We were delighted by the dolphin performance and its cast of hundreds!

Dolphins are said to be one of the most intelligent animals in the world. One remarkable dolphin tale was the dolphin 'thank you." Our cruising friends were anchored in a bay off the coast of Venezuela where they saw an injured dolphin with a fishing line tangled around its fins. They managed to free it. That evening the dolphin found shiny bits of stone and metal on the ocean bottom, picked them up and deposited them in our friend's dinghy, which was tied some 20 feet off their stern.

Another curious event happened to friends who were caught in a storm off the coast of the Tehuantepec. Their boat was taking so much water they thought it was going to sink so they abandoned ship and took to their life raft. The storm abated but they were miles off the coast. For three days they drifted in the boiling sun. Their water was gone, and they were not sure they could make it another day when two dolphins glided up and started pushing their raft. Our friends said they could not have been pushed more than 20 or 30 feet but come dawn the next day they were rescued by a Mexican fishing boat. They swore the dolphins were trying to push them into the path of the rescuers.

Tehuantepec Gulf is the body of water that is on the Pacific side of the narrowest part of lower Mexico. Because Chivela Pass, the mountain gap across the isthmus is low, winds that build up in the Gulf of Mexico funnel through the Gap, concentrate and can become very fierce. And, because the water is shallow huge 20-foot waves can build up. Also, the high winds that are funneled through pickup sand from the beach and can literally sandblast a yacht on the Pacific side.

We were scared to death as we approached our Tehuantepec Gulf crossing and we tried to stay right next to the beach to avoid being caught in the huge waves. As it turned out we caught a calm day and about halfway across I decided to leave the beach and head directly for the other side. There was no wind, so we motored.

As we got to the open water, we saw the most extraordinary sight. There were hundreds of sea turtles resting on the surface and on the back of every turtle was a bird. We assume the birds were there to rest and to pick growths off the turtles' backs. As we would approach a turtle it would dive, and the gull would fly off. The sea turtles and their passengers were an unexpected thrill.

Eating Rat

I think rats are so underappreciated.
—Robert Sullivan, NY Times

10 a.m. Time to tune in.

Our cruising community got on the ham radio every morning to exchange information. The island, San Jose, off the Pacific coast of Panama, was often mentioned in the conversation. The chatter included a discussion of Gerta and Dieter, a German couple who had arrived by sailboat, moved ashore and set up camp. They were raising papaya, other fresh fruit and, most interestingly, rats to eat. Other cruisers had tasted the rats and said they were delicious. Eating rat was an adventure Betty and I hadn't had in our 12 years of cruising. We were intrigued.

San Jose has a beautiful volcanic bay sprinkled with white sand and deep blue water dotted with rugged rock formations and we decided to stay a few days with the prospect of sampling a rat dinner. The island had a freshwater lagoon that was only yards back from the beach, which was a big attraction for us as we had no water maker in those days and our freshwater supply was always very dear. We went ashore in the afternoons to bathe in chest deep water, which we thoroughly enjoyed until the day Dieter asked if we had seen the alligators. That was the end of all bathing for Betty.

I made a deal with Dieter to trade lamb chops we had in our freezer for a rat all dressed and ready to eat. When the appointed day came for the lamb chop/rat exchange, Dieter's face was a mile-long. He apologized because he could not deliver the nice fat rat he had promised. The night before, it had produced babies. Alas, I have never eaten rat.

But I did have guinea pig for dinner one night when I was in Peru with the grandkids. It was served whole, including the skull and shiny teeth. Problem was it was so spiced up I really couldn't tell what the meat tasted like. The grandkids thought it was gross!

George's 35th Birthday

What is 20 gallons of water worth?

It looked like a little bit of paradise when we sailed our 44-foot cutter, Expectation, into the azul waters of Aqua Verde, a remote bay in the Sea of Cortez. And, better yet, what looked like a picturesque Mexican village was hugging the shore. We had no more than dropped our anchor when we were joined by friends sailing two other cruising boats.

Our passengers were Betty's son, George, and his then girlfriend Kristy Lee. And it was George's 35th birthday although we had not yet figured out how to celebrate the occasion. Seeing the village and hearing the sound of bleating goats gave me inspiration.

"Let's see if we can't get the villagers to put on a goat roast." Once I made sure our anchor was holding and everything was shipshape on Expectation, I launched our dinghy and headed for shore to see what kind of a deal I could make with the locals. Approaching shore, it quickly became apparent that what had appeared to be a very picturesque village was, in fact, a very poor one.

The natives that greeted me were very friendly, but before I could ask about the possibility of a goat roast, the woman that seemed to be in charge asked me if we would give them some water. Apparently, their water supply was brackish and fresh water was a valuable commodity. The problem was that fresh water was also a very valuable commodity on a cruising boat. Our tanks held a total of only 150 gallons, and we sometimes had to make that last for as long as a month. As a frame of reference, we would easily use more than that in a single day when we were ashore.

Essentially, we used our freshwater only to drink. We washed our dishes in saltwater and had learned how to take a bath in only six glasses of water. We would dive in the ocean, come back on deck and wash ourselves with saltwater soap, then dive back in the water to rinse off. Back on deck we would get the salt off by rinsing in three cups of precious water.

Feeling sorry for the villagers, we did collect 20 gallons for the cause. A very reasonable price was agreed on for the goat roast and we were allowed to select two young goats for the sacrifice. The goats were hung upside down from a tree, their throats were slit, and the women collected every drop of blood in pans. At the appointed time, our group was back on shore with beer and tequila to celebrate George's birthday. The local women served an incredible meal of homemade tortillas, beans and perfectly roasted goat on tin plates. We had brought plastic silverware from the boats. It was a wonderful birthday, and the meal would have been a tribute to any fine dining room. Our group staggered back to the boats by moonlight. We hoped it had been a memorable birthday for George.

Sailing through Life: Ninety-three years of adventure

Lake Powell and The Grand Canyon

Newfoundland, Priscilla, at Lake Powell

Part of her soul ... gloried in the sheer bodacious unnaturalness of it. Putting a great blue-green water park smack down in the red desert complete with cactus, trading posts, genuine Navajo Indians, and five kinds of rattlesnakes was theater of the absurd at its most outrageous. — The Rope by Nevada Barr

I had taken the hair-raising shortcut over the 12,000-foot Independence Pass, which, at that time, was unpaved and no guardrails to protect us from the 500-foot drop-offs. We had towed the 16-foot inboard/outboard motorboat all the way to Aspen from Kansas City. It was early fall of 1968 and time to go exploring in the boat except there was only one place to use a boat near Aspen, the newly formed Lake Ruedi, which while picturesque and unspoiled, was ice cold year around and limited in scope for a multiple day adventure.

I had heard there were great adventures to be experienced on the Colorado River and I decided to take my son, Jeff to Utah. But, when Jeff and I arrived at Moab, Utah, we were told that the Colorado was too low to navigate at this time of year although if we went farther west, we could try the newly formed Lake Powell, so west we went.

Arriving at the northernmost boat ramp on the lake we saw that there was a big problem: the water at the bottom of the ramp was crowded with huge floating tree trunks. The challenge was figuring out how to get through this mass of wood to the open water. Since the wind was calm, we were able to launch the boat, push aside logs, and reach open water at last. The water, although murky where we launched, cleared as we motored farther south along the magnificent shoreline. For three days we explored the sandstone cliffs that turn from pink to purple as the sun rises and the narrow slot canyons, going ashore each night to camp. We discovered another launching ramp called Bullfrog, which, on later trips, became our principal launching site, since it was on a more attractive part of the lake and the water was crystal clear.

Although we did a lot of exploring on that first trip, we saw less than a dozen other boats—a far cry from later years when we would see more than that in an hour on popular parts of the lake.

Lake Powell was formed when the Glen Canyon Dam was built across the Colorado River, backing up thousands of acres of water and forming a lake with more shoreline than the western coast of the United States. At some places, the depth is over 500 feet. The exploring was fantastic; there were some areas where you could hike up to caves that had petroglyphs from ancient Indian tribes. There was also an acre-sized area where the ground was littered with large pieces of petrified wood.

This first trip inspired a fascination with Lake Powell that lasted many years. Betty and I really started exploring in earnest when I bought a one fourth interest in what I thought was a perfect Lake Powell boat, *The Aspen Four*. This boat had a small galley, a table that seated four, which converted to a bed, and, best of all, a huge, cushioned platform in the stern that made for a perfect outdoor sleeping area. We often explored the lake with other couples and would find a sandy spot to nose ashore. Our friends slept in a tent on the beach while Betty and I slept in the boat.

Two particularly memorable experiences come to mind. One was when Tita and Xander Kaspar set up a tent and Tita surrounded their tent with an extremely heavy hemp rope. When asked about this, Tita told me it had kept away the snakes. To which I responded, "Great and it also kept away the elephants!"

The other instance was when we pulled up to a small island where Barbara and Carson Bell set up camp. The wind came up strong enough that we drifted off during the night without waking up. Imagine their shock to wake up in the morning and find themselves on a tiny island without a boat in sight!

After Betty and I were married in Tucson in 1977, we had our reservations and our bags packed for our honeymoon in Hawaii. At the wedding party we learned that several of our guests had chartered a houseboat and were going directly to Lake Powell. We had been having so much fun that they did not have a hard time convincing us to cancel our trip to Hawaii and join them with our boat. It was a fabulous few days, but we felt terrible when, after we got back to Aspen, we learned that our good friend, Chris Hemiter, had planned a huge surprise party for us at his home in Honolulu.

The Friendship Cruise

The Marine Store in Moab told us about The Friendship Cruise, which is a cooperative effort of the Chambers of Commerce of Green River, Utah and Moab, Utah. It is held every spring, covers 184 miles, and makes some of the most remote river areas in the U.S. available for exploration; making a trip that is extremely risky to do on your own into a safe and scenic adventure.

The following year, Jeff and I signed up. We launched our boat at Green River, Utah, and explored the Green River south to its confluence with the Colorado, just a few miles north of where the Colorado begins to form Lake Powell. We then turned north and ran the Colorado upstream to Moab, where our trailer was awaiting us, having been towed from Green River by the Chambers of Commerce. We passed examples of "Navajo Tapestry," deep purples, burnt red and oranges, and shiny blues on the sandstone walls that had taken centuries to form. It was the river trip of a lifetime.

Although the number of boats on the lake increased exponentially, there were still plenty of remote areas to explore. One of our favorite adventures was going down a new canyon where the sheer walls on both sides were several hundred feet straight up. The channel would get narrower and narrower until both sides of the boat were rubbing against the walls, and you could go no farther. We had to push our way back along the sides of the canyon to a place where it was wide enough to use the engine.

Our Lake Powell adventures ended when we got involved in ocean sailing and it wasn't until several years later that I decided it was time to explore the Colorado River as it roars through the Grand Canyon. I arranged to do it on a powered raft because, being a purist and floating the canyon using only oars called for too many slow days for our young group. I invited Lee Lyon who brought one of his granddaughters, Kim, Sara, Jackson, Jeff and Candy's son, Steven. It was an exciting three-day trip. Our guides would find a wide sandbar each night and we would set up camp while they prepared a delicious dinner. Lee managed to throw a little spice in the mix by introducing the kids to the joys of the bourbon bottle. We caught some fish, sang campfire songs and enjoyed hot, sunny weather. If you are brave, you could cool off with a 42-degree dip in the freezing cold Colorado River.

One afternoon is engraved in my memory forever. There were storm clouds forming so we hiked up under a huge overhang to have our lunch. It rained cats and dogs for about 15 minutes while we ate and then the sun came out again. We returned to the rafts and, as we started back down the river, magnificent waterfalls were plunging off the canyon walls. It was short-lived but unbelievably beautiful. One of those sights you never forget.
The trip ended just before we entered Lake Mead and we were taken out of the canyon by helicopter. This was about as thrilling as anything in the canyon when we zoomed just above ground level between the towering canyon walls.

Monarch Butterfly Wonderment

Monarch Butterflies

An adult monarch butterfly weighs less than a gram yet has one of the most incredible migrations of any animal. Monarchs, whose lifespan is normally only four to six weeks, spend their summers in Canada and the northern part of the USA. Then, for reasons that no one understands, a fifth or sixth generation monarch will decide to make the 3000-mile trip from its home to a pine forest in the state of Michoacán in central Mexico. On this journey, the monarchs feed on plant nectar and the milkweed plant that makes them poisonous to their predators.

Although this migration has been going on for thousands of years, it was not known to the outside world until 1975 when it was discovered and publicized by a Mexican entomologist. Just one year after the monarch migration was discovered, Betty and I were on an auto trip through Mexico and stopped in Morelia to visit the furniture plant we had invested in. As we were getting ready to start our drive south to Mexico City, we read about the discovery of the monarch migration in the local English-language paper. Fascinated, we decided to see this phenomenon for ourselves. Arriving at Angangueo, the closest city to the pine forest where the butterflies go for the winter, we learned that there were no paved roads to the sanctuary. The only way to get there was to buy a ride in a pickup truck. After some typical Mexican negotiations, this was arranged, and we found ourselves standing with eight Mexicans in the bed of the truck as we jostled over a deeply rutted dirt road.

About half a mile from the pine forest, we began to see monarch butterflies along the roadside, growing ever more numerous as we approached the forest. At the edge of the forest the air was literally filled with beautiful yellow and black monarchs, and as we entered the pine forest, there were so many of the tiny monarchs hanging from the limbs of the trees that the branches were bending over from their weight. The ground was literally covered with butterflies so you could not walk down the path without stepping on thousands of them. A single monarch flies in silence, but when a thousand are flying together it sounds like the beating of a muted drum. The spectacle was truly like nothing we'd ever seen!

We had the opportunity to make a return visit in 1979 and what a difference. There was a paved road right to the edge of the forest and a visitor center offering guided tours and selling souvenirs. The monarchs were just as spectacular as they had been on our first visit, but the paths were more defined and there were, of course, rules. But the sight was equally spectacular.

Our third and final visit was two years later. Several friends were visiting us at our home in Puerto Vallarta. Somehow the subject of the butterflies came up, we shared our pictures, and the pressure was on to make a return visit! At that time, I had a small airplane and a great pilot, Charlie Parker. Although

Charlie has lived in Mexico most of his life and was married to a Mexican, he had never seen the butterflies so nothing would have it, but that Charlie would fly four of us to see the phenomenon. We landed in a different city and hired a cab for the 30-minute drive to the pine forest. This time we did not start at the visitor center but at the bottom of a rather long, steep hill that led to the forest. I guess we were sneaking in the back door. Our friends thought it was spectacular, but we knew different. The clusters of butterflies were not as dense and there were fewer in the air and on the ground. Perhaps we had come too early in the migration but the trip, while exciting for our friends, was a real disappointment for us. And now that I have lost my sight, that is one experience I will never have again.

Postscript: On February 10, 2020, two men were killed near the sanctuary. It is believed they were murdered because they were involved in protecting the sanctuary from cartels who wanted to log the valuable trees.

Sailing through Life: Ninety-three years of adventure

Morocco: Marrakesh, the Market, the Volkswagen

To visit Morocco is still like turning the pages of some illuminated Persian manuscript all embroidered with bright shapes and subtle lines.—Edith Wharton

Driving opens a whole different world. When my daughter went to Morocco in 2017, it brought back memories of that completely different Moroccan adventure that Betty and I had taken over 30 years ago. Whereas Kim and her group traveled by air and stayed in nice hotels, our trip was made in a Volkswagen Pop-Top Van with a porta potty for the toilet and a black plastic bag we could hang on a tree limb to have a sun shower.

On the second day, we hired a slim, heavily mustached, 20-year-old dressed in blue jeans and a khaki shirt. His English was impeccable, and like almost all Moroccan guides his name was Mohammed. He took us to a local fair that was like visiting a different universe.

There were 20 horsemen in full tribal regalia mounted on magnificent Arabian horses on a field (approximately 250 yards long and 50 yards wide). They gathered at the end of the field and at some unknown signal charged en masse firing their rifles in the air all at once. It was spectacular![1]

After watching this performance repeated several times, we noticed several huge Arabian tents nearby, and with typical American audacity, asked Mohammed if we could see the inside of one. He opened the flap to reveal a group of 25 or 30 men sitting on cushions on a magnificently carpeted floor. Although they seemed to be engaged in a serious discussion, they stopped. They were as surprised to see us as we were to see them. There was absolutely no common language, but they let us know that we were welcome to a cup of tea, which we politely refused and exited.

Our trip had started in Paris, and we explored parts of France and Spain with our friends from Canada, the Bells. The two weeks the Bells were with us we stayed in hotels.

After we had dropped our friends off in Barcelona, the real adventure began. The crossing of the Straits of Gibraltar went smoothly, and Moroccan customs were slow but hassle-free. For the first two days, we were not even able to secure a map. Before we met Mohammed, we just headed south on the only road that seemed to be going that way.

Mohammed gave us a highway map and we proceeded without incident to Marrakesh and located a campground that was basically an open field with primitive toilet facilities. We were the only occupants, although there was space for at least 50 campers. In the week we spent there, only a few tent campers joined us and one day a huge double decker [k1] bus pulled in. We were never invited inside. Apparently, it consisted of sleeping cubicles on both levels and there must've been toilet facilities because they never used the primitive bathrooms and only stayed two nights.

The city of Marrakesh is as flat as a pancake, so I delighted in exploring it on the bicycle we carried on the back of the van. Twice we hired a driver to show us the local sights, which were interesting, but the most fascinating thing in town was Jemaa el-Fnaa, the central square, where there was action night and day. When I biked over in the morning the square would be full of colorful stands selling fruit juice and pastries. In the evening,

Betty and I would return to the square, where the smell of a slow-cooked tagines, herbs and spices permeated the air.

Betty pointed, "Oh look, there's a devil stick juggler, and a fire eater, and over there is a dentist actually pulling that poor man's tooth! "

There are acrobats and contortionists and snake charmers. It is a mosaic of color, chaos, people, culture and history.

I was particularly fascinated by the water sellers, who each had a beautiful ornamental bag over their shoulder for selling what you hoped was pure water. Water sellers must have been essential in the days before bottled water, there was still a handful of them who seemed to be making a living. I thought the bags they sold the water in were so unique and beautiful I had to have one, so I started negotiating because, in Morocco, you negotiate for everything. I was willing to pay his asking price, but as soon as we started bargaining the other water sellers gathered around to kibitz and offer advice. We negotiated with gestures and sometimes we wrote numbers on a pad. It was all in great spirit and I was having so much fun I returned for three days in a row to continue the negotiation.

Sailing through Life: Ninety-three years of adventure

The Moroccon water purse I purchased.

Behind the square there is a maze of small shops selling everything imaginable, a surprise at every corner. Everyone wanted to bargain, and they especially wanted to make a deal for my bicycle. The day before we left for the coast, I bought my water bag[k2] . I cherish it to this day.

The road to the coast was two lanes and very windy. We were shocked when our left rear tire blew out. We could only get partially off the road, and I became very worried when the rather cheap lug wrench that came with the van would not move the lug nuts and, in fact, stripped one. A goat herdsman came along and offered assistance, but of course, could do nothing. I thought it was curious that as soon as he stopped his goats climbed a nearby tree to observe from the branches. Yes, a tree full of goats.

We were not unsafe where we were in daylight, but it was getting dark, and I knew we would be very vulnerable at night as there was no way we could get the van farther off the road. Then an expensively dressed man in a fancy Mercedes was kind enough to stop and offer help. We had no common language so after failing to get our lug bolt off, he indicated he would go for help. I had deep reservations, but less than a half hour later a tow truck arrived with the tools to change our tire and we were on our way.
We camped on the street that night and went to the garage the next day to get a new tire and all our lug bolts lubricated.

The rest of our trip was anticlimactic and while we found the coastal area nice it could have been anywhere; it was not nearly as interesting as Marrakesh and the market.

[1] We later learned that the flurry of horses, riders, bright colors, dust and gunpowder smoke in a simulation of a cavalry-based military charge is the Moroccan tradition of Fantasia, also known as lab al baroud (Arabic for "gunpowder game") or Tbourida,—a celebration of the region's history and of the bond between horse and rider.

A New Year's Eve to Remember in Guatemala

There were seven cars behind us, all waiting for the forms to come so we could cross from Mexico into Guatemala. The Guatemalan authorities had run out of the forms permitting foreign cars to enter the country. They had sent a runner to Guatemala City, approximately a 12-hour round-trip, to get new forms.

As I celebrate my 88th New Year's Eve, I can't help but think back to my most memorable one. It was 1987 and Betty and I were driving our motorhome to Guatemala. We had had an easy trip from Aspen through Mexico and were planning on being in Guatemala City to celebrate New Year's Eve. Then we came to the Mexico/Guatemala border. No foreigners could cross.
After all, it was New Year's Eve and everyone was disappointed, but a comradery developed among us stranded strangers and we started sharing a bottle of wine and someone even had a bottle of champagne. Everyone realized there was nothing we could do until the forms arrived and so we shared stories and made the best of it there on the roadside. About 11 p.m., the forms arrived, and we were cleared to enter Guatemala.

People, wearing some of the most colorful costumes we had ever seen, walked beside the mountainous highway. The scene was like a vibrant bouquet of blue, yellow, red, and bold pink flowers flung along the highway. We later learned that the fabulous costumes were actually everyday Guatemalan dress and Guatemalans walk from village to village. Exhausted and feeling the effects of our roadside party, we drove about an hour, when we spotted a motel that looked like the Guatemalan version of an outdated Holiday Inn. Not wanting to leave our camper unattended, we asked the proprietor if it was all right to park on the edge of the highway near his establishment. With approval, we spent our first night in Guatemala soundly asleep just off the highway.

Imagine our surprise to wake up on New Year's Day to hear whispering and giggles and to see a group of curious, brown-eyed Guatemalan children peering in our windows.

This was the beginning of an enchanting month exploring Guatemala.

The Panama Canal

Sailing across the Continental Divide.[8]

We are in a third world country about to embark on an all-day adventure. We have our permit from the canal authorities, paid our $186 transit fee, been assigned an advisor and given a departure time.

I have transited the Canal four times—once on a cruise ship and three times in the most interesting way, on my own yacht where I am responsible. Since the fee is based on tonnage, they lose money on yachts as the fee includes the advisor's pay.

We need four line-handlers on board and four links of rope at least 125 feet long. From our close-knit yachting community, we soon have our four volunteers, line-handlers and the additional required rope. The line handlers take their stations, one on each side of the bow and one on each side of the stern. Minutes later, our advisor arrives by water taxi, and we are on our way to an adventure that only a select few yachts experience.

Named one of the Seven Wonders of the Modern World by the American Society of Civil Engineers in 1994, the Panama Canal opened in 1914, 10 years after the U.S. began construction. The French had started to build the canal in the 1880s but had to give up after encountering engineering and financial problems. The canal is 51 miles long and consists of three locks on both the Atlantic and Pacific sides with Gatun Lake in the center. Amazingly the lake provides all the water to raise the level of the locks at both ends.

It's 1987 and we are making the transit center lock, which is unusual because it is not taking maximum advantage of the lock space. Attendants on the lock secure each line and the line handlers take in the line as each of the three sequential Gatun locks fill, lifting us to Gatun Lake. As we enter the lake, we are now sailing some 90 feet above sea level.

The 25 miles across the lake, the longest part of the transit, is clearly marked with buoys and is a time to relax. We stop only for a freshwater swim and to clean our propeller. Then we serve our advisor and crew gourmet sandwiches for lunch. The advisor refuses wine or a tip for his services but the rest of us enjoy a glass of wine. As usual, we do not have enough wind to sail, but our engine is fairly quiet, and we distinctly hear the cacophony of sounds from the jungle as we motor along. It sounds like the roar of tigers, but we suspect it is monkeys. Many areas of the jungle are nature preserves where rare tropical birds nest and where the U.S. astronauts take their jungle training.[9]

Whichever way you are transiting, you start with three up locks that take you to Gatun Lake, cross the lake and then enter the three down locks on the other side. Since the lake is freshwater, some boats spend the night there and clean their bottoms. We never did this.

On our second 1987 transit, we were tied to another yacht with three pairs of yachts behind us in each lock. This kept everyone on their toes. We made another transit tied to a tug and one other with a ship. When you enter the locks with a ship, it finally dawns on you how huge they are in comparison. You feel like a mosquito on the back of a rhinoceros!

There is a world of difference between the cities on the opposite ends of the canal. Panama City, on the Pacific side is sophisticated with excellent restaurants and an international Airport. We felt safe leaving our boat at the Anchorage to go ashore for dinner. In contrast, Colon, on the Atlantic side was the armpit of the world. Dirty, riddled with crime and ugly buildings. The good news was that the Panama Canal yacht club had docks, a decent restaurant and was surrounded by a 12-foot fence with barbed wire at the top. When in Colon, everyone always docked at the yacht club.

One night Betty and I and another couple were returning to the yacht club after dining nearby, as we were walking down the road to the club entrance three men came out of the dark and went after us with knives. We ran for our lives and were fortunately saved when a guard at a storage yard came out and fired his gun in the air, scaring the thieves away. I was the slowest runner, and they were so close that the guard asked me if I had been cut! After that we were even more careful. When I went down that same road in broad daylight to find a taxi for departing friends, I took off my watch and wore only short pants and a T-shirt. I even turned the pockets of the pants inside out so a thief could see I wasn't worth robbing.

Transiting the Panama Canal is exciting and an enjoyable adventure everyone should experience.

Pig Roast

Nick and Robbie at a Pig Roast

The uniqueness is the presentation.

After all the guests had arrived, usually about 20 or so, and we had had a drink or two, we gathered on the lawn by the little house. The beautiful, shimmering golden-skinned pig with an apple in its mouth, cherry eyes, and a lei of daisies around its neck nestling in parsley on my father's handmade platter was presented to our delightfully awed guests.

This exquisite production took skillful construction and master planning, in addition to tending the roasting pig all day. Shortly after my father built his Lake Lotawana cabin, he designed and built a unique barbecue oven on the hill just above it. This was a large structure built out of native stone and wasn't for grilling a few steaks but for serious barbecue. The lowest part was a fire pit that was large enough to hold three or four full-size split logs. The heat and smoke from the logs were funneled through a chimney at the rear of the structure. The smoke and heat traveled under a large open cooking area that had a grate at the bottom to hold the meat while roasting and was lined by glazed tile that gave a smooth, easy to clean surface. As the heat and smoke passed under the cooking area, the amount that was introduced was controlled by two baffles that could be regulated by levers (handles) on the outside. If you wanted more heat, you turned the baffles so they were vertical and if you wanted less, they could be closed so all the smoke went directly up the chimney. The cooking area was approximately 3' x 4', large enough to accommodate a 50-pound pig.

One of the hardest tasks was securing the pig. Pig farmers sell meat by the pound, they do not want to sell a small pig. We dealt directly with the farmer and paid a premium to buy a small pig. The next problem was finding someone to prepare the pig. Most butchers were not concerned with appearance. We wanted a pig with its head still intact, with ears, and no cuts on the skin. We negotiated with the farmer then loaded the live pig in the trunk of our car and delivered him to a butcher who would prepare him to our specifications.

We packed the pig's ears in dough to protect them and propped the mouth open so he could have an apple in his mouth and cherries in his eyes. To slow roast the animal, constantly baste the skin to keep it from cracking and to obtain a good color was an all-day job. Since a 50-pound pig does not have enough meat to feed a large crowd we would cook a couple of large briskets of beef with him and we knew when the briskets were done, the pig was cooked. The tricky part was getting the animal out of the barbecue pit and onto the special serving board in one piece. A cooked pig tends to fall apart. It took two men and careful handling.

"Securing the pig is the hardest part." My sister, Carol, reminded me of the 200-pound pig episode. One year, Walt

Meininger asked my father to roast a pig for a party he was throwing. When Walt brought it, it was a 200-pound pig and much too large for our oven. Walt and my father found a local farmer who would sell a small pig, but they had to catch him. It was winter, frost on the ground, and the pig pen was slippery. They slipped and fell and were covered in barnyard crud, but they captured the pig they wanted.

A pig roast brings to mind a whole pig, the roasting, the eating, the comradery and the festivity. A properly roasted pig is a spectacular sight and well worth all the effort.

Finally, remember that no enormous cooking project will be as simple as you imagine. You see a whole pig, and you imagine the roasting, and the eating, and the joy and camaraderie that goes along with it. But don't forget the transportation, the setup, the fuel management, stray sparks and coal and ash, grease, estimating cooking progress and correcting your schedule, and of course the cleanup.

If you're up for tackling all those challenges this Independence Day and roasting a whole pig—perhaps on a spit! What could go wrong?! — more power to you. This is a free country, after all. But remember that freedom also means the right to turn to your humble household oven, to buy your pig in pieces from a butcher as God intended, to set your dial to 300F and completely nix the chances of turning what should be a happy holiday into an Iraq War-style misadventure. Or, hey, there's always the old, not too complicated standby of the backyard grill, some beers, and some choice beef cuts. But only if you must, patriot.

Robberies

Being robbed hurts—not physically, but from what it does to your pride.—John Boyega

I have had my fair share of robberies. The first one I remember occurred in Chicago. After Robbie and I had packed the car for a trip to Kansas City, we had stopped in downtown Chicago for a late evening snack at the Prudential building. We were walking down the dark street to our parked car when Robbie noticed that someone was messing with it. We both realized at once that we were watching a break-in. It made me furious and without thinking I charged at the thief just as he jimmied the car door open. By good luck, he was no bigger than me and was concentrating on his theft. In my fury I was able to surprise him and knock him to the ground. Then, while he was still disoriented, I shoved him into a nearby telephone booth and held him there while Robbie called the police. It never occurred to me that he might have a gun.

The police were fairly prompt, took our statement, and took the thief into custody. We exchanged information including the name of the prosecuting attorney who would probably be handling our case. The drive to Kansas City was uneventful but the more we talked about the incident the more determined we were to get this guy off the streets so he wouldn't be robbing other people. When we got to Kansas City, we called the prosecutor's office and were very disturbed to learn how our justice system operates. He told us that if this case followed the usual pattern the thief would get a lawyer who would get the judge to give him a postponement if we came back for trial. He would be allowed three postponements so the only way we were going to get justice was to make the thousand mile round-trip to Chicago four times. Losing faith in our justice system, we gave up.

Some years later, Betty and I were robbed three times in one year. The first incident was in Corsica when we were traveling in our VW Pop-Top camper. Being conscious of thievery, we parked our van in a crowded parking lot while we went to lunch. It was a typical Corsican lunch, a very leisurely three-hours with two bottles of excellent wine. We were in great spirits, until we returned to the van and a virtually empty parking lot. Our van had been broken into and my camera case stolen. I was sorry to lose the camera but even sorrier to lose the three precious rolls of undeveloped film shot over the two days we had spent extensively photographing the Benedict home in Cap Ferret. I had hoped to give the pictures to the Benedicts as a thank you for their hospitality.

Later, on that same trip, the van was broken into again, this time while parked on the street in Paris. The thieves took our carry-on bags with our passports and airline tickets. Fortunately, we were not flying back to the states for a couple of days, so we had time to get new passports and tickets. Six months later we were surprised to receive a letter with our tickets from a French lady who, ironically, had found them when her stolen car was recovered.

That winter we suffered our third robbery. We had left Expectation, our 44- foot cutter, at anchor in the bay on the French side of St. Martin while we went ashore for dinner. Expectation was locked up, but sailboats are notoriously easy to break into and the thieves had gotten our expensive binoculars and other electronic gear. There is something unnerving about having your space violated and we were very upset. The next morning, we went to the French police to report the robbery, and, to our astonishment, they had everything in their custody. Apparently, our thieves had left our belongings on the beach while they went to rob another boat. They plundered a huge pile of cash from that boat and took off rather than take the chance of being caught on the beach with our stuff.

Reports of piracy at sea made having a weapon on board seem like a good idea but the problem is you have to declare your weapons at every foreign port or face criminal prosecution. It can be a hassle and a lot of paperwork. My solution was to buy a sawed-off shotgun, paint the stock red and put it in a case in our head with a sign on it "flare gun, for emergency use only." Of course, the shells were real shotgun shells. We never declared it, were never questioned when the boat was inspected, and luckily, never had an occasion where we felt we needed it. Later I acquired a pistol, which we hid under the huge bed in the aft cabin, and we never had to use it either.

Now that I can't see I would be an easy target for thieves. Hercules is a guide dog – not a watchdog – and he would probably lick any thieves that came along just like he does everyone else. Hercules does not have an enemy—he even loves the three cats that live outside our front door.

Swimming with Sharks

Have you ever been nose to nose with a 10-foot hammerhead shark?

The bright, sunny morning became one of thrilling possibilities, when my good friend, Stan Starr, called and proposed we go to the Cocos Islands off the coast of Costa Rica. These islands are known as a gathering place for large hammerhead sharks who congregate there for reasons that no one knows.

Stan owned a 38-foot powerboat that was already in Costa Rica on its way from Panama to the U.S. I suspect I was invited because I am a diver and, one of the cardinal rules of scuba diving is to never dive alone. This is a rule no one wants to break, especially when diving with sharks.
With pounding heart and in high spirits, I accepted Stan's invitation and we headed to Costa Rica. The name of Stan's boat was POSH, which he explained came from the old sailing days when people traveled by square Riggers between England and India. To travel POSH meant that your cabin was on the preferable land side of the ship both ways—port out, starboard home.

When we arrived in Costa Rica, we purchased provisions for the trip, checked the equipment and were off. The seas were high and right on our nose, so the night was a rough one. By morning things had calmed down some and we cooked a hearty breakfast. Our navigation was good, and we were safely anchored off the island by noon the next day.

There are a million things to learn about scuba diving, but just three basic principles are essential: never panic and hold your breath going to the surface, always keep breathing, and never rise faster than your bubbles.

Every scuba diver carries a weight belt, which, theoretically, balances the buoying effect of the scuba tank and your body to create equilibrium in the water. The trick is to achieve the proper balance. If you put on too much weight, you're constantly battling to keep from sinking to the bottom, and if you put on too little weight you are constantly fighting to stay down. A little too much is better than too little. I hadn't been diving for over year, so I had to guess what amount of weight to take. The good thing about weight belts is they come with a quick release so if you need to get to the surface in an emergency, you can instantly drop the belt.

My guess on the amount of weight I needed was close, so I just had a little negative buoyancy. We entered the water together and headed for what looked like a lagoon on the coast of the island. The water was crystal clear, and after a 15-minute swim we spotted the tall dorsal- finned, gray-brown sharks in about 40 feet of water. We headed for them and hoped they weren't hungry!
I vacillated between trepidation and exhilaration as we started our descent to swim with these huge beasts.

Before long we had reached their depth and were swimming alongside them. They ignored us even though we were so close we could have touched them. We decided this was too dangerous, but in retrospect, I regret not touching one. Wouldn't it have been an extraordinary coup to relieve a hammerhead of one of his barnacles?

After 20 minutes or so we headed to the boat. Back on POSH we washed our equipment, put it away and were just opening our first beer when we noticed that we had been joined by a large National Geographic vessel. Apparently, they had come to photograph our sharks. Unfortunately, I was never able to find the program. But that's ok, I swam with our sharks.

Sailing through Life: Ninety-three years of adventure

Wanderlust

To move, to breathe, to fly, to float, to gain all while you give, to roam the roads of lands remote: To travel is to live.
—Hans Christian Andersen

It was a pleasant summer day, and we were jouncing along in our Model A Ford over a rutted section of a dirt highway on our way to the Lake of the Ozarks, 150 miles from our Kansas City home. I could see that we were about to hit a stretch of pavement and I leaned forward in anticipation.

As soon as we were on the paved road Dad sped up and exclaimed, "We're going a mile a minute!"

I remember many such road trips with my parents and Dad always being excited when we hit paved sections of the road. Dad, an expert driver, had built two racing cars from scratch before he was 21.

I must have been born with a passion for travel. My memory bank is full of pictures of traveling with my parents by automobile.

The Model A was replaced by a conventional sedan long before air-conditioning and every one of our cars carried a plastic bag of water tied above the front bumper to refill the radiator, which sometimes overheated and boiled over. No air-conditioning meant driving with the windows open so, by the end of the day, we were so grimy that the first order of business after stopping was a hot shower.

Sailing through Life: Ninety-three years of adventure

One of the longest of our many trips was from Kansas City to Maine. For several days I was dreaming of swimming in the ocean. When we saw the first Maine beach, I raced to the water and dove in. What a shock when I hit that ice-cold water!

The summer I was fifteen, I went on a trip that, in retrospect, changed my life. That summer I traveled with a sailing group from Lake Lotawana, outside Kansas City, to Lake Okoboji, in northern Iowa. We were a pretty ragtag group since this was the first time, we Lotawana sailors had ever traveled with our boats. We were using a crude collection of farm trailers instead of specially designed boat trailers. While we were unloading, a beautiful Chrysler convertible with wood paneled sides, pulled up to watch the unloading. Two of the most beautiful women I've ever seen stepped out of that convertible. One was Robbie Gibbon who, after a lot of ups and downs over the years, became my wife.

The following fall when I was sixteen, I crossed the Atlantic on the Queen Mary to begin my year as an English-speaking Union exchange student at Haileybury College in Hertfordshire England. There were 22 of us exchange students on board. In those days, the Queen Mary was a three-class ship, and we were, of course, assigned to the cheapest, Tourist Class. Our berths were in the bowels of the ship with cabin class level above and the very ritzy first class on the top deck. The stairways had barricades to prevent any upward movement, but they were easily bypassed, and we could pretty much roam the ship at our leisure. I found first class a little stuffy, but the people in Cabin Class seemed to tolerate us when we passed the barricade to visit. We did not take our meals there, but we thoroughly enjoyed their comfortable movie theater and the snacks they served.

My trip back to the USA on the Queen Elizabeth was more of the same except that my confidence had grown, and I spent more time in Cabin Class, where I especially enjoyed the snacks that were served every afternoon.

The British have a more enlightened school vacation policy than we do in the U.S. Our short Christmas and spring breaks allow for a long summer vacation originally intended for the students to have time to help with farm work. For some crazy reason we continue to stick with this silly policy although, I understand, there is some change finally taking place. In England you have almost a month's vacation at Christmas, a month in the spring and about six weeks in the summer. This gives students time to explore the continent during their breaks and their summer holiday is not so long that they have forgotten what school is all about. I am hopeful that American educators are beginning to see the picture.

I wanted to learn to ski so the first place I went on my Christmas holiday was Lauterbrunnen, Switzerland. The leader of our group of ESU exchange students had chosen it because it was reasonable (cheap) however we found that it was not really a ski resort at all but a summer resort with snow. Having been on basically wartime diets in England, we reveled at the food and the goodwill of our hosts though our ski training consisted of doing the herringbone while walking uphill for 30 minutes to snowplow back down to the bottom in three minutes, then to repeat the process. One of our group was hurt one day, wandered down to the railway station and found large groups of skiers heading to higher altitudes and the ski resort of Wengen. The next day we said farewell to our gracious hosts and boarded the train for Wengen. What a different world: charming village with active shops, ski lifts, instructors and, most important of all, GIRLS. It was a delightful place to learn to ski.

Later that same trip I met my father at St. Moritz. He was a good sport and skied with me until, skiing fast and showing off,

I accidentally skied into deep snow and broke my wooden skis. I was lucky not to break my stupid legs. Dad and I decided to hit the beach and headed for Nice, France. What a disappointment. The weather was so cold we had to wear our overcoats. And the beaches were all rocks, not sand. This trip was when my father discovered the French motorized bicycles called VéloSoleX that we rented. Dad was so entranced with them that he secured the exclusive rights to sell them in the USA. Unfortunately, that was one of his unsuccessful ventures as the bikes were a big success with the younger crowd, but the police insisted you had to be sixteen and have a driver's license to ride one even though they were no faster than a regular bike with an enthusiastic rider.

My college travel was pretty routine—spring break visiting Robbie's parents' condominium in Florida and trips to Sioux City to visit her in the summer. I also had the opportunity to travel with my father to his plants in Leicester, England, Paris and Milan and then later to Luxembourg for the opening of the factory he built there to serve the European Union.

Robbie and I went to Europe twice. Betty and George Byers traveled with us on part of both of these trips. On the first one we picked up a Volkswagen van in Rome and drove it north to Paris. I enjoyed the sightseeing but got terribly irritated with Betty because she wanted to explore every cathedral we passed. Many years later, after my divorce and George's death, Betty and I were married and began a life of traveling in earnest spending 8 to 9 months each year cruising the world on our sailboat and later exploring almost full-time in our RVs.

Whale Watching

Nick and baby whale

There is no sight more majestic than seeing a 60,000-pound humpback whale leap clear of the water.

When Betty and I had guests at our Puerto Vallarta home, one of our favorite winter activities was to take them out on Banderas Bay to observe the humpback whales. The best time to hit the water was right after dawn, fortunately, that's about 7:30 a.m. These huge beasts make one of the longest mammal migrations in the world, 6,000 miles. And they are mammals—they breathe, produce live infants that they nurse and are, in every way, gigantic mammals.

The humpbacks that come to our bay have migrated from Alaska to find calm, warm waters to breed and bear their young. We occasionally saw whales sounding from our balcony and nothing was more exciting than to see the spectacle of a huge humpback leaping clear of the water before returning with a gigantic splash. Sometimes the same whale jumped over and over again. No one is sure why the whales put on this performance. Some speculate that it is the males showing off to impress a female, but others claim that they are doing this to rid their body of barnacles. In any case it is one spectacular sight!

We left the marina right at dawn and we almost always encountered a huge pod of dolphins on our way out to the whale grounds. The dolphins always put on a show, surfing right in front and beside our bow—close enough that you could almost reach out and touch them. The dolphin show was enough for a great day in itself! But we had come to see whales and there was no telling where they might turn up.

Because whales are mammals they must surface occasionally to breathe, so we looked for the spout of water from their blowhole. A special thrill was seeing a mother with a newborn calf at her side. Mothers with calves seldom left the water like the huge males. The secret was to be close enough for a great view but not too close to disturb the whales. For some reason they liked to perform in the early part of the morning and by 10 a.m. the show would be almost over.

Interestingly, the scientists tell us that the humpbacks in the bay do not eat while they are there. Humpbacks have no teeth but take in their food of plankton and small fish by filtering tons of water through their baleen, a kind of filter in their mouth. They are not aggressive and there are rare reports of them defending a swimmer from a shark attack using their huge flippers as weapons.

We frequently saw huge manta rays lying on the surface. We could approach fairly close before they would dive and occasionally, we saw one leap clear of the water. Were they doing this for the same reason as the whales? On rare occasions we ran across a pod of eight or 10 spectacularly beautiful killer whales. Killer whales are not whales at all but are a type of dolphin that kill their prey by ramming into it.

One summer when I chartered a cabin cruiser to explore Alaskan waters with my grandchildren, we came across a group of about 20 humpbacks, each the size of a school bus, working together for a meal. They were on the surface in a circle thrashing and blowing air from their blowholes. They continually made the circle smaller and smaller as they concentrated the krill until they finally broke into a concerted mass to feed. It was a singular demonstration of animal cooperation.

A completely different whale experience was the two times we took my Pilatus airplane to the coast of Baja California where the gray whales come to the lagoons to breed and have their young. The Pilatus with its unusually low landing speed is the perfect plane to land at the small dirt strips close to the lagoons. We would land and hire a Pongo, (small outboard motorboat) and go out on the lagoon to get very up close and personal with the gray whales. They had no fear of the boats, probably because the boats were of no danger to them. Sometimes a young whale would come right up to the boat and let us pat him while his mother watched from 20 to 30 yards away like a mother would watch her child at a playground. Someone took a picture of me rubbing the tongue of a baby whale. Just ask, I will show you. I still carry that picture in my wallet.

Sailing through Life: Ninety-three years of adventure

WATER, AIR, AND LAND

Water

No pessimist ever discovered the secrets of the stars, or sailed to an uncharted land, or opened a new heaven to the human spirit.
—Helen Keller

In my sailing career I've been wet, tired, and even a little scared, but I've loved every minute of it. All my life I have been good at sports, but never great. Sailing is the one possible exception. I wouldn't call what I've accomplished "great"—but maybe "pretty good."

A word about sailing terms. A regatta is a series of sailboat races usually held over several days. A class is a type of sailboat that conforms to certain dimensions and weight restrictions, which theoretically means that all boats in one class are the same. I grew up sailing the "C" class, which is the smallest type of scow boat. I always believed in one design sailing because if the boats were identical, the outcome of the race was primarily dependent on the skill of the sailor.

If I were to be left to my own devices, I would choose to sail a Laser or a Finn, which are single handed boats. You don't have to depend on anyone else for decisions – it is all on you.

Sailing through Life: Ninety-three years of adventure

The Beginning of My Sailing Days

Childhood on Lake Lotawana

> *There is NOTHING, the Water Rat says in The Wind in the Willows, "—absolutely nothing—half so much worth doing as simply messing about in boats."*

I love the excitement and the competition of small boat racing where a lapse of judgment or a slow reaction can cost you five boats in the blink of an eye!

I could swim at 4, run my own little outboard motorboat at 5, and was about 8 when my parents bought me my first sailboat. It was an open cockpit 12-foot catboat (single sail). I wish I had a picture of it. I loved that boat and spent hours learning the fundamentals of sailing.

Unfortunately, it was a type of boat that filled with water if tipped too far in a heavy wind and the only remedy was tow it to a dock, pull it up and empty it. Someone on the lake always saw my plight and phoned the house and Mom got in the outboard and towed me to shore. She was always a good sport about it.

In those days, there were two racing fleets on Lake Lotawana, the Snipes and the C-Scows. Our next-door neighbor, Chuck Schwindler, was one of the Lake's top "C" sailors and I hung around him like a puppy dog. I was dying to crew for Chuck, but my friends said you had to be 16 to crew and that was a long way off. However, when I was 12, my dream came true. Chuck's regular crew was sick, and he asked if I would fill in for a race. Would I! We did well together, and I became his regular crew, winning often. I loved the competition and learned a lot about sailing and life from Chuck.

Chuck was known as "Light-Wind Charlie" for his ability to sniff out the breeze when there was very little wind. Part of that was skill, the other part was that Chuck was a slight man so, between the two of us, we were by far the lightest crew on the lake. If the wind was too strong for the two of us, we took on a third crew and were still competitive.

In one unforgettable race, we were sailing up the lake toward the yacht club and we were a quarter of a mile ahead of the next boat with one more lap to go. We easily had the race won but as we approached the club, we realized that somehow the rounding buoy was missing. We were running out of lake. Bob Peet, the judge, yelled from his boat, "Make your own buoy." So we turned at the place where the buoy should have been and headed downwind. The judges came up behind us and set a temporary buoy for the rest of the fleet.

We were going downwind, more than a quarter mile ahead, when suddenly Chuck said to me, "We're going about." We hardened on the wind and headed back. I couldn't understand what was wrong.

"Chuck, why are we going back? We're going to lose the race!"
"We went around the imaginary buoy the wrong way."

By the time we returned to the temporary buoy, unwound, and headed back downwind we were in sixth place and I was despondent. We had suddenly gone from a quarter mile ahead to a quarter-mile behind. But Chuck wasn't about to give up. It was just our kind of wind, and we started to catch boats, one after the other. On the final windward leg we closed in on the lead boat, which was trying to cover us, but Chuck did two quick tacks right at the finish line and won the race. I can still hear the cheers from the crowd at the yacht club.

Of course, none of them could figure out why we'd gone back. I think they assumed we were just giving the others a chance, but I knew I had witnessed an outstanding example of good sportsmanship.

Learning to Race

Small boats H-12 Cove on Lake Lotawana

We looked like the Beverly Hillbillies with boats. The Lotawana "C" Fleet felt they were pretty hot, but they'd never really competed with the fleets on any other lakes. In 1946 the group decided to make the 350-mile trip to Lake Okoboji in northern Iowa to see how we would fare against another fleet. Since none of the boats had traveled, we didn't have proper trailers. Some were hauled on farm trailers that repeatedly broke. I don't recall everyone who went but I know the group included Dick Dickey, Bill Linscott, Joe Birmingham, Bill Wicker and several others. We took five boats total.

The Okoboji group couldn't have been more hospitable. They didn't laugh at our crude trailers nor what were, in fact, our crude boats.

Back then, we kept our boats in the water, which made them heavy and required constant cleaning to keep the slime off the bottom. At Okoboji, they sailed their boats dry. In other words, they took them out of the water on a lift after every race. We were also a little more interested in comfort. Our boats had floorboards and metal lined drawers to hold the ice and beer. No one was concerned about weight.

It was a fun weekend but to say that we stunk up the sailing course is putting it mildly. The Okoboji sailors, including Jerry Huse and Bob Schneider, left us in the dust. They were better sailors and they had far better equipment.

We only had three or four trailer breakdowns on the way home, but we certainly had our tails between our legs. Actually, it was the best thing that ever happened to Lotawana sailing because we found out how bad we were and how far we had to go in order to compete in the big world of sailing. From then on people started buying lifts to take their boats out of the water, reading sailing books, and, more importantly, competing with other lakes.

I was head over heels in love with sailing. Occasionally Chuck let me borrow his boat for a race and I was able to do well. I was dying to get a boat of my own but there was no money.

At that time, everyone on Lotawana sailed Johnson sailboats, which were made in White Bear Lake, Minnesota. When we went to regattas, (a regatta is a series of races over several days), we found there was another brand of boat, the Melges.

I met Harry Melges and his son, Buddy (see my essay on Buddy Melges) at a Wisconsin regatta. I watched Buddy sail what I thought was the most beautiful "C" boat in the world. I had to have one and finally persuaded my parents into it after my freshman year at Northwestern. The boat was named Creeper.

It had a pink deck (my dad called it "Titty Pink"). It was beautiful and it was the first Melges on Lotawana.

Back then, the boats were of wood construction with single-planked bottoms. Leaking was a consistent problem until the wood swelled after the boats were in the water. Johnson solved this by making a double-planked boat that didn't leak but was fairly heavy. I loved my Melges, though, as it was light. So, I was willing to put up with the leaking problem.

Each lake had a letter designation for the sails. Okoboji was P and Lotawana was MO. My sail number was MO-3. Creeper and I did well right from the start. My two major nemeses during the early years were Bill Linscott and Joe Jack Merriman among some other good sailors on the lake.

During summer vacations from Northwestern, I competed in the local races and tried to go to as many regattas as possible. Paul Koontz, home on vacation from Princeton, was my regular crew. Paul drove out from Kansas City every Saturday afternoon and Sunday morning to race, and he went to a number of regattas with me.

I'll never forget when Paul and I competed in the embarrassing regatta at Lake Geneva, Wisconsin. It was embarrassing because the Lake Geneva sailors were excellent. Not only did we not win, I was embarrassed to be beaten for the first time by a girl! Jane Pagel was one tough sailor.

On the way back we stopped at the S.A.E. house at Northwestern for a free night's lodging. I wanted Paul to see some of the seedier nightlife in the Chicago area, so I took him to Calumet City. As we walked in the door, an experienced Nick told Paul, "I'm going to the men's room, but while I'm gone, don't buy anyone drinks." I wasn't gone ten minutes, only to find Paul with a topless performer on his lap. She had about five drinks lined up in front of her. Paul was trying to find out why a nice young girl like Cindy was into that line of work. There are some things they didn't teach you at Princeton.

That summer, with Paul's excellent crewing, we won both the Saturday and the Sunday series as well as the Labor Day regatta. And, yes, more and more Melges boats started appearing on Lake Lotawana.

Winter Sailing—
Frostbite and Freez'n Fun

Iceboats on Lake Lotawana

"Cold! If the thermometer had been an inch longer we'd all have frozen to death." —Mark Twain and I, Opie Read

Summer sailing season just wasn't long enough! In the early 60s, my great friend, Lee Lyon, and I organized "frostbite sailing." Each winter, we left a fleet of Butterfly sailboats at the Lotawana Yacht Club and every Sunday morning for three winters, no matter the weather, a group of seven or eight of us drove out from Kansas City together, rigged the boats, and sailed a series of short races, followed by liquid libation if our hands weren't too numb to hold a drink. I remember one winter we never missed a weekend. A few times we broke thin ice to sail, but we got the job done.

We had some great competitive sailing. Of course, there was the danger of tipping over and ending up in the freezing water but, to the best of my knowledge, that never happened in these races. On a good Sunday, we could get in six or seven races. Because we sailed short races, we got the thrill of the start and the excitement of close-passing competitors more frequently than normal.

A typical sailboat race would be started by a committee boat, the boat where the members of the organizing committee watch and judge the race, setting a starting line between itself and a buoy that marks the other end of the line. A gun would be fired 10 minutes prior to the start, then five minutes and finally the starting gun. Everyone wanted to be as close to the starting line as possible when the final gun sounded without being over the line.

If you jump the gun you had to go around the buoy and start over again, which meant you started last. We did not have the luxury of a committee, so we used what is called a rabbit start. In a rabbit start, one boat is designated the rabbit and crosses all the other boats in the fleet on port tack. They try to cross behind him as close as possible on starboard tack and, when the last boat has crossed the race is on.

It can get cold in Missouri. When the lake froze, we went ice boating. My boat, Freez'n Fun, was all black. On a good day I could hit 60 miles per hour. When you're in the open wind and only six inches above the ice, 60 mph feels like the speed of light.

The days of great ice boating were few and far between as the conditions had to be just right. Not only must the lake be frozen solid, there couldn't be too much snow on the ice, and there had to be enough wind. However, when it is good there isn't anything more exciting. I can still hear the chatter of the ice boat runners digging into the ice.

Ice boating is much better on the northern lakes, where they have organized racing. The big boys have been known to hit 100! We raced a little, but the boats were all so different that it really wasn't a race at all, still skimming across the ice at high speed is a thrill that I will always remember.

In addition to racing, we did drive our cars on the lake when it was really solid. One guy hit a thin patch of ice and his car fell through and he had to be rescued. You want that done quickly, as a man does not last long in 30° water. He was rescued, but how did he explain that loss to his insurance company?

When I was young, my family would occasionally stay at the lake house overnight during the winter. But, since the house got very little use during the colder months, the pipes were drained. This meant that in order to flush toilets we had to chop a hole in the ice, fill up buckets with water, and carry them up the hill. You really notice how much water is used when you have to do it that way. We had a rule that there was no flushing until something serious was deposited in the toilet.

There wasn't a furnace, but my father solved that issue by building an airspace next to the fireplace flue that used a fan to pump hot air into the bedrooms. We were fairly comfortable even when the temperatures were near zero outside. And, when conditions were right, the ice-skating was phenomenal.

What a pleasure it would be to return to those heady days!

Racing Days

Nick and Robbie

While we all love the sensation of connecting a series of perfect tacks and jibes, it's the people we sail with what's most important. Our relationships are those upon which the sport is built...—Bill Buchholz (US-3314)

Total blind luck, but I can boast that I only sailed one Star boat race in my life and I won it.

After graduating from Northwestern, I went to work for my father in the Chicago area selling construction equipment. There was no place close to sail a "C" boat. Rather than give up sailing, I signed on to crew for Dick Stearns, one of the top Star sailors in the United States. I'd have to check the records, but I believe Dick had won the World Championship a year or so before and winning the World in the Stars (an Olympic Class) is a very big deal. I think The Star is one of the most beautiful sailboats built, and because it is a keelboat it can handle any weather.

We sailed out of Wilmette Harbor where there was a hot fleet, traveling to local regattas. Competition was tough but we were usually first and never worse than third.

Dick called one Sunday. "I can't make the race today. You go ahead and take the boat. Good luck."

This was the first time I'd ever skippered a Star in competition. There was a big wind shift on the first weather leg, which I caught just right, and from then on, the race was a series of broad reaches, so it was easy for me to defend my lead and I had a lucky win.

When Robbie and I moved back to Kansas City all our weekends and vacations were taken up with sailing. By this time, the Lotawana fleet had a number of good sailors including Dwight Westholt, Lee Lyon and Fritz Rudabush. We joined the Inland Lake Yachting Association and traveled to regattas all over the Midwest. We even started a fall regatta of our own on Lotawana and attracted top sailors from all over the Inland. Buddy Melges (later Mallory Cup Winner, Olympic Champion, America's Cup Winner) was a frequent visitor who stayed at our house.

Robbie was my crew and, when the wind was high, we took on various third crews, including Betty "Buckets" Byers, who lived next door with her husband George and their kids, Jeni and George. A great camaraderie developed between the sailors from various lakes where the regattas were held. If we went to

Okoboji, we stayed with the Huse. If we went to Minnetonka, we stayed with the Hurds and so it went. Since none of us had any money, it made economic sense and we developed lasting friendships.

Traveling to regattas was time consuming. I was occasionally able to talk Robbie into driving and towing the boat; then I could fly to meet her and get an extra day at work. That all ended with a regatta at Lake Maxinkuckee in Indiana when a wheel came off the trailer 150 miles from the lake. She left the trailer and the boat at a filling station and met my plane more than a little distressed.

Since we had come all this way and didn't want to miss the regatta, I borrowed a trailer and spent the night going back to retrieve our boat. Bleary-eyed from no sleep, I was back at the launching pad the next morning where I managed to add to the calamity and dropped the contents of our drawer into 30 feet of water losing our stopwatches, tools, etc. On top of that I didn't sail well so it was a complete disaster.

I worked harder at it than most during my sailing years at Lotawana and won my share of club championships and local regattas. At the national level, I didn't do so well. I finished near the top in several Inland regattas, including the biggest one of the summer, but a win eluded me. We did manage to win two Inter-Lake championships, which was the next best level of competition.

Those were extraordinary years of competition and companionship.

Big Butterfly

Lee Lyon, left, preparing the mast and centerboard

"Big boats get the glory, but the dingy makes the sailor."
— From the movie, "Wind"

From the time I was born, our family spent much of our summers at Lake Lotawana, a beautiful man-made lake located about 30 miles east of Kansas City. I loved the sport of sailing, and it was probably the only sport that I ever pursued successfully. The most popular boat on the lake at that time was the C scow, a 20-foot catboat that was sailed by a crew of two or occasionally three in heavy weather.

When our kids approached sailing age, I wanted to pass on my love of the sport to them. A "C" boat was too much for small kids to handle and the X boat, which was the typical training boat on other lakes, was clunkily designed and not a scow at all.

I set my mind on finding a boat that would be a better trainer for kids who were going to grow up to become scow sailors. A friend told me about the Butterfly, a miniature, 12-foot version of a "C" boat.

Although an adult can sail a Butterfly single-handed, the national rules required a crew of two or more and a 250-pound minimum crew weight. There was no one selling Butterflies in the Kansas City area and, even though I was not in the boat business, I managed to become the local dealer. I was not in it for the money so I sold boats to families around the lake at just over my cost and became known as the Big Butterfly. Lee Lyon, my co-conspirator in the training, was called The Little Butterfly.

Every Saturday, we held sailing classes for the kids on our Lake Lotawana lawn at H-12. We would usually start with a one-half hour of ground school, then put the kids into the boats to learn how to turn them over and right them so they felt comfortable and safe in their boats. We then ran a series of short races to help teach them sailing techniques and the rules.

I had a special trailer built to pick up the boats at the factory and to go to regattas. The trailer held three Butterflies with all the masts and booms on a top rack. We could get an additional two boats on top of the car if necessary. Two adults can pick up a Butterfly and move it around (each weighed 150 pounds) but it took a bunch of ten–to–twelve-year-olds to do the job. Those kids were determined and would swarm underneath a boat like ants and carry it to wherever it needed to go.

It hadn't been long after the Butterfly Fleet was established when I decided to try a competition. Lee and I hauled a bunch of kids and boats to the National Butterfly Championship at Wauconda, Illinois, in the early fall of 1966. With my son, eight-year-old Jeff, as crew, I competed and won my first national championship.

Low points won, and I finished 3-1-1-3-1 for a total of 11.4 points. Dick Meyers of Oshkosh, Wisconsin was second with 57.4, Lee Lyon was seventh with 79 and Dwight Westholt from Lottawana was tenth with 105.7. Being a modest guy, I don't want to dwell on the point spread between me and the second-place guy. But it was 46 points!

Jeff and I won the Nationals at Lotawana in 1967, and three more championships followed, the last being on Lake Ruedi after we had moved to Aspen.

The Butterfly Championships in the Midwest drew over 100 boats, but we thought the fleet of 67 that came all the way West to Ruedi was great—by far the largest single sailing fleet that's ever been on that lake.

I thought we were going to lose that championship as we had tough competition and there were just a few points separating the top three boats. The final race started in very light air and Jeff and I were well back in the fleet—somewhere around 25th place—when we got to the last windward mark. There was an offset buoy about 150 yards away before the boats headed downwind to the finish. Normally you would turn at the mark and head directly for the offset. Knowing Ruedi and its fickle winds, I looked up toward the dam and saw a breeze coming in.

So instead of tacking, I kept sailing towards the dam. I caught that breeze first and went from 25th to 1st place in a matter of a couple hundred yards. When the wind piped in, Jeff and I were tough to beat. We went on to win the race and the regatta.

That was the last time I sailed a Butterfly, the last race I would sail on Ruedi, and a happy end of my sailboat racing career.

National Racing

One summer I said to Lee Lyon, "I have an idea."

Scow sailing was pretty much confined to the Midwest. There were four different classes: C, D, E, and A. The scow sailors in our region were probably as good as any in the country but I had a craving for the "big-time."

A shadow passed across Lee's face, and he replied, "Uh-uh, not me. Find someone else. My toes are still frozen from last winter."

"But Lee, you're the man for the job. We have to go to the Finn National Championships."

"That's an Olympic class!"

"Yes, and we're going to do it."

Actually, Lee is an avid sportsman, so once I planted the seed, I just waited for it to grow. Lee agreed to charter some Finns and tackle the competition.

A Finn is a single-handed boat (no crew), and it's a lot to handle, especially off the wind. In heavy air you might wear five sweatshirts under your lifejacket and dunk yourself in the water to get them wet. The process would add 20 pounds or more of weight, enough to give you some good leverage. I remember one of the Finn National Champions saying to me "the fatter the head the faster the boat."

Lee and I practiced on the lake all summer and went to a couple of small regattas where we did fairly well. The eliminations for the Nationals were on Lake Lanier, outside Atlanta, and that's where we met the big boys. To make things even, everyone switched boats after each race.

This was rugged sailing made worse by a series of thunderstorms that were passing through the area that weekend. As a storm would pass, the wind would get completely out of control and we would stand, holding our boats chest deep in the water, for as long as an hour until the wind became "sailable" again.

I was holding my own until the wind really came up on the last day. I used a hiking stick to steer, with everything but the calves of our legs hanging outside the boat. On that last day I broke my hiking stick, turned over, and finished "just out of the money" for the Nationals. I decided to save my hiking stick for the mountains.

My other adventure into National sailing was in the Laser class, another highly competitive (Olympic) single-handled fleet. Lee couldn't resist when I told him I had chartered boats and we were going to sail in the National Championship in San Diego. We brought our wives, registered at the Coronado Hotel and hitchhiked down the beach where more than a hundred sailors were preparing for the regatta. It was the big-time and these guys were good.

The funny thing is we were always picked up by the first car when hitchhiking. This surprised us so we finally asked a navy noncom in a VW why he had stopped for us. He said, "I just wondered where two old duffers in funny hats, shorts, and carrying big yellow duffle bags could possibly be going."

This Championship was just before I underwent my first cataract surgery, and my eyesight was terrible. Nothing like Mr. Magoo on the racecourse!

The wind was unbelievable. There was just a spit of land between the bay and the ocean so it was like sailing in the ocean without waves, although they could build up in time. The wind was usually fairly light to moderate in the morning but would pipe up strong in the afternoon.

After the first day they split the fleet into the Gold Fleet and Bronze Fleet, based on that day's results. I made the Gold Fleet! I was good in light to medium air and did well to windward in heavy air. I recall one race where I rounded the weather mark in second or third place and by the time, we finished the reaching leg I was fifteenth! Were those guys ever fast on the reach.

If I remember correctly, I finished in the low 20s. We had a great time, though, and it was a wonderful introduction to laser sailing, which I always enjoyed. When we moved to Aspen, I introduced laser sailing to Ruedi and eventually gave two lasers to the Ruedi Yacht Club that they are still using today.

Ocean Racing

Ocean racing is like standing in a cold, saltwater shower tearing up $100 bills!

It's day two of sailing nonstop in a speeding boat pounding wave after wave, and the reality of ocean racing conditions has set in: sleep deprivation, always wet, physical exhaustion, fear, no hot meals, no privacy, stuck on board. This is not one design racing.

My good friend, Jim Briggs, had invited me to join his crew to race in the SORC (Southern Ocean Racing Circuit.) Jim sailed a 44-foot sloop, Yahoo, that had been competing successfully in ocean races for several years. I was in my twenties and had been racing small one-design boats successfully for five years and I was eager to find out what the other part of the sailboat racing world was like.

I met Jim and the rest of his crew in Miami for the first race of that winter's series, the Miami to Bimini race. There were seven of us, although three men could handle the boat in most conditions. The additional crew members allowed those off-duty to get some rest as the race lasted for days, not hours. Three, or occasionally four, crew members would be on deck for a three-hour watch while the rest tried to get some sleep. But sleep was not easy when you were still soaking wet from you last watch and the boat was pitching with every wave. And, you always had to be ready to scramble topside for a sail change or other emergency. It's still 24/7.

Twenty large sailboats jockeying to be the first to cross the line when the gun sounded was the most thrilling part of the three-day race for me. I felt honored when Jim had me take the helm for the start of the race. He knew I was known for my good starts in one design sailing. Maneuvering a 44-foot boat is completely different, but I managed to get us a decent start.

Within two hours I realized how meaningless the start actually is in a race that lasts for several days. The fleet had separated so much that only four other boats were in sight. By nightfall we could not see the lights of any boat. What a contrast to one design sailing where a long race might last three-and-one-half hours and you could always see your competitors and knew exactly how you were doing against the rest of the fleet.

That is not to say that ocean racing is easy. The crew, often sleep-deprived, is constantly working to adjust the sails for maximum speed in shifting winds, and the skipper is working hard to lay a course that will take maximum benefit of the currents and anticipated changes in the weather.

But, when it is all said and done, a yacht design for light winds really does not have a chance if it is blowing hard for most of the race and the boat designed for heavy winds has little chance if the winds are light.

By the time we were approaching Bimini the winds had picked up to 30 mph with higher gusts, the seas were rough and everything in the boat was wet. As Jim maneuvered Yahoo across the finish line and then through the narrow channel to the docks, I had a moment of apprehension.

We had finished a respectable third in a fleet of 20.

There had been no time for anyone to prepare a real meal during the race. We had existed on sandwiches and fruit juice. Once we had the sails stowed and we were securely tied up to the dock, the whiskey came out and I experienced one of the legendary ocean sailing celebrations firsthand. In the afterglow of strenuous physical effort and teamwork, we began exchanging jokes and telling sailing stories. What a fantastic party, but I decided this was my first and my last ocean race.

The Missouri Yacht Club

Missouri Yacht Club

A "yacht" club in name only, the original Missouri Yacht Club was located in Kansas City. It was on the Missouri River at the foot of Main Street and the members were powerboaters who enjoyed cruising the river. The Missouri was muddy, subject to flooding and not terribly interesting. After a while membership dropped and the club was virtually abandoned.

With a vision for a yacht club, Neligh Coates and Candy Houston, who were among the first to build homes on the newly formed Lake Lotawana, organized a small group of Lake residents to explore the idea. There was much contention among the group, mostly financial. Some wanted to do everything on the cheap while others wanted a more elaborate club. Finally, the founding group agreed to go ahead, rented an abandoned farmhouse on lakeside property and did minor repairs. The newly formed Missouri Yacht Club hired Mr. and Mrs. Queen to be the managers/cooks.

Kerplink! Kerplunk! Splash! Shortly after the Club opened, it rained. The roof was leaking like a sieve right on the fried chicken and mashed potatoes. The Coateses, the Houstons and two other guests were soaking wet. Mopping up couldn't handle the amount of water pouring from the ceiling. The only solution was to drill holes in the floor and allow the water to run out. That was the night a decision was made to build a real clubhouse.

The budget was set at $50,000 and the original clubhouse, which essentially was the same as exists today, was completed for $46,000. Neligh Coates was the first Commodore and, many years later, I was also Commodore.

As Commodore, I was the guy in charge. The problems were similar to restaurant ownership, cleanliness and quality of food. I had to act as the go-between the members and the staff and the members were not always reasonable. The fried chicken was too dry or cold. Mashed potatoes were lumpy or too salty. It was impossible to please everyone.

I drew great satisfaction from knowing that most of the members were happy with the club and appreciated how hard the staff worked.

And the sailboat races! The time a race took depended upon the length of the course the committee set and the wind velocity. A race might be as short as one-and-one-half hours and as long as three hours. The summers in Missouri are sweltering hot and the sailors worked up a good sweat. Nothing tasted better than a nice cold beer after two or more hours of concentrating on getting the best out of your sailboat and making the right tactical decisions during the race.

When I was racing there were two classes of boat races at the same time, although they were started 10 minutes apart. The faster C class race started first followed by the slower Snipe class. Occasionally, the judges made the Snipe course shorter, and the Snipe races would finish first.

The races always ended at the club. Those people interested in the races watched from their powerboats and then, in a leisurely mood, congregated on the lawn in front of the clubhouse to watch the sailboats battle for positions at the finish.

After the race, the sailboats were tied up at the dock, while the sailors with a beer in hand, discussed the tactics of the sailboats during the race. The sound of laughter bubbled up through the mood of community.

Boats and Ships

I have been fortunate to have boats of all kinds and sizes in my life. It all started on Lake Lotawana, a man-made lake thirty miles east of Kansas City. While I was growing up, my family spent a lot of time there during the summers.

There are hundreds of types of boats, all of which can be classified as powerboats, sailboats or ships. I've enjoyed many experiences on all kinds of boats but if I had to pick a favorite it would be sailboats. I spent some of the finest, most exciting times of my life on them. But I've always been happy to spend time on the water, regardless of the vessel.

Powerboats

My first boat was an aluminum outboard that had a 5 hp motor.
The Kansas City Star ran an article on me operating it when I was five years old, along with pictures of me riding a surfboard and swimming. As I got older, I graduated to a 9-1/2 hp motor on the same boat. This motor was just powerful enough that if you got the boat real flat in the water it would plane, which meant the speed would more than double.

Eventually my parents bought a Century twenty-foot inboard. It had a wood hull and a beautifully varnished mahogany deck. These boats were truly a work of art but the wood planked bottom would shrink if it was left out of the water for an extended period of time and would leak like a sieve when put back in, so to keep from sinking it had to be pumped until the bottom planks swelled shut again. It also had to be covered when not in use to protect it from rain and sun damage. I wish we had put that boat in storage; it would be a classic worth a lot of money today. My parents later bought a fiberglass version of the same boat which, while not nearly as striking, was pretty much maintenance-free.

Around that time my father brought Skippy to the lake. Skippy was the boat he had built as a young man for use on the Missouri River in Kansas City. She was fast with a 50 hp outboard motor but not a good ski boat and required constant maintenance. Dad soon determined that Skippy was no longer practical, so she was permanently retired.

The year my twin sisters were born my parents bought a 36-foot cruising boat they called The Carol Jean, named after my sisters, which they used to entertain business associates on the Lake of the Ozarks. It was not fast but a very comfortable boat with a galley, excellent berth for sleeping, and lots of deck space for sunning. In those days you could cruise for an hour and only see one or two other boats. Later, the lake became popular and small boats buzzed around like mosquitoes.

In the mid-1960s, a new fad developed on Lake Lotawana—the float boat. They were large floating platforms built on two pontoons, powered by an outboard motor that was remote controlled by a console in the middle of the platform. They were great for getting around the lake and could accommodate ten to twelve adults comfortably on easily stored folding chairs.

My father decided to buy one but, being Neligh Coates, he had to go one step further. The Coates's float boat had a bright yellow and white canopy, nice indoor-outdoor carpeting, a barbecue, a bar, and geraniums in hanging baskets. The only problem was that Dad would sometimes get oblivious to his surroundings and interfere with some of the boats while watching the Sunday sailboat races.

The first powerboat I owned as an adult was a gift to Robbie and me from our good friend, Jim Briggs. Jim was Vice President of Outboard Marine, the manufacturer of both Evinrude and Johnson outboard motors. They decided to experiment with getting into the boat business. Jim sent us one of the experiment models of their first product, a fiberglass inboard/outboard boat, to evaluate. We used it at the lake and eventually tried to return it but Outboard Marine had decided against going into production so Jim told us to keep it—a very nice gift! When we moved to Aspen we towed that boat over unpaved Independence Pass, which had no guardrails at the time. It was a hair-raising adventure. We also towed that boat all the way from Aspen to Baja, California (see my essay titled "Baja Adventures" for that story).

I went in on a fourth interest in a powerboat called The Aspen Four. It was a 26-foot inboard/outboard based at Lake Powell. It was a perfect lake boat. It had a small galley, a forward sleeping birth, and a huge upholstered rear platform that made for a great outside sleeping area. It was fast enough to explore the lake and small enough to go down the canyons where the canyon walls were 75 to 100 feet straight up on both sides.

The final powerboat worth mentioning is the catamaran we purchased in California and towed to Puerto Vallarta. It was the perfect boat for whale watching because it was fast, with twin 60 hp outboard motors, and extremely stable because of its catamaran hull. Typically, the problem with whale watching is that when a whale is spotted everyone rushes to the side to get a close look at the beast, but a catamaran can handle that without any danger of swamping.

Sailboats

When I was about 10 years old, my parents bought me my first sailboat. It was a dinghy that taught me the art of sailing. It was a good boat to learn with except that if you let it tip too far in a good wind it would fill with water and would then have to be towed to a dock to be emptied out. On Lake Lotawana, this involved someone ashore calling my mother, who would come with the motorboat to the rescue. A real pain in the ass for her, but she was always a good sport.

Before too long I became fascinated with competitive sailboat racing. The boat of choice on our lake was the C class Inland Lake Scow, the smallest class of Lake Scow. This class had been developed in the late 1800s for use in the sheltered waters of the Midwest Lakes. Scows are flat bottom boats and instead of centerboards they have Lee boards on each side of the hull; essentially it is like having two hulls. This type of boat is sailed slightly heeled over so the lower bilge board acts like a centerboard. Being light, scows are extremely fast but they are not made for big waves. I had several C boats throughout my life. The first was called Creeper, another was Fim de Mundo, named after a bar in Estoril, Portugal where Robbie and I had some wild nights and even met the future King of Spain.

The boat that meant as much to me as any was the Butterfly. I discovered the Butterfly when looking for the perfect training boat to teach my kids how to sail. In those days, Midwest youngsters were trained in what was called an X boat. The X boat was not a scow at all, but rather a sort of lumbering sloop. It was a terrible training boat, especially for future scow sailors. When I learned about the Butterfly, a fiberglass 12-foot C boat, I made a deal to be the Kansas City area dealer and started selling boats at just over cost to get a local fleet developed. It turned out to be the perfect choice and before long we had a fleet of twelve Butterflies on Lake Lotawana. I had a special trailer made that would carry three boats. With the trailer and two boats on top of my car I could bring back five at once from the factory.

Sailing through Life: Ninety-three years of adventure

My good friend, Lee Lyon, and I would gather all the kids on my lawn every Saturday morning for ground training and then put the kids in their boats to teach them the fundamentals of racing. My daughters each had one; Candie's was called The Red Baron and Kim's was called Snoopy. The kids were good learners and some of them became top sailors in several classes.

Lee and I took the boats and kids to regattas all over the Midwest. Butterfly racing rules required a crew of two and a minimum of 150 pounds. Although at Lake Lotawana, the Butterfly was primarily a training boat for kids, at many of the other lakes Butterflies were mainly sailed by adults. So I started competing and won five national championships, usually in fleets of 50 to 75 boats. There was a tradition that the national champion could pick the site of the next regatta. I won the national championship at Lake Lotawana just before moving to Aspen, so I was able to designate Lake Ruedi, about 40 miles east of Aspen, for the following year. That year I sailed and won my final national championship.

When I moved to Aspen a group of men met to organize the Aspen Yacht Club. Everyone had their own opinion, but I strongly believed we should all sail the same boat, even if it was a bathtub, so that we could have real competition. Lefty Brinkman had a dealership for the Skipjack class so a bunch of us bought those. Bad choice! I hated that boat so much; it was eventually the reason I got out of sailboat racing altogether. A group of us went to one regatta on the James River in Virginia and I took Lee Lyon as crew. It was a great trip and we met some interesting people but screwed up on the racecourse and finished second.

Lee Lyon and I had some adventures in other classes. One year we decided to try for the Olympic team in the Finn class, a single-handed boat and a real brute in high winds. To get more weight out when the winds blew, we would wear as many as four sweatshirts which we dipped in the water to give us an extra 50 or 60 pounds of ballast. Fortunately, the class required everyone to wear a life vest.

Lee and I did well enough in the regionals in Illinois to qualify for the semifinals in Atlanta. That's where we met some real pros and experienced some thrilling sailing when thunderstorms came through. We both did okay but didn't quite make it to the finals.
Another year I chartered two Laser class boats to sail in the national championship in San Diego. Lee and I sailed in a bay on Coronado Island, which was only separated from the ocean by 150 feet of sand. That was some of the finest sailing I have ever experienced. A fairly mild wind would come off the ocean in the morning, then as the sun heated the sand, the wind would increase yet remained constant so you didn't have to play the wind shifts at all. We were competing against some of the top sailors in the country and I could hold my own against them on the windward leg but when we went off in a reach these guys could fly. I would go from second or third at the windward mark and eight boats would pass me on the reaching leg. It was great sailing, but we didn't finish in the money.

Next was the Morgan Out Island 41. Betty and I purchased it with Barbara and Carson Bell. The Morgan was part of a charter fleet based in St. Thomas, US Virgin Islands. Usually these charter boats were restricted to the Virgin Islands so, knowing we would get bored sailing only the Virgins, we made a special deal which allowed us to sail it anywhere in the Caribbean during our annual month of use (see essay XX).

My final boat was a Peterson 44 called The Sea Nymph. It was the perfect cruising boat for two people. Betty and I had originally purchased a small interest in it. Being a partnership boat with several partners who were not sailors, The Sea Nymph was not well maintained, so every time we used her, we had maintenance problems. However, she served as our introduction to the cruising life, and we loved it! It had a very comfortable center cockpit with benches on both sides that were long enough for an adult to sleep on, when necessary, a huge aft cabin with a comfortable king-size bed and head (bathroom), a nice galley with a huge refrigerator/freezer, a comfortable lounge area and a very comfortable forward cabin for guests. The Peterson 44 had originally been designed as a racing boat, so it was fast and a great boat to sail.

When two of the partners dropped out, we started looking to buy our own cruising boat. We hired a yacht broker, went to boat shows, and even went to Europe to look at the Bowman 57, which sounded like a good deal. After ten minutes on the boat, we knew it wasn't for us. So, we decided to purchase the other half interest in The Sea Nymph, had it totally refitted and updated, and renamed it Expectation.

We started spending more and more time cruising and ended up having twelve great years of adventures on Expectation. We would pick it up each fall and cruise a different area of Mexico or the Caribbean for seven or eight months, then leave her at a different port for the summer. We were fortunate to be able to hire Deloris and Lynn Bolkan (see my essay on the Bolkans on page XX) to arrive at wherever Expectation had been left the previous spring to add any new electronics we had bought and get her in top shape so we could arrive and start comfortably on another season of cruising.

Over the years, people would always ask about the storms we encountered and the dangers from pirates and other hazards. To me, the hard part about cruising was not the sailing but the maintenance and repair of the engine, the refrigeration system, the windlass and all the other mechanical systems involved.

Ships

My first experience with a ship was when I boarded the Queen Mary in New York in the fall of 1947 to England to start my year at Haileybury College as an English Speaking Union exchange scholar (more in *My Year in England* essay). The return trip the following spring was on the Queen Elizabeth. I also enjoyed my time on many cruise ships including one voyage from San Francisco to Miami through the Panama Canal. Other delightful cruises were in the Caribbean. I always preferred the medium-size cruise ships—500 to 600 passengers—to the 4000 passenger mammoths.

Cruising

Not For Sissies

Expectation Voyage

The pessimist complains about the wind; the optimist expects it to change; the realist adjusts the sails. —William Arthur Ward

There were challenges and danger and discovery and freedom and the sea and sunsets and hard work and the people.

Water? Look, they have fresh water! It was the days before water makers, so whenever we got to a place where there was fresh water we went ashore in the dinghy, filled our collapsible jerry jugs, hauled them back to the boat, lifted the jugs up onto the deck, and emptied them into our tanks. Then we made another trip or more until the tanks were full. Cruising Mexico, there were small marinas in La Paz and Acapulco, but other than that you were on your own. I'm sure that lifting those heavy 40-to 45-pound water jugs out of the dinghy and onto the deck is the reason I had to have my right shoulder replaced some years later. In our early cruises, sailing in Mexico was anything but luxurious.

Eat out? No restaurants. We cooked three meals a day. Need some groceries, maybe some fresh fruit, and veggies? There were very few grocery stores except in the major ports. Hard to believe? Even Puerto Vallarta only had one grocery. To get groceries, we took the dinghy ashore to a road and then hitchhiked, catching a ride in the back of a pickup truck with maybe 5 or 6 locals, to a village where, if we were lucky, we bought a few vegetables, and, if we were really lucky, we might find paper towels. I remember paper towels were a very precious commodity.

Sailing of the type we were doing was not a sport for sissies, and it wasn't that good on marriages. I can't tell you how many people we met who had left California—one couple without charts, just a road map—with their dream of sailing off into the sunset forever. By the time they had reached Cabo or La Paz, many of them weren't speaking and boats were for sale at bargain prices because the couple had broken up. In some ways it was like a little Peyton Place in that they were also switching partners.

The ones who stuck it out were special and we met many wonderful people who became great friends. Chuck and Doris Mace, retired school teachers, sailed for eight years that I know of, in the heat of Baja without refrigeration. Suzanne and Jim Austin, wonderful sailors on Whisper, could always find dinner with a spear gun. Steve and Nancy Loye had their first baby in San Carlos so she could be a Mexican citizen and then made the long trip to the South Pacific with her before she was old enough to walk. Carlos and Magaly Caprioglio (she a Chilean, and he an Argentinian) were always great fun and such a help whenever things Lynn and his wife, Deloris, had built the biggest sailboat ever built in the state of Oregon, from scratch! The wonderful thing about it was that they didn't know how to sail at the time.

Lynn had worked as a logger and decided that the logging life was not for him. He wanted to immigrate with his family to Australia. They thought the best way to get there was to build a boat and sail there, although they had never sailed.

It took Lynn and Deloris 10 years to build and rig Endless Summer, a 72-foot Ferro cement boat. Lynn had to get a special permit from the U.S. Forrest Service to cut the tree for the mast.

Their work included making the sails, which were beautiful.

When I asked Lynn how he learned to make sails, he replied, "I read a book." I have the greatest admiration for him because I could read every book ever published on sail making and wouldn't be able to do that job. I think Lynn could build a computer from scratch if there was a book on it.

By the time Endless Summer was finished, their kids were grown and had left home so they never made it to Australia. Instead, they headed for Mexico with $25 in their pockets.

That year, Lynn helped us out with a couple of problems, and we became great friends. Eventually a pattern developed: Lynn would meet us in the spring to help put the boat away, and before we headed out in the fall, he would arrive for two weeks to a month early to take care of a list of repairs and additions, do the varnish work, and get the boat in first-class shape. I was getting busier with work, and it was harder and harder to take time off; Lynn and Deloris's help prolonged our sailing days by several years.

In 1987, Betty and I decided to head for Panama. We sailed from Acapulco to Puerto Escondido with our good friend Mary Ann Rivas, where we were met by Patty and Jack Ferguson (Patty is Betty's niece), who were going to sail with us to Costa Rica.

For several years, we'd been hearing horror tales of the Gulf of Tehuantepec, which is the narrowest point of land in Mexico. Storms build up in the Gulf of Mexico and funnel west across the isthmus, building up huge winds. Because the Gulf of Tehuantepec is shallow, the waves can be tremendous. We kept meeting boats that had come all the way from California but were turning back because they had taken such a beating in the gulf.

On one boat, the skipper had gone nuts and had to be locked in his cabin by the crew. Another boat we met had been sandblasted by sand coming off the beach, and there wasn't a bit of varnish or paint left on her. In Panama, we heard of a boat that was swamped in the Gulf and the crew of three had to abandon ship in a life raft. After several days in the raft in the blazing sun without water, they were about to die when some dolphins approached them one night and pushed the boat south. It was maybe only a few yards but the next day they were rescued by a Mexican fishing boat. To this day they'll swear that the dolphins were trying to push them to where they would intercept with their rescuers.

You can cross the Gulf in one of two ways: either right next to shore—as sailors say, "with one foot on the beach"—so if the wind comes up, the waves won't have too much of a chance to build before hitting you; or far out to sea where it's deeper and the wind is somewhat dispersed.

It was with no small amount of trepidation that we approached the Gulf. The night before, we had anchored in the Bay of Huatulco (which was just a sleepy little village then but later became a major Mexican resort).

On the day we started out it was calm, and we were following the beach, knowing that a Tehuantepecer, as the wind gusts were called, could come up at any moment. Halfway across, I decided that we were safe, and we should cut the corner and head directly for Puerto Madero. Not only was the sea flat, but there were turtles lying on the surface everywhere, resting, we assumed, from the last Tehuantepecer. Almost every turtle had a bird on its back. As we would approach within 30 or 40 feet, the turtle would dive, and the bird would fly away and look for a new landing spot.

Our crossing on the glassy sea was absolutely uneventful.

The excitement on the trip came when we were crossing from Mexico to Costa Rica off the coast of Nicaragua, which, because of the war going on, was a definite no-no for cruisers. As usual I was taking the daylight watch and also as usual, we were trailing a fishing line, hoping to pick up a Dorado or something else for dinner.

I was alone when I caught a brilliant 40-pounder. I got him on deck and was preparing to remove the lure when he flopped and threw the other hook from the lure into my leg, all the way in one side and out the other—did that hurt! I thought I had been stabbed with a red-hot poker.

I yelled for Jack because the struggling fish was pulling at the hook in my leg and making matters worse. Jack got on deck and got the fish off the lure, so I just had a lure sticking out of my leg.

Fortunately, the barb had gone all the way in and out, so Jack was eventually able to cut the barb off and we removed the hook without trouble. Everyone thought I was going to die from infection as the hook was a little rusty, but we proceeded on to Costa Rica without problem. The Dorado was delicious! And we sailed on.

Our Early Cruising Life

Live in the sunshine, swim the sea, drink the wild air.
— *Ralph Waldo Emerson*

One of the best things about sailing is the freedom. That whole, wide ocean is yours to meander…no phones, no faxes, no crowds. No doctors, either.

Being a small boat racer, I thought that sailing a cruising boat sounded just about as dull as dirt. But good, racing buddies, Sally and Bud Hurd, kept raving about the great times they had cruising the Virgin Islands.

Thus, in 1979, Betty and I decided to give it a try. We enticed good friends, Barbara and Carson Bell, to join us and chartered a Morgan Out Island 41 from Dick Jackney of Caribbean Yacht Charters based in St. Thomas, U.S. Virgin Islands. We had a fabulous time and Dick convinced us that these boats were going to make good rental income and appreciate with time. We bit, and with the Bells, bought one. The deal was that we could use it free one month a year for five years and I threw in the provision that we could take it out of the Virgins as I was worried we might get bored sailing only the Virgins for five years. This was the first yacht that we named Expectation.

The Morgan was not a great sailboat. It was more of a floating condominium, comfortable but slow and not good on the wind. In those days charter boats came with minimum equipment: a VHF radio and a depth finder, no navigational equipment and no windlass! Still, we had some wonderful adventures with Expectation.

And about the "no doctor:" one year, Betty and I were sailing Expectation with Jeff and his girlfriend, Kerry, off the west coast of Martinique when we ran out of diesel on a flat calm day. Jeff hadn't been feeling great, but we had to get some fuel and I didn't feel I could leave the boat. So, we loaded Jeff and Kerry into the dinghy and sent them ashore in the blazing sun. They came back with the fuel and fortunately, the engine started up without bleeding. This was a minor miracle since, in those days, I didn't know diesel engines had to be bled to restart after running out of fuel.

Jeff felt terrible when he got back to the boat and by the time we reached Fort-de-France, he had a high fever. We anchored in the bay and went ashore in the dinghy looking for a hospital. We finally found the hospital except there wasn't a soul on duty that spoke English. All they could do was agree he was sick and give him some pills.

The next day Jeff was so sick he couldn't keep anything down and became delirious. We were deeply concerned because there was no way we could get him ashore in the dinghy. I went ashore and was finally able to locate the American Consulate, which fortunately was open, and they gave me the name of an English-speaking doctor. Not only was the doctor a nice lady but she was willing to make "boat calls."

She agreed Jeff was a very sick boy and gave him a shot. Since he needed three a day for the next three days, she left us with the shots and showed Kerry how to administer them. In fact, she had Kerry practice on an orange. Kerry got it right away and soon Jeff was his old self again.

Sometime later, we were on the beach in Martinique when we met an American doctor. Jeff described his symptoms and the shots he was given, and the doctor just shook his head.

He said, "We don't use that medicine in the States anymore. It tends to cause blindness."

On another trip, we were anchored near a tiny island close to Martinique when Betty developed a terrible toothache in the tooth where she had had a root canal procedure in Aspen just a few weeks earlier. We found the local dentist in a dirt-floored office. He said that some dental work was a success and some a failure. She had a failure. He pulled the tooth!

Our most memorable trip on the original Expectation was from St. Thomas to St. Martin's with Carson and Barbara Bell. We hung out for four days in the Virgins waiting for a serious storm to pass. I spent some time examining my chart (a type of map that shows all the places where you might be lost). There were high wind warnings and reports of two ships lost in the Anegada Passage. The Anegada Passage between the Virgin Island and St. Martin's can be one of the roughest pieces of water anywhere.

The wind comes unimpeded all the way from Africa and then funnels between the two islands, developing huge seas.

We were at the Bitter End and getting impatient. It seemed that the wind had calmed some so I suggested we just stick our nose out to see how bad it was. Once we left the island and it started to get dark, there was no way we could come back without navigational equipment. We were committed to the crossing. What a night!

The Morgan didn't have a dodger so every wave came over the bow and hit the person trying to steer. One wave brought a good size fish that hit Carson in the shoulder and flopped around the cockpit before we got rid of it.

Below deck it was a nightmare. It was raining salt water everywhere. The boat had never seen rough water and leaked like a sieve. At one point, Barbara was lying in bed with two garbage sacks around her, trying to keep dry. Because you had to turn away from the compass every time a wave hit, and the big waves were constantly throwing us off course, steering was impossible. I steered as long as I could but finally was exhausted and turned it over to Carson who, at his prime, wasn't a great helmsman. We floundered on, motor sailing through the night.

When dawn broke, we should have been within sight of St. Martin or Anguilla, but there was nothing except ocean. The wind had calmed down and we sailed on until I finally spotted an island ahead of us, which, although I'd never seen it before, I recognized by its unusual conical shape to be Saba. We were miles south of our course.

Having missed St. Martin entirely, the closest protection was St. Barts, and we motor sailed into the harbor by mid-afternoon. By then the wind had died down and the sun was out. We anchored, looking like drowned rats.

The first order of business was to get things dry. Everything in the boat was soaked: the bedding, clothes, my camera—everything. We brought as much as we could up on deck and hung it on the lifelines to dry. We were just settling down when a harbor boat came out and a man on board starting yelling that we had to leave, "The ferry's coming!" he shouted repeatedly.

I turned the key to start the engine. Silence. We tried everything we could think of to get the engine turned over but had no luck at all. By this time the man on the patrol boat was going crazy yelling at us, "You have to move, you have to move!" We soon saw why. A huge barge was coming at us and the wind was blowing it right down on our position. Since the barge had unloaded its cargo, its side was higher than our mast. I could see barnacles the size of baseballs on its towering walls.

All we could do was let out every inch of rode (anchor line) we had and hope for the best. The ferry passed so close that everything on Expectation shook. I couldn't believe that barge didn't catch our line, but it passed safely. We celebrated with the stiffest drink anyone could make. The drowned rats lived to toast another day!

The next morning the charter company sent a mechanic over who found a short in the ignition system, obviously from all the saltwater we had taken during our crossing.

Another trip across the Anegada was memorable for its beauty. Lee Lyon had joined us as crew, the night sky was full of stars as it can only be when you are out of sight of land, the wind was perfect to sail on a smooth broad reach and for two hours we had a whale following us only 20 yards astern. It's nights like those that make you forget all the rough passages.

 Five years of cruising on Expectation and we were hooked for good. We eventually had 12 more wonderful years of cruising on our new Expectation.

The Expectation

Expectation

Little did I know that reefing, wind blowing like stink (very strong), and 150 candles were the beginning of a new way of life.

In 1981, Betty and I and Monty and Sally Goldman, friends from Aspen, were all in San Francisco. The Goldmans called and asked if we'd like to go sailing with friends of theirs. It was a beautiful San Francisco day with the sun shining and a brisk wind on the bay. We gladly accepted.

The boat was a Peterson 44. I liked everything about it. It was comfortable, fast, and had good lines. When we returned to the dock, Betty and I decided that if we ever got another boat, this would be the one.

We had only been back in Aspen a few days when my friend, Dave Baxter, said he was partners in a boat called the Sea

Nymph and one of his partners had dropped out and they were looking for a replacement. The Sea Nymph was a Peterson 44. The boat had a mortgage, five partners, and it only cost a couple of thousand to "join the club."

The Sea Nymph summered in San Diego and each winter it sailed the Sea of Cortez. The group hired an attendant who stayed on the boat, maintained it, and sailed with some of the partners who were not sailors themselves. Back then, we called him a BN (Boat N——); now, we'd probably call him a sailboat maintenance technician. When a sailing partner would use the boat, the attendant could take a week or two off.

That winter, we decided to sail the Sea Nymph with Valerie and Steve Arelt as our guests. On this trip, Valerie discovered she was a landlubber—defined as anyone on board a boat who wishes she was not.

Our first attendant was Dave Muckinhern from Aspen. Because we didn't feel we needed a crew, we gave Dave a couple of weeks off after he showed us how to operate the Sea Nymph's systems. Shortly after the Arelts arrived in La Paz, we left for one of the islands about 25 miles north.

The wind was strong, but the Sea Nymph sailed beautifully. Because I hadn't learned about reefing, I had too much sail up, and we heeled over farther than necessary with our rail in the water. I knew we were fine, but Valerie panicked, thinking we were going to tip over.

Disaster occurred when we were about an hour out of La Paz sailing hard on a starboard tack. I happened to look ahead and saw that the leeward side stay was just dangling loose. If we had come about at that time, we would have lost the mast. I didn't want to further alarm Valerie, who might raise her fist to the grey sky and curse me and my children for ten generations.

Fortunately, I was able to fix the side stay, and we proceeded to Isla San Francisco where Valerie recovered, and we anchored for the night.

The water was calm, and we broke out the drinks, ready to relax and enjoy the evening. Then, while we were cooking dinner, the stove went out. No one had thought to check the propane. It wasn't going to be a fun trip if we couldn't cook or make coffee. We decided to come back the next morning.

Lo and behold, the engine wouldn't start the next morning. The wind was blowing like stink and because we were only a hundred yards offshore, getting the anchor up with a slow manual windlass and sailing out of there without going aground was a bit tricky, but we made it. We turned back for La Paz.

For me, it was a glorious sail. For Valerie, it was a nightmare. We were off the wind, zipping along at hull speed, but when you sat in the cockpit and looked back, the waves were huge. It looked like they were 15 feet high and each one was going to crash over the stern. Of course, as a wave got closer, the stern rose, and we would surf down the face of the sea at great speed. Valerie curled into a ball, muttering, "I can't die, I have two little babies at home."

There is a long dogleg channel at the entrance to La Paz Harbor. It would have been impossible against the wind without a motor, but the wind was with us, and we managed it nicely. As I approached the fleet of some 50 boats anchored off the town, I radioed to get some instructions for the best place to anchor and to warn other boats that we had no engine hence our anchoring might be a little perilous. Everyone in the harbor monitors their radio and they were all on deck, panicked that this runaway boat in a 25-knot breeze was going to wipe them out. I tried not to let anyone know how nervous I was about this maneuver—but I was plenty scared.

As it turned out, we sailed behind a number of boats, rounded up into the wind, Steve dropped the anchor perfectly, and it was "no sweat." We even heard cheers from the other sailors, and some came over to congratulate us on such a good job.

Steve and Val were supposed to spend the night on board, but they couldn't get off fast enough. They checked into a hotel and Barbara and Carson Bell, who were there to meet us, moved on board. That night was Betty's birthday and we decided to party at a local restaurant.

Considering Steve and Val were overjoyed to be alive and in one piece and Carson and Barbara were delighted to be on vacation, we over-celebrated like seldom before.

My memory is of Barbara, who rarely drinks to excess, staggering out of the bathroom where she'd thrown up, saying, "I need to get some air." She disappeared for a while; then Steve and Carson went to find her. I will never forget walking outside and seeing Steve and Carson holding her up. They could barely walk as they dragged her across the ground like a survivor in a battlefield movie.

Carson had ordered a huge cake for Betty's birthday—maybe 150 candles. As they brought it to our table it was obvious that the Bells and Arelts were finished for the night and had to go to a hotel even though all their gear was on the boat. I took them to the hotel, which left Betty sitting at an empty table with a huge birthday cake. A group of Mexicans nearby felt sorry for her and invited her to join them for a drink. Somehow, I managed to get back to the restaurant to pick up Betty and we made it back to the boat alive. Oh, what a night to remember.

A few years later, Dave Baxter called me to say that our partners in the Sea Nymph, none of whom I had met, were having a financial disaster in the oil business and had to drop out of the boat. Dave said he couldn't afford to own half a boat and thought it best to put the Sea Nymph up for sale.

By this time, Betty and I were bitten with the cruising bug. Since things were going well with Coates, Reid & Waldron, we started looking for a boat for ourselves. Boat shopping from Aspen isn't easy. We hired a broker and initiated the search. David Hooks, a broker from Marblehead, found a Bowman 57 in France. We knew the Bowman was a fine sailing boat, the price seemed right, so we flew to the Riviera with David to take a look. We were sure we were going to buy the boat.

Poor David. We hadn't been on the boat five minutes when we looked at each other and said this wasn't for us. We knew it was a good boat and plenty big enough, but we felt the accommodations below were not as good as the Peterson 44.

We decided we liked the Peterson 44 better than anything else and made a deal to buy David's Sea Nymph interest and recondition the boat. She was in rough shape (partnership boats always are.) We hired Billy Cast, better known as "Captain Billy," to do a complete renovation of the Sea Nymph. We bought new rigging, a power windlass, new instruments, a total refinishing—the works.

Expectation was the name of a boat we bought as part of a charter fleet in St. Thomas, U.S. Virgin Islands. We had sold that boat, but we still liked the name Expectation and we had never run across another boat with the same name.

We changed the name of Sea Nymph to Expectation. We decided against Expectation II as we thought it was a little trite and would require too much explanation to other sailors.

Sailing through Life: Ninety-three years of adventure

The Maiden Voyage

Harrowing sailing adventures are to men what childbirth is to some women: if you remembered how awful it was you would never do it again!

In the summer of 1983, Betty and I had bought out all our partners in the 44-foot cutter, the Sea Nymph. We wanted to do some serious cruising and to do that we decided to totally refurbish the boat and rename it Expectation. Expectation had been the name of our Morgan Out Island 41 we had purchased as part of a charter boat fleet in St. Thomas, U.S. Virgin Islands. The first Expectation had introduced us to the cruising life we loved, and we decided to keep the name.

The refurbishing took place in San Diego. We hired Billy Cast (Captain Billy) to do the job because he also owned a Peterson 44 and knew the intricacies of the boat. Terrible mistake! Billy was a nice guy, but he hadn't the faintest idea how to keep a schedule and was rather disingenuous about reporting his progress.

One of the items of new equipment I was most proud of was a Satnav, a satellite navigation system. Previously I had relied on a compass, the depth finder and dead reckoning for navigation. The Satnav, a forerunner of GPS, determines the boat's position from satellites at least every four hours and sometimes more frequently. Every four hours is not a problem on open water when you're only traveling six or seven miles an hour.

The original plan was to complete the refitting by October 1, then take the month of October to do a shakedown cruise and final adjustments. In anticipation of this, I had invited my son,

Jeff, and good friends, Paul Koontz and Dave Smart, to join us on the maiden voyage. Paul and Dave were under the impression that I was an experienced Bluewater sailor because I had told them about the sailing Betty and I had done in the Caribbean. What I hadn't told them, and, in fact, didn't even think about, was that almost all our sailing had been in warm Caribbean waters with very predictable moderate winds.

To allow a little leeway, I had scheduled the guests' arrival for November 10, and they were right on time. Regrettably, not only had we not done our shakedown cruise, but the final work was not completed. Everybody pitched in to do what they could and on November 20, I decided it was now or never as everyone had commitments back in Kansas City. We could do the final small tasks underway.

I had been told that the traditional winds were from the north and usually fairly light this time of year but the wind in the protected harbor told us that we should expect fairly strong winds out of the south so we prepared by putting up the smaller staysail instead of the regular jib and put a double reef in the mainsail.

Late in the afternoon of November 20, we left the harbor and discovered that it was indeed rough out there. Our greatly reduced sail area meant that we were not heeled over too far, however, almost every wave was breaking over the bow and it was going to be a rough ride.

We soon found that the ports had not been properly sealed and the main salon was getting a nice saltwater bath. And the crew was feeling queasy!

Fortunately, the chart table where the Satnav was installed was staying dry.

When I checked the engine room, I found the automatic bilge pump was not working. The sawdust from the construction had not been cleaned out of the bilge and was being sucked into the strainer causing the pump to fail. The only solution was to go down into the hot engine compartment to clear the intake every 10 to 15 minutes. Not a comfortable job.

Later that evening, I looked up and could see that the side stay on the starboard side was loose and flapping in the wind. If we had come about onto a starboard tack, we would've lost the mast. The wind was blowing 45 knots, waves were breaking over the forward deck and I had to go out there and secure the side stay or we could lose the mast. As I made my way along the deck, it was like riding a roller coaster. I was soaked and cold but managed to reach the stay and somehow anchor it. It turned out that Billy had forgotten to install the cotter keys, an essential for keeping the stays tight.

I don't know what we would've done if we had lost our mast out there.

We had attached a windsurfer to the lifelines on the port side and, sometime during the night, a giant wave swept the windsurfer overboard and there was no hope of a recovery in those conditions.

The autopilot that was doing most of the steering was working but draining the batteries and to compensate I was hand steering as much as possible. Eventually our batteries got so low that we decided to run without lights and to check the compass heading by flashlight!

It was a night from hell, and everybody was seasick except Jeff and me. I decided to head for the Mexican island of Guadalupe with the thought that we could anchor there, regroup and make repairs. It was dawn as we were approaching the island and I was extremely concerned about a reef that the chart showed to be just off the harbor. Fortunately, the wind had let up considerably and switched to the north, so we were before the wind as we approached the island. At the last moment we were caught by a wind shift, the mainsail accidentally jibed, and the force of the jibe ripped the sail in two. Then we had a moment of panic when the engine would not start, and we were approaching the reef. Fortunately, the engine caught just in time, we avoided the reef, and with a great feeling of exhilaration, dropped anchor in the small bay.

The calmer weather had revived the crew and we were able to breakfast on last night's 's sandwiches. Then everyone pitched in to make repairs. Paul Koontz, the renowned breast surgeon, was the only one who knew how to sew so he was assigned to repair the sail. The rest of us got busy caulking portholes and cleaning the engine room. About that time to men paddled out to us in a dugout canoe with their rifles in 6 inches of water at the bottom.

 They purported to be the local customs officials. They wanted to see our papers but, since the papers were all in English, we suspected they could not make heads or tails of them. They were friendly enough, examined our documents, accepted a cold beer and were on their way.

Two hours later most of the repairs had been finished except Paul's, who, at his doctor rate, had sewn $10,000 worth of stitches in the sail but was less than 1/5 finished. We decided to put the sail in its bag and see if we could get some sewing assistance ashore.

We all piled into the dinghy with the wounded sail and headed for the beach and the village we could see above the shore. There was one large problem on the beach: a group of elephant seals the size of small houses were between us and the village. Each was easily 2,000 pounds of unknown danger. There was nothing to do but hold our breath and walk right through them. I later learned that the following year another yacht made the same stop and one of the elephant seals felt threatened by their dinghy, attacked, and destroyed it.

The friendly villagers were patiently waiting for our arrival. I explained our problem with my pidgin Spanish and sign language. It was obvious when we showed them the ripped sail. One of the women looked at it, indicated she could fix it by the next day and proceeded to rip out thousands of dollars of Paul's handiwork right in front of him.

When we returned the next day, our sewing lady presented us with a fully repaired sail. That repair lasted as long as we had that boat. She wanted $100 but seemed delighted when I offered her $70.

By then the winds had returned to normal, everything was working, and my wonderful crew and I headed south before the wind. We decided to stop at Magdalena Bay for drinking water and hopefully some of the cheap lobsters we had heard about. We backed up to the pier, filled our water tanks and made a deal on enough lobster for a feast. The sail from there to Cabo San Lucas was before the wind and we were even able to fly the spinnaker for the first time on Expectation.

We hated to see Paul Koontz leave us at Cabo, but he had to get back to surgery. We would miss his dry sense of humor. Seems like sometimes you did not get the joke until five minutes later.

Sailing through Life: Ninety-three years of adventure

Ashore at Cabo we saw a cockfight. A cockfight is 20 minutes of betting followed by 20 seconds of feathers flying. One bird is down but the only way you could really tell what had happened would be to film the fight and view it later in slow motion.

That night we met two young women from Aspen and Jeff invited them to sail the final leg to Puerto Vallarta with us. A shipboard romance was kindled between Tonya Younbblat, one of the women, and Jeff. In fact, Jeff was at the helm while we were flying the spinnaker that night, got off course with romance, and wrapped the spinnaker around the forestay. A mess but not fatal.

It was just before dawn when we were approaching the Bay of Banderas and I knew there were dangerous islands at the head of the bay. Since Billy had been there before I told him to take the helm as we entered the bay. I laid down in the aft cabin to get some rest, but I could hear what was going on at the helm. Someone was calling out the depths from the fathometer and I heard 30 feet, 25, 20, 15 and, knowing we drew almost 7 feet, I was wide awake and headed topside as 10 was called. Just then the helm was swung to the right, away from shore. Billy explained that it was his "barking dog" theory of navigation. You want to cut the corner of the bay as close as possible, so you head in until you hear the dog's bark. Then you know it is time to go to deeper water!

Betty was at the dock when we landed and not at all happy about our female passengers. Despite everything, it was a story book ending. Jeff and Tonya were married and gave us Keegan and Sasha, two great kids.

More Sailing Adventures

Sailing anywhere has its hazards and there were several occasions when we could have lost the boat if things hadn't happened just right. One day, we were anchored in the harbor at Careyes very close to some major rocks. It was a touchy place to anchor, but it was a clear day and Lee Lyon was on deck, so I asked him to keep a sharp lookout while I went below to do some chores. Half an hour later I came back on deck to find us literally inches from the rocks with Lee engrossed in his book.

He said his attention wandered when he got to the part where it said, "and she arched her back."

I think it was that same trip when I was ashore, out of sight of the boat, a little kid came running up yelling,

"Your boat is on fire!"

I got back as quick as I could and found that indeed it had been on fire—the generator had overheated. Luckily, Betty was there and was able to put out the fire. We found a Mexican mechanic to rebuild our generator. That spring, we installed an automatic fire extinguisher in the engine room.

One winter, Betty invited Jeni and Kyle to Vallarta for a week and I decided to invite some stags to go cruising. The group included Jim Moran, Willie Jordan and Dale Eubank. We had a whole series of disasters.

My guests took the dinghy and went exploring one afternoon. I had warned them about the surf, but they didn't listen. They flipped the dinghy, soaking the engine (outboards don't run when full of saltwater.) It was a long row back only to spend the rest of the evening taking the motor apart to clean it.

On the last night of that trip, we did an overnight from Careyes to Vallarta. It was overcast, there was no moon and no lights along that shore – in other words it was black as stink! The wind came up to about 30 knots, we ripped our jib and the engine quit. To restart a diesel that has sucked in some air you have to bleed it, which involves opening various lines to let the air (and always a fair amount of diesel fuel) out. In a rough sea, we take off all our clothes to do this as it is akin to taking a diesel bath in a very hot, pitching, crowded space.

Dale was helping me, but fifteen minutes in he started to turn green and asked to be excused for a minute. Dale is quite a guy—he went on deck, threw up, and came back to help me get the engine started. And just in time, too. I went topsides and found that we had been driven so close to shore that I could hear the surf breaking. We sailed away from another close one!

In 1980 we chartered a boat on the French Riviera with Barbara and Carson Bell. The highlight of that trip was our time in the harbor at St. Tropez with our little sailboat moored among the mega yachts.

One day we were walking along a beach on one of the French islands. There were trees, then a sandy area, then more trees. As we came out of the trees onto one of the pocket beaches, we saw this gorgeous French gal lying on her back stark naked. We didn't bother her, but Carson was so fascinated he walked right into a broken tree branch and put a hole in his forehead. He bled like a stuck pig.

In the summer of 1982, I took a stag group—Fritz Benedict, Ron Gray, Lee Lyon, and Willie Jordan—on a cruise from San

Diego to Catalina and the Channel Islands. We got to Catalina without incident and were enjoying great camaraderie as we started the overnight sail to the Channel Islands.

My eye had been bothering me a little, but that night it got badly inflamed. The pain was excruciating. It was obvious that I needed a doctor and soon.

We bypassed the islands and headed for the nearest port, Santa Barbara, where Fabi Benedict's relative, Herbert Bayer and his wife lived. As soon as we hit the dock, the gang immediately got me to the emergency room of a hospital where I was fortunate to find an excellent ophthalmologist on duty. He gave me shots and IVs to fight the infection and told me that in another twelve hours I would have probably lost that eye. It was an infection caused by a bad contact lens.

I was one sick puppy and since there was no way I was going to get out of the hospital for a few days, the crew took the boat back as far as Newport Beach. Most of them didn't know very much about boats except Lee who knew how to sail and was a good navigator because he had flown in World War II. If it hadn't been for Lee, I'd have probably lost the boat, as the rest of the crew got heavily into the rum bottle and were so drunk by the time they arrived at Long Beach that they were lucky the harbor master allowed them to go ashore.

With heavy antibiotics I recovered nicely, and Betty and I picked up the boat at Newport and sailed it back to San Diego.

Land

Yachts on Wheels

Pea Green Princess

Bliss was exploring the world with my adventurous wife, Betty. We explored four continents, North and Central America; Europe; and Australia and New Zealand. We camped in our Volkswagen Pop-Top in Morocco (see Morocco essay), Africa. And adventurous it was from exquisite beauty to a burned vehicle to "we need the snow tires."

We were just a couple of hours out of Guatemala City, when we crested the hill. As we started down the long steep hill, magnificent Lake Atitlan unfolded before us in rich blue waters and then, across the lake, were majestic conic-shaped volcanic mountains. We camped in a beautiful, lush meadow bordering the lake. It was not a campground, just an open meadow. Often, we were the only campers there. Our view was the emerald-blue Lake Atitlan and the volcanoes on the opposite shore. One morning I was sitting outside our RV, the lake was absolutely calm, and I watched as an Indian canoe ghosted along in front of me, volcanoes forming the backdrop. A photograph could not have captured the breathtaking beauty — it was more beautiful than a Monet painting.

Betty and I always thought of our RV as a yacht on wheels. It did not have the romance of the water nor all the disadvantages of corrosion from saltwater, the lack of repair facilities and the difficulties of finding fuel either. It did have the freedom of the open road. We could always answer the question, "What's on the other side of that mountain?"

Our first RV was a Volkswagen Pop-Top, the Pea Green Princess, that we purchased in Frankfurt, Germany. We parked the Volkswagen and spent our first night in the turret of a castle overlooking the Rhine River. I will never forget waking up that first morning and looking out over the Rhine and seeing the dynamics of the bustling German economy. There was a busy highway, the river with barges and boats and tugs going in both directions, and on the opposite bank, dual railroad tracks with trains also going both directions.

We drove the Pea Green Princess for three weeks and then shipped it back to the U.S. where we used it as a second car, and as planned, an easy way to enjoy the wonderful local campgrounds and do some trout fishing.

When we decided to try some more adventurous trips, we purchased a Winnebago Mini, the White Shark. It was diesel powered—I should say it was diesel underpowered because the diesel engine was not powerful enough to handle steep hills in drive gear and we would have to shift down to make it. I remember one hill at Lake Atitlan in Guatemala where I didn't think we were going to make it even in low gear. Somehow, the White Shark managed to creep to the crest. Yet it was a big improvement over the VW as it had a full kitchen and bathroom with shower.

Pea Green Princess

Propane flame throwers? We stepped up to a class C motorhome (an RV on a Ford truck chassis.) It had good power and was very comfortable. We were returning to Aspen from a winter in Puerto Vallarta with most of our clothes, computer, jewelry, etc. We were about three hours north of Puerto Vallarta, when we stopped to change drivers and noticed smoke coming from the engine. We had a fire extinguisher, and I immediately tried to unlock the hood to fight the fire, but the release latch was far too hot to touch and there was no way to use the fire extinguisher through the radiator. I struggled to enter the van to rescue our belongings, but the smoke was too dense and all we could do was remove the motor scooter from the rack on the back and watch the vehicle burn. I was afraid the propane tanks would explode, but as they heated up, the propane would flare out like a flamethrower.

    Two American, mango buyers drove up just as the Mexican fire brigade arrived from a nearby village. What a sight. The firefighters apparently had gotten their oversized uniforms from U.S. firefighters, and they were far too large. It looked like the seven dwarfs had come to fight the fire which, by the time of their arrival, was nothing but a smoldering frame on the highway. All our clothing, computers and shaving/makeup kits were gone. The firefighters tried to charge us for damage to the asphalt but our new American friends, who spoke perfect Spanish, intervened for us.

In the meantime, Mexican women were poking through the carnage picking out gold pieces and precious stones that had survived the fire.

By now we were totally hooked on RV life, and we purchased a series of class A motorhomes, which are essentially buses with kitchens, bedrooms, etc. Our last class A, Bertha, had a slide-out to substantially enlarge the living room when parked. A couple of times we started driving without retracting the slide-out, but we always caught it in time.

The modern Class A motorhome has all the conveniences of modern cars except for a few challenges. We had to grow accustomed to the size and remember to swing wide on corners because the rear wheels take the shortest route.

Betty destroyed a taxi in Puerto Vallarta. She had not driven since autumn, and just two blocks from where the RV had been stored, she cut a corner too close. It could have been a legal nightmare, but we were still in a city where we had employees and attorneys. The insurance company handled it.

One year, we were late starting south. When we left Aspen, we had to go a different route through Denver on I-25 to Colorado Springs. It started snowing and the wind was blowing hard. We had no snow tires and between the wind gusts and poor traction, it took everything we had to stay on the road. We were warm enough inside, but our waste tank was frozen. We skidded at the filling station, hit the waste tank on the median causing it to split open. At least the contents were frozen! We were able to get to an RV shop for repairs before the tank thawed. A small complication compared to what might have happened had we been blown off the road by two of the most dangerous threats for an RV: high wind and poor traction.

Exploring in a motorhome gave us unlimited opportunities for travel as we did not have to worry about hotel reservations or really anything except planning the next day's adventure. In those days Walmart allowed RV overnight parking in their lots, so we did not even have to worry about finding a campground. Many RVers solved the parked transportation problem by towing an automobile, but we thought this was too much trouble. Instead we carried a motor scooter on a forward rack and a bicycle on the back. We had a generator for power and basically all the comforts of home. In those days we felt completely safe traveling in Mexico and Guatemala and would frequently spend the night on a town square, parked across the street from a police station. Our evening entertainment was sipping a drink as we watched the Mexican couples do their courting-dance walking around the square.

One of our most memorable trips was from Aspen to Toronto where Barbara and Carson Bell joined us on our way to Montréal and the Maritime provinces before ducking down to Maine for lobster and other seafood delights. We hired a guide in Montreal and Quebec City, a necessity when you are driving a big motorhome.

People were amazed that Betty could drive these 36-foot monsters well into her 80s. Betty's friends were in total shock at her lifestyle. Most of Betty's Kansas City contemporaries thought an exciting trip was their annual two weeks in Florida at the same resort they went to year after year and probably was the same resort where their parents had vacationed. How thankful I am to have married someone adventurous enough to spend 12 years on a sailboat and then move into almost full-time RV living.

It was a sad day when we finally decided all good things had to come to an end and we sold Bertha, our last motorhome, to move into a retirement community in San Antonio.

Vans, Convertibles and a 50-year Model A Infatuation

Model A

If you don't look back at your car when you park it, you own the wrong car. —9GAG

When I was 14 my father sat me down at the kitchen table one Sunday morning and told me he had a proposition for me.

"Son, " he said, "when I was your age my father made a proposal to me, and I would like to make the same deal with you. If you will refrain from drinking and smoking to age 21, I will give you $1000 to buy a new car."

Remember, in those days you could buy a decent car for $1000! However, I got a nice surprise the year I was leaving to attend Northwestern. Dad was so proud of me making the honor roll and other honors at Peddie that he presented me with a very used Plymouth. It had originally been a demonstrator car for one of his salesmen. As a demonstrator car it had a huge trunk designed to carry a masonry saw. The removal of the equipment had left it with a huge backseat.

Not the hottest vehicle on campus that fall, but I was one of the few freshmen who had their own wheels. Plus, the huge backseat made it very popular for double dates. That car served me well for all my time at Northwestern and there were occasions when three couples would squeeze in to attend a party in downtown Chicago.

After Robbie and I were married and living in Glenview, just north of Chicago, I decided it was time for an upgrade — something sporty. We bought a well-used, red MG convertible that gave Robbie transportation while I was at work and a fun vehicle for us to take our new daughter, Candy, to explore the Chicago area in style.

When it came time to move to Kansas City, we sold the MG and bought a traditional Ford station wagon to make the move and serve as our family car for several years.

On one of my business trips to France, I became enthralled with the Renault convertible. When I decided we needed a second car, we imported a shiny blue Renault, another totally impractical yet fun car. As our primary vehicle we continued with conventional station wagons.

Sailing through Life: Ninety-three years of adventure

When we learned we were moving to Aspen, we knew we needed a more powerful vehicle to carry all our stuff and tow the 16-foot inboard/outboard powerboat we were taking with us. We bought a big GMC van but made the mistake of taking the shortcut over 12,000-foot Independence Pass. That was one of my more hair-raising rides as, at that time, Independence Pass was unpaved and there were no guardrails to protect you from 500-foot drop-offs. It would have been an exciting trip without a huge powerboat behind us but with the boat it was a real hair raiser!

After a few years in Aspen, I got the convertible bug again. My good friend, Irv Hockaday, was on the board of Ford Motor Company and Ford had acquired Jaguar. Irv said he could get me the friends and family price. Soon there was a shiny Jaguar convertible in our driveway.

One of my fondest car memories had always been driving to the Ozarks at about age 10 with my father in a Model A Ford convertible. I'll never forget him finally getting off the dirt road and hitting a stretch of asphalt. With the accelerator to the floor, he would scream with delight when we hit 60 miles an hour, "We're going a mile a minute!" To him it was like breaking the sound barrier. My father knew quite a bit about cars, having built one from scratch out of junkyard parts at age 16.[k1]

One night I was talking to Dad on the phone from Aspen. "Dad, I loved that Model A we had when I was growing up and I have been thinking about getting one."

It was just a week later that he announced that he had bought one for me – well not exactly – he had made a deal to buy one using my money. A few weeks later the car arrived in Aspen and I arranged to be the chauffeur for the grand marshal and proudly led the Fourth of July parade[k2] , something I continued to do for almost 20 years.

It turned out that my Model A was not as well restored as the seller made it seem, and for that reason, I looked into car restoration professionals and found one in Pueblo, Colorado and made a deal with him to restore the car. It turned out to be a bad choice as he did not do a great job and it took far longer than promised. Years later, I decided to get a complete restoration and add all the options that were available on the original cars. The main additions were spare tires built into both front bumpers. This time I did my homework and found a fine restoration mechanic in Denver who did an outstanding job in a timely manner.

After I lost my eyesight and could no longer drive in the parade, I reluctantly sold the Model A to a friend of Kim's who is now lovingly looking after it in Michigan.

My hope is that I live long enough for self-driving cars to be available so I can once again own an automobile.

Air

I Can Fly!

3 Passenger Stinson Plane

What I like best about flying is the freedom it affords to navigate an ocean of air and see the Earth from a wider perspective. I never tire of the beauty of the Earth by day or the sky by night.—Chesley "Sully" Sullenbeger on National Aviation Day

Should I tell my parents?

I hadn't bothered to tell my parents because I wasn't sure how they would feel. When I finally had the courage to reveal that I had bought an airplane and learned to fly, I was pleasantly surprised that they did not have heart attacks or even object to my new adventure. I'm sure my father had done more dangerous escapades at my age! In fact, my father was rather enthusiastic about the idea… And in retrospect this was not surprising because by the time my father was my age, he had built a roller coaster in his backyard and two racing cars from scratch.

Like most kids growing up during World War II, I was fascinated by all planes. My father's tales of seeing 1930's stunt pilots perform dangerous aerobatics like flying upside down captured my imagination, too.

Sailing through Life: Ninety-three years of adventure

It all began in 1952, when I was a sophomore at Northwestern, a friend suggested we buy an airplane together. Since I had saved a little money from summer jobs, I decided to give flying a try. We scoured the ads looking for a plane and eventually found one at Palwaukee Airport, just northwest of Chicago. In those days Palwaukee was a small field that had no control tower, one dirt runway and a rather informal flying school. We found a three-passenger Stinson offered for sale at $650. Three-passenger?

Only if they were midgets. It was actually a two-passenger plane with space behind the seats for a little luggage. The plane was 16 years old with a green fabric skin. The only instruments were an altimeter, a compass, and gauges that showed the RPMs, the oil pressure, and the engine temperature — no radio and no navigational equipment.

We were able to negotiate the price down to $500. Who could go wrong investing $250 in a real live airplane that was airworthy?

My friend and I paid the flight instructor $10 an hour for flying lessons. The first thing we were taught was how to prop the plane because it didn't have a starter. One person would sit in the cockpit to handle the controls while someone else would grab the propeller with both hands. The person outside would raise one foot in the air, then pull down on the propeller while swinging the raised foot back to create momentum. That would swing the prop person safely back from the propeller. On a cold day this might take six or more tries before the engine came to life.

Without navigational instruments, our cross-country flights were done using detailed maps that showed highways, railways, and rivers. Railways and rivers were the easiest to follow as highways could be confusing sometimes. By following railroads and rivers, I was able to successfully complete my solo cross-country flight to Indianapolis and get my pilot's license. After that, I would take the plane up on weekends just for the joy of flying and to improve my piloting skills.

I had a long weekend in the spring of '53 so I decided to fly my new airplane to Kansas City to show it to my folks. Chicago to Kansas City is a little over 400 miles by air so, at a little over 100 miles an hour I could make it in just over four hours with one stop to refuel. The weather was good and the flight to Kansas City was uneventful except that I noticed that the engine was running a little hotter than usual. Stateline Airport was a grass strip just south of Kansas City and I found it easily.

The next morning, I took my father for a flight. We climbed to about 500 feet, but I could see that the temperature gauge was rising just about as fast as we were. It was obvious that doubling the payload of the plane was having a very negative effect on performance. Breaking out into a sweat, I was thinking about returning to the field as soon as possible, but my father was having the time of his life. Everything looks different from the air, and he was exclaiming how great old Charlie's farm looked from up here and that he'd never realized that there was a lake over there. He was totally oblivious to our crisis. So, he was terribly disappointed when I told him we had to abort the flight after less than 15 minutes. We managed a safe landing. Then I had to decide what to do.

With important classes on Monday, I headed back to Chicago. Because the plane was losing oil, the airplane was overheating, and the oil pressure dropped. What should have been a one-stop flight turned into a three-stop flight and every stop took longer than usual as I had to add oil. Adding oil meant each time I stopped, I had to descend, get into a landing pattern, land, taxi to the service facilities, find someone who could sell the oil to me and someone to prop the plane to get me started again.

I hadn't realized how much time those stops had consumed until the sun set well before I got to Chicago. Without any night landing experience, I still felt I had to press on. My one advantage was the crystal-clear evening. The bright lights of towns made them easy to spot, and I could see the aircraft beacons from a long way away.

I'd been sweating on the flight with my dad, but now I was wringing wet with perspiration and my heart was racing by the time I approached Palwaukee for that first night landing. I landed smoothly, and you never saw a more delighted guy tying a plane down.

A crack in the crankcase had caused the problem. We had it repaired and continued to fly the plane quite a bit on weekends. During that year we owned the airplane, I had some touch-and-go moments mostly as a result of learning while doing. With only one runway and no control tower and no radio communication at our airport, I had to be very alert for other airplanes that might be trying to land.

Crosswind landing is always tricky even with radio contact. On my first crosswind landing, I had two options. I could approach the runway crabbing into the wind so I could line up with the runway and then straighten out just before landing. Or I could fly the wing low. To fly the wing low, I used my rudder to line my nose up with the runway, and ailerons to correct for left/right drift all the way from final approach to touchdown. I had to be very certain that the wing tip didn't touch the ground.

Essentially, I was slipping the plane through the crosswind in order to keep myself lined up with the runway. Touch down! I had just executed another landing.

I eventually accumulated 100 hundred hours in that little plane.

The following spring a windstorm hit Palwaukee where the plane was tied down and badly damaged the tail and some of the fabric. We sold the plane for $300 as we were getting close to graduation and didn't have the money to repair it. Not bad for all the use we got out of it.

It was many years before I bought another airplane, but in the meantime, I found my flying experience very useful. I had continued to rent Cessna 150s and 172s, just enough to keep my proficiency up. Then I moved to Kansas City to work for Clipper. We had a big business selling saws and diamond blades to contractors who were doing new highway construction. The contractors used our equipment and blades to cut contraction joints in new concrete.

Many of these jobs were in remote areas and I found that if I rented a plane, I could visit them quickly. Sometimes I would land at a nearby airport, but I often landed right on new pavement not yet opened for traffic. In those days, it was not uncommon to land at a small field where there were no rental cars and have the field manager or one of the mechanics lend me his car for a couple of hours—no paperwork and no charge!

I gave up flying when we moved to Aspen in 1967. Mountain flying is a lot trickier than flatland flying and I had little need for an airplane in my real estate and property management business. Just flying back and forth to Denver was still exciting, as in those days Rocky Mountain Airways was flying Cessna 310s with a single pilot. Because I knew how to fly, I was always given the co-pilot's seat and occasionally the pilot would let me take over the controls for part of the flight.

Aspen was a great place for glider flying and I took some lessons, but I was too busy working to become proficient.

Mexico, Real Estate, and Gonzo Gordo

Plane Pilatus PC 12

When Betty and I started the remodel of our home in San Miguel, Mexico, it seemed like a plane was the logical way to get back and forth between Puerto Vallarta and San Miguel. The drive was a hard 10-hour trip through Guadalajara, but by buying a Cessna 210 we could make it in two hours flat. Fortunately, the airport in San Miguel was only ten minutes from the house.

Before long I decided we needed a plane with a bigger payload than the 210 and made a deal with Aspen Aviation to buy their 206, which had a belly pod for extra storage. That plane was a real workhorse, it carried a ton of stuff, and we loved using it.

When I first started flying in Mexico, I thought I would hire a pilot to fly us back and forth while I slowly picked up the skills again. Too much had changed in the way of navigation and radio procedures that I knew it would take a while to get the hang of it. However, I soon discovered that I was more comfortable with an experienced pilot flying, especially when he would point out "a plane right over there" and I couldn't find the plane. I figured my eyesight was not up to being a safe pilot, although I was seeing almost 20/20 out of my right eye.

We hired a series of pilots without incident until one day a fellow by the name of Rodolfo came over from Puerto Vallarta to pick us up in San Miguel and fly us back. He'd never been to San Miguel before and had a little trouble finding the airport. On the way back we had a pretty good headwind, and I could see we were getting low on fuel. He seemed to think we were all right and we proceeded on.

There are very high, rugged mountains just as you approach Vallarta, and it wouldn't be a good place to land a plane. As we cleared the mountains and were lining up for our approach to Vallarta, I could tell Rodolfo was a little nervous, and I found out why as we touched the runway, the engine stopped—out of gas. We had to be towed to the hangar. That's as close as I ever want to call it.

I purchased a Pilatus, PC 12, after I became involved in Mexican real estate. The Pilatus has such a slow landing speed that a crash would not be fatal, and we used very small airports like the one in San Miguel de Allende.

I never qualified as a pilot. Instead, I hired Charlie Parker, the perfect pilot and adventurous companion.

We had the plane repainted and came up with a sitting goose symbol on the tail and called it Gonzo Gordo (the fat goose) because that's what she looked like. On the pilot's door was the slogan, "Never too fat to fly."

I trusted Charlie, but when we left the dirt field at San Miguel de Allende with a heavily loaded plane, I was wide-eyed and uncertain. Were we going over or under the high-tension wires at the end of the field?

Terror! One night on returning from Mexico, we nervously watched huge, black thunderstorms building up. We decided to land as soon as possible. We headed for Phoenix. As we approached, the field was dark, the rain was coming down in sheets, and the wind was pitching us uncontrollably. Charlie was calm, but I was sweating bullets. To maintain control, Charley literally powered us onto the runway. I had never been more frightened. The storm got worse, and just like that we chose to spend the night. I headed to the bar and ordered a stiff cocktail.

To me the Pilatus was, and still is, the perfect airplane. The Pilatus is essentially a glider with an engine. It is roomy, mine had six comfortable seats and room for tons of cargo that is easily accessed from the ground through a huge cargo door. It only requires a single pilot whereas a jet requires two. It is pressurized so we flew as high as 28,000 feet in comfort. The Pilatus is not as fast as a jet, but the difference is not significant and for most flights, we were less than 20 minutes slower. It was a sad day when I had to sell the Pilatus, but the good news was its value had held up and I lost very little on the sale. I was 14 when I wanted to be a pilot. I'm now 90, and I still want to be a pilot, but I'd rather be 14 again.

More Airplane Adventures

"Life is inherently risky. There is only one big risk you should avoid at all costs, and that is the risk of doing nothing."
—*Denis Waitley*

Dick Stearns, the guy I crewed for in Star boats, had his own plane, and occasionally, during the wintertime, we would fly up to Wisconsin to watch the ice boat races. Watching ice boat races from the ground is difficult because the boats are very fast and far away most of the time that it's hard to tell what's happening. It's a whole different experience when you watch them from the air because you can see exactly what's going on.

One day, Dick and I flew up to Pewaukee to watch the races. We landed on the frozen lake after the last race and talked with some of the sailors for a while. Then a strong wind came up and made the takeoff extremely challenging.

Turning a single-engine plane is done by braking one wheel. Unfortunately, the sun had melted the ice enough that it was as slick as glass. When Dick braked to turn, the wheel kept skidding on the ice, and we continued to get closer and closer to shore. It looked like we were going to be in real trouble as we were running out of both daylight and sea room.

Finally, Dick said, "Hang on!" gave it full throttle, and we literally flew around the corner, missing docks by no more than ten feet. Another exciting day.

Midwest Hospitality

Renting an airplane? Borrowing a stranger's car?

I'll never forget one summer when our French manager, Jacques Martinoni, was visiting us. The contractors weren't cutting joints in France at that time and he wanted to see an actual operation. Since there was a job going on in southern Iowa, we rented a plane and flew to Iowa. Jacques was nervous about landing on the pavement, but there was a small airport about 10 miles away and we landed there. In my usual fashion,

I solved the problem of ground transportation by borrowing the manager's car.

Jacques couldn't believe it. In France, renting airplanes was practically unknown, and he'd never heard of someone going up to a complete stranger and asking to borrow his car for a few hours—and being handed the keys. It was a great example of Midwest hospitality for Jacques.

Aspen

When we moved to Aspen in 1967, I knew my piloting days were over because mountain flying requires special skills and more practice than I had the time or the money for, so I gave up something that had given me a lot of satisfaction over the years.

However, it was still exciting just flying back and forth to Denver, as in those days Rocky Mountain Airways was flying Cessna 310s with a single pilot. Because I knew how to fly, I was always given the co-pilot's seat and occasionally the pilot would let me take over the controls for part of the flight.

Hot Air Balloon Racing

A famous woman World War II pilot, a hot-air balloonist with a huge walrus-mustache, the Rocky Mountains, and balloons of every imaginable color and shape. My first ever balloon ride was about to begin.

Hot air balloon races started in Snowmass in 1975 and our good friend and pilot extraordinaire (she had ferried bombers to England during World War II) Betty Pfister called.

"Nick, will you sponsor a balloon in our inaugural Snowmass Balloon Race? You get to fly with the pilot if you sponsor, and do I have a pilot for you!"

This was how I was introduced to J. J. Garcia, one of the great characters of the balloon world. J. J., handlebar mustache waggling with each word, while a serious pilot, was always good for a laugh.

The first year J. J. showed up in Snowmass with an all-girl crew wearing tight T-shirts that said, "J. J. can't get it up without us."

The next year J. J.'s all-girl crew had T-shirts that said, "J. J. gets it up and we chase it."

Balloon racing is really a misnomer because the purpose of a balloon race is to keep all the balloons as close together as possible to make a great spectacle. And they do make an incredible sight. Each balloon is designed by its owner and everyone tries to make their balloon stand out by picking outrageous colors. The first year or so all the balloons were the traditional shape, but later they started appearing in every shape possible. One was Snoopy, the dog, and another might be Superman, or even Van Gogh's head. The shapes were as varied as the owner's imagination!

Ballooning can be dangerous, too. The real enemy of hot air ballooning is wind. Light breezes are fine, but even a 15-mile per hour wind can put things out of control. Three people were killed in a tragic balloon accident very near our home in Woody Creek. The balloon was caught in a gust of wind that dragged it into a powerline. Fortunately, accidents are fairly rare.

What a thrill that first flight was—floating through the sky with the silence only occasionally broken when a blast of hot air was released into the balloon to gain altitude. You must remember that the pilot actually has very little control of the balloon. He can gain altitude by adding hot air and lose altitude by releasing hot air from a vent at the top of the balloon. Motion from side to side or forward and back is strictly up to the air currents, and it is remarkable how the air may be flowing one way at 500 feet and a totally different way at 750 feet. To the person on the ground, it may seem that there is no wind at all. That is the reason most balloon "racing" is done in the early morning with dew still on the ground.

Getting the balloons launched is a big operation. J. J. traveled with his balloon stuffed in a huge bag that he stored inside the basket that carried the propane tank and when flying, his passengers. These baskets are beautifully made and extremely strong so they can hold up in a crash landing.

Getting started is a big operation. The uninflated balloon is stretched out on the grass and it looks like it goes forever—remember balloons are at least six stories high. Regular air is blown in to open the airway up before the hot air flow is started. As the balloon begins to fill with hot air it starts to rise, the crew gets in, which in our case, was usually J. J. and three passengers. The ground crew leans on the basket to keep it from taking off prematurely, and when everything is ready, releases us and we are off.

Since the objective of the race is to keep the balloons as close together as possible, they invent games to do this. They might give each balloon a 3-foot stick with a nail in the end and put up a 3-foot hydrogen colored balloon held in place by a string attached to the ground. The objective is to see which balloon can maneuver close enough to pop the balloon. Or they might give everyone a sandbag and see who can maneuver close enough to drop their bag on a target on the ground.

Sailing through Life: Ninety-three years of adventure

After I had made a few flights, I found the spectacle beautiful but ballooning not very exciting.

A couple of years later, the Snowmass Balloon Race organizers introduced another race that started at the Aspen Airport. The objective was to see how far you could get down the valley with the ultimate goal being Glenwood Springs, some 45 miles away. When you're only control is up or down, and you can only go up if your fuel lasts it was a real challenge.

I thought it was terrific. Because we were moving slowly and silently, sometimes less than 100 feet up, we were seeing things that I never saw from my airplane. The elk and deer did not know what to make of us as we drifted silently above them.

We left the airport at dawn and were having a beautiful flight, when as the ground heated up from the rising sun, the wind started picking up. J. J. started a frantic search for a field without power lines or trees. He found one and started dumping air.

"Hang on!"

Everyone was gripping the sides of the basket as we started to crash. No one wanted to be thrown out of the basket on impact. The basket hit the ground with a bang and was pulled along toward danger as J. J. dumped air. Fortunately, no one was hurt. The all-girl crew showed up to help us pack the balloon into its bag and put the bag in the gondola (basket) for transportation home.

"We're o.k."

We opened the champagne to celebrate our survival! That was

my last flight. We moved to San Antonio, and when I lost my eyesight, I knew ballooning was no longer for me. But I do have those wonderful memories.

THE MENAGERIE

Growing Up at the Lake

Most children fondly remember a dog or a cat from their youth. I remember snakes. Not that I haven't had more ordinary animals, but my choice of pets has run to the exotic. Growing up at Lake Lotawana, there were many opportunities to acquire some rather unusual pets.

At about age ten, I developed a fascination with snakes, and they were plentiful at the lake. Most were harmless. I collected king snakes, garter snakes, salt-and-pepper snakes, and at one time I had a six-foot black snake. I was always alert since my father had killed at least a dozen poisonous copperheads while building our house.

By this time, my parents had built a second house on our property. The original house, which they built entirely with their own hands, was over the water with a boat slip underneath. The new house, which had three bedrooms, was built above it, and I was given the little house as my "room." I kept my snake collection down there in cages, and it wasn't unusual for one of the snakes to stage an escape. It only took my mother one time running across an escapee to refuse to do any more cleaning in the little house. I was on my own.

When I was thirteen, my parents decided that I should spend the bulk of the summer at camp. First, they sent me to the Boy Scout camp at Osceola, Missouri, an area that was alive with snakes. I came home with a pillowslip holding six or seven, including a fairly good-sized black snake. My parents met the bus and took me home, where Mom did the laundry and packed me up to leave that night on the overnight train for Camp SoSo on the upper peninsula of Michigan.

At the train station I hooked up with my counselor, Pud Hamilton, who was busy saying goodbye to his love of the moment, Barbara Thorne. Pud and I were to share a lower berth. We'd just pulled out of the station and he was engrossed in writing a letter to Barbara.

"Hey Pud, would you like to see my snake collection?" I casually asked.

He muttered something that I took for yes, and I opened my pillow slip to show him the snakes. A wide-eyed, open-mouthed Pud leaped out of the bed, spilling the pillowslip, and letting the snakes loose and slithering all over the compartment. A snake could hide in a million places in a Pullman car, and I was only able to recover about half of the collection. Pud didn't sleep a wink that night.

One pet that I particularly remember was a mole. We kept Davey in a cage with about 6-8 inches of dirt on the bottom. He would burrow in the dirt as moles are prone to do, and every morning I would pat down what Davey had dug up the previous day. He loved peanuts so I would push two or three into the dirt to give him something to work for every night. Moles don't like daylight, so once the novelty of watching him make the burrows from above wore off, he wasn't much fun, and we returned him to the wild—not our lawn.

A baby racoon's mother had been hit by a car. One of the employees at the lake brought the orphaned raccoon, Bandit, to me to raise. Raccoons are extremely intelligent and very clean. While Bandit was young, he was easy to handle and made an excellent pet. Bandit would take a morsel of food in his front paws, wash it and then daintily eat it. As Bandit grew older, he apparently got tired of the cage and tried to take a chunk out of me anytime I got too close or tried to handle him. Unfortunately, Bandit was also returned to the wild.

Then there was this cute little goat I saw on a neighbor's farm and bought as a Mother's Day present for my mom. Billy was great fun and very friendly except you did have to be very careful bending over near him as he loved to give you a butt on your hindside. As Billy got older, he took a great liking for Mom's flowers and that distressed her to no end. His fondness for flowers led him to banishment back to the farm from whence he came.

Kids Need a Pet

Priscilla, the Newfoundland dog

As I got older, we had an occasional dog, but I really wasn't too involved with pets. I was soon going away to school and busy with sailing in the summer. After Robbie and I were married and had moved back to Kansas City, I decided it was time to get a dog for the kids. At least that was my story!

For some reason, I decided that the dog to get was a Newfoundland and started researching the breed. My good friend, Joanne Lyon, had shown dogs and was an expert on the subject. She advised me to get a purebred, for, as Joanne put it, "They don't eat any more than the mongrels." I took her advice and found Little Bear Kennels in Connecticut. On a business trip back East, I went to the Little Bear Kennels and bought a Newfoundland puppy we named Little Bear's Priscilla. Priscilla was a purebred, but she wasn't sold as a show dog, just a good pet puppy.

In those days you could bring a small dog in the cabin of the plane with you and carry it in your lap. There's nothing cuter than a Newfoundland puppy. Everyone on TWA had to stop by to pet Priscilla and "ooh" and "aah" over her. I remember we made it without a bathroom incident.

Watching a Newfoundland grow is like watching one of those time delay movies—you can almost see it happen. It wasn't long before Priscilla was over one hundred pounds and a loving, loyal, and resourceful dog. Because of her size, most people were afraid of her, but the only damage Priscilla ever would have done to anyone would be to lick them to death. She was the world's friendliest dog.

I took Priscilla to a local Newfoundland breeder to have her groomed, and he asked if he could take her to the dog show in St. Louis the following week. I didn't see any harm in it, so off she went. Lo and behold, she came back top Newfoundland in the show. This was remarkable, as young dogs seldom win best of breed.

In order to become a champion, a dog must accumulate fifteen AKC points in at least three different shows before three different judges. Priscilla already had a big step up the ladder with this win, so we let the breeder show her in shows over the next six months and finish her championship. She could now be called Champion Little Bear's Priscilla. Regrettably, we never saw her shown.

Priscilla moved to Aspen with us. She relished the cold weather there. I built a pen for her across the street from the office, but as the snow would come down, she would pack it until she could step over the fence and head for the Red Onion, a local restaurant, where they always had a handout for her. In fact, Priscilla became a great favorite of the animal control people and the fines became serious, doubling each time.

We were living in a Chateau Roaring Fork apartment and we fed Priscilla on the balcony just outside our front door. Sometimes we'd come home at night and find that the tourists staying in the building had left as many as 5 doggie bags next to her bowl. She became a very fat Newfoundland.

From doggie bag gifts, she progressed to carrying her bowl in her mouth and visiting the adjoining apartments, scratching on the doors. Imagine opening your door and seeing a big happy Newfoundland outside, holding an empty bowl in her mouth—how could you resist giving her a treat?

Priscilla was coal black and blended in with the asphalt pavement of the Chateau Eau Clair where we had moved, and one tragic day a tourist ran over her. It was a sad, sad day, and I think of her still.

I had never been much of a cat lover, but when we were living in Kansas City the kids brought home a stray cat and named her Carmel. Someone once told me that thousands of years ago, cats were worshiped as gods, and they've never forgotten it. Carmel, if not worshiped, was certainly loved. She was an affectionate cat and would even come when called. She got along with Priscilla just fine.

Carmel hated riding in the car. On our move to Aspen, we had a long drive ahead of us, so we sedated Carmel to make it possible for her to tolerate the trip. We stopped for the night at a motel in Denver and let Carmel out to do her duty. Unfortunately, she wandered off and we couldn't find her. We spent half the night roaming the streets looking for her, posted notices, and asked the people at the motel to please let us know when she turned up. Disconsolately, we had to leave the next morning as the kids had to start school in Aspen.

That evening we got a phone call that Carmel had been hit by a car and killed. Undoubtedly, she was so drugged up she didn't know where she was or what she was doing. I never thought I would mourn the loss of a cat, but I did mourn the loss of Carmel.

The Feathered Ones

"Wouldn't fresh eggs taste wonderful?"

From that simple question asked at the breakfast table in Woody Creek, Robbie and I decided to raise chickens. We had a chicken coop built with six inside boxes for laying and a fenced yard for the chickens to explore. We got lucky because someone suggested we contact Tom Whiting for layers. Tom supplied the perfect chicken – a French breed called ASA Brown. Whereas normal chickens would scatter and do almost anything to keep from being picked up, the Browns would come right up to you and try to untie your shoes. They laid large, beautiful brown eggs that we collected in small baskets that held four or five eggs. We gave them to friends who remarked how different a fresh egg tastes compared to a store-bought egg that could easily be three weeks old. We probably spoiled eggs for many of our friends.

We also managed to get six Mallard ducks to populate the small pond on our property. Their wings were clipped initially, but once situated and getting fed daily they were never going to leave. We built a small island on the pond that kept them safe from predators. Remarkably one of the females laid and hatched eggs, which we did not realize until we saw her swimming around the pond followed by six ducklings.

When we left for winter sailing, we boarded our ducks with our friend, Dave Marlow, the famous photographer, whoever since is known as Ducky Dave.

Jeff's Exotic Animal Ventures

After losing Priscilla and Carmel, pets par excellence, most of my association with animals was vicarious through my son Jeff, who had a small ranch in Snowmass Creek outside Aspen. Jeff collected exotic animals. The price curve on most exotic animals is the same—a perfect bell. The animals start off low, and then become "the thing to buy." Prices rise rather rapidly. Eventually everyone who wants one has one and the prices start back down again.

Jeff's Llama

Picnicking with Llamas

I loved the idea of hiking and camping in the mountains but hated carrying a heavy pack. I'd seen pictures of people camping with llamas and encouraged Jeff to start a herd. I financed the business, and Jeff bought some good llamas and started competing in shows. Similar to a dog show, the llamas were judged for confirmation and the quality of their wool.

At the height of the market, an outstanding llama could cost from $30,000 to $50,000. We had some pretty good ones, doing well on paper, until the bubble burst, prices went down, and Jeff sold his herd except for a few favorites for packing.

We could go camping for several days with the llamas carrying everything but our daypacks. An elegant llama picnic was inviting a dozen or so friends to hike to a remote location where we had wine, cheese, and other culinary delights. The llamas themselves were quite the entertainment. If you held a treat in your mouth, the llama would take it, in effect giving you a big kiss.

With their very soft feet, llamas are sure-footed on the trail, and, when well trained, are easy to lead. It is said that leading a well-trained llama is like leading a balloon. There are few limitations. A llama can go anywhere a man can go without using his hands.

People worry about llamas spitting, and they do when angry or fighting over a female, but I have spent hundreds of hours with them and never been spit on once.

To supplement the packing rental income, Jeff taught a team to pull a buggy and sold llama rides around downtown Aspen. In winter, his llamas wore little barium-studded booties, designed by Jeff, to give them traction on the icy streets. Imagine the elegant Llama, head held high, pulling a buggy in his fancy booties.

Wallaby at a Cocktail Party

After llamas, Jeff decided to raise wallabies—a type of miniature kangaroo. A newborn wallaby is about the size of a bee and lives in its mother's pouch for three to four months.

As the wallaby begins to peek out and occasionally leave the pouch, it can be taken from its mother and raised by hand. This isn't easy, because at first you have to feed it every couple hours night and day, but hand-raised this way a wallaby will become a wonderful pet.

Jeff raised one named Hannah. I would take her to cocktail parties where she was always a huge hit, hopping around on the floor and then back into the sack that served as her pouch. There was something wrong with the soil conditions on the ranch; adult wallabies did fine and bred easily, but as soon as the babies started getting on the ground they would die. Jeff eventually had to dispose of the entire herd.

Reindeer and Movies

Jeff's last venture into exotics was reindeer. Literally thousands of reindeer inhabit Alaska but importing them was difficult because they had to be quarantined when they came through Canada (a long, difficult, expensive process).

Jeff solved this problem by chartering a DC6 to fly them directly from Alaska to Aspen. Talk about a rodeo—you haven't seen one until you've seen the unloading of wild-eyed reindeer off a DC6 onto the truck to take them out to the ranch.

It was tumultuous! Reindeer going every direction, much like herding cats. One escaped from the airport during an unloading. There were unconfirmed reports of sightings for a couple of years, but he was never recaptured. Unfortunately, reindeer can't live in the wild in Colorado. The lichen that grows in Alaska is an essential part of their diet. A loose reindeer would eventually die, and this one either succumbed to its diet or predators.

Supplementing the herd's feed with certain vitamins solved this problem for Jeff's herd.

Jeff would sell the reindeer to people who wanted to keep them as pets. He also had a prosperous business renting reindeer to various zoos at Christmastime. It's incredible that zoos didn't have reindeer. After all, they are a native animal, but some zoos wanted just Christmas exhibitions.

Reindeer were hauled as far away as Florida. Jeff also dressed up as Santa Claus and went to private parties and shopping malls during the Christmas season. He trained a team of six to pull a sleigh. It was great fun to take the kids sleigh-riding around the ranch.

Jeff provided reindeer for movies. He rented the sleigh team to Rob Reiner for a Castle Rock Pictures production. In another movie venture, he took a herd of one hundred up the Castle Creek Valley for several days to film scenes for a Disney movie, White Fang 2.

Imagine one hundred reindeer with their antler racks and their high-stepping gait stampeding down a mountain valley! I went up one day to watch the action and witnessed the stampede of one hundred reindeer (stand-ins for caribou). It was quite a thrilling production.

Eventually, Jeff developed the largest reindeer herd in the lower 48 states—over 200. Prices were starting to fall when he decided to move to Puerto Vallarta and sold the entire herd. He got out just in time. In 2002 various quarantine regulations were implemented to control chronic wasting disease, prominent in some of the elk herds in Colorado. That killed the reindeer market.

Alice and Claudio

Claudio, Nick, and Alice

When I was part owner of a ranch outside of San Miguel de Allende in Mexico, we had a herd of Dorper, Peleway and Black Belly sheep, plus rabbits, chickens, and quail. None of them exotic, but not exactly household pets either.

Most people have dogs or cats as house pets, but we had a rabbit and a rooster that ran freely in our San Miguel home! Alice, the rabbit, would frequently pass through the bedroom on one of her explorations. Claudio, the rooster, would perch on the back of the sofa during cocktail hour begging for peanuts. Fortunately, Claudio was house broken to the point where he would only do his business in the garden. I love the crow of a rooster at the break of dawn, but some of our guests did not appreciate the crowing. So, in those cases, Carlos, the house man, would have to put Claudio in the garage at night.

THOUGHTS, MEANDERINGS, AND CONTRIBUTIONS

Sailing through Life: Ninety-three years of adventure

Lucky to be Blind?

Nick and Hercules

The other day I told a friend that I was fortunate to be blind. He was startled until I qualified this by saying I was fortunate to be blind today rather than back in the 1860s, the time when my great-grandfather was blind.

At 18 years of age Jefferson Coates was shot through both eyes on the first day of the battle of Gettysburg. He suffered for three days in the July heat laying in no man's land as the battle raged around him. It is a miracle that he survived in the days before antibiotics. Jefferson recovered, learned Braille and how to make brooms for a living. He returned to his native Wisconsin, married and drove a horse-drawn wagon all the way to Nebraska where he homesteaded, built a sod house, ran a farm and even served on the school board – all as a blind man. It's an amazing story of courage and perseverance.

I count my blessings for being blind in today's world. I have a wonderful seeing-eye dog that will safely walk me anywhere I want to go. I can listen to almost any book published on my phone or on the wonderful device provided by Blind Services. I can say a number to my phone, and it will read me articles from the local paper, the Wall Street Journal or any newspaper in the country.

I can communicate with friends all over the world on a computer that reads my emails to me and transcribes my replies by simply talking. I can pick up my phone and say, "call Jeff" and it will connect me with my son in Mexico. If I need to go to the doctor the local transportation company will take me anywhere in town for just two dollars. And I live with the expectation that if one of my grandkids ever goes blind, by that time they will have the medical expertise to replace a retina. What a wonderful world we live in!

Sailing through Life: Ninety-three years of adventure

Hercules my Guide Dog

Nick and Hercules at Independence Pass

By Bob Meyers

I have a blind friend whose blindness was progressive over about ten years and is now almost complete. He totally relies on a guide dog. His wife died several years ago so his life has become somewhat narrowed and his guide dog, whose name is Hercules, has become extremely close to my friend.

I recently wrote him a letter and inserted a short story that I had written about my mother who I had interviewed on video tape when she was 88 years old. Some of those clips are very powerful and resonated with him. He had an unusual take on this issue and considering his circumstances of living alone with his guide dog Hercules, wondered what would happen if we could interview his dog. This got me thinking. Those of us that like dogs often try to anthropomorphize them. This means we try to make them like humans. It somehow brings us great comfort to think that our dog knows what we're thinking and acts in ways that are not just self-serving for the dog but actually almost like friends, sort of a give and take. We take their attention but would also like to take their thoughts, just what are they thinking or not. For a moment let's just pretend that they do think, and they dream, those involuntary movements that they have are reactions in their dreams. As we know dreams help us solve the problems of the day when we are unconscious at night. So what would I say or what would I ask a dog during an interview?

I might ask...when you wait for me to come home is it really that pleasurable when I walk through the door? I might also ask is it all about food or do you really like me for myself. These are the same questions that we might ask any friend or relative. But a dog, what might a dog say?

Looking for an answer, I went to the only dog that I know that I'm friendly with ...my daughter's Samoyed. Her name is Lucy. I said Lucy... "I'm trying to figure out what you might be thinking." She immediately nuzzled up to me shook head slightly to the left because that's what she does when she wants a treat. I said, "Lucy I'm trying to get into your head, let's forget about these treats for a minute." Lucy then nuzzled up to me with her toy and shook it vigorously left and right then dropped it at my feet, hoping I would throw it, which I always do. Once this was done, we went through the ritual of throwing a ball in the backyard with her retrieving it. Is Lucy really wondering what I'm thinking? Is there any reason that I should wonder what Lucy's thinking? No, Lucy is just an emotional response, a food response, and maybe also my best friend when it comes to these items. I can't give treats to my friends, they don't appreciate them, when I throw balls, they do not retrieve them, and they certainly will not take my hat and shake it rapidly left and right when I pull it off.

So what is a dog thinking? It probably makes no difference. We make them happy…they make us happy…no strings. It would be nice if all of life is like that, I like dogs!

Marijuana: A Gateway Drug?

In spite of living in Colorado, the crown jewel of marijuana experimentation, my experience with the drug is very limited. In 1972, I went to a friend's party, where there were a number of young people present. I unknowingly participated liberally in the delicious brownies that were served only to find out later they were heavily laced with marijuana. I had also had a couple of glasses of wine and left the party feeling unusually friendly. On my way home I ran into some friends and remember dancing on their kitchen counter—and I'm a terrible dancer. I somehow managed to stagger across the street and into bed, thinking I would wake up with a world-class hangover. The morning found me only a little ashamed, but alert and with no other ill effects.

In 2011, my grandson had a minor interest in a medical marijuana business and I had him send me a sampling of marijuana candy—for experimental purposes only! At that time Betty and I were living in our motorhome in a park outside of San Antonio and I tried the candy on two separate occasions, did not like the effects, and threw the box away.

Colorado has legalized both medical and recreational marijuana, there is a big debate about whether it is a gateway drug to cocaine, heroin and other more addictive substances. The jury is still out, but the indications are that this is not the case. Other studies have shown that it could be a substitute for some opiate prescription drugs that often lead to heroin - let's hope that trend continues. For years, I have taken the position that all drugs should be legal. We've been fighting the war on drugs for over 60 years and are losing. Our prisons are full of people who did nothing worse than abuse their own bodies, hundreds of millions of dollars are being made by the drug cartels, and thousands of people are killed in the drug wars. We should make it legal, collect the tax revenue, and devote our country's efforts and dollars to drug education and rehabilitation.

And that's the way I see it.

Aspen

When the Door to Opportunity Opens, Walk Through It!

My first door of opportunity opened when I was fired from my job in 1967! It was a door that would lead to many others.

When I was young, my father had invented the masonry saw and founded Clipper Manufacturing, which began in his garage and went on to be an international business with headquarters in Grandview, Missouri, and factories in seven foreign countries. I worked in the family business and continued after it was sold to the Norton Company, a New York Stock Exchange member. It was a match made in hell and it did not come as a surprise when I was fired.

Condominiums? Skiing? Luckily, another door opened when I received an offer from a friend of mine from Northwestern University to partner with him and build a condominium in Aspen, Colorado. I had heard of Aspen but had never been there, and the concept of condominiums was completely new to me. It seemed like it might be a fun experience and it wasn't hard to convince my wife and three kids to live and ski in Aspen for a year. We rented our Kansas City home, packed our bags and pets (Priscilla, the Newfoundland dog, and Carmel, the cat) and were off!

Luck and timing are everything. Our first 48-unit project was a huge success. The concept of owning a second Aspen home you could rent when not using it made so much sense that we were able to sell the entire project by word-of-mouth—no realtors involved and an advertising budget of less than $500.

None of the buyers wanted to live in their unit. So, another door opened, and I immediately found myself in the property management and rental business. Satisfied customers and referrals led to the success of two more condominiums and then an office building. Resale market? When I noticed that units were being resold by local realtors, I decided to get my real estate license and went on to become quite successful selling condominiums. Shortly thereafter, another door opened when Kay Reid, owner of the largest home-sales firm in the area, approached me about buying her business. This was a huge door that I eagerly walked through! I bought Kay's business thus becoming the largest real estate and property management business in the Aspen area; we were the second-largest employer in town, after the Aspen Skiing Corporation.

Later, just down the valley, a new ski area, "Snowmass Village," opened. My good friend, Fritz Benedict, proposed that we build a shopping center on the land he owned at the base of Snowmass Mountain. The timing was perfect, and I was able to rent the entire shopping center before it opened.

Doors opened even while vacationing! On one of my vacations in Puerto Vallarta, I ran into an Aspen acquaintance at a local bar. Before the night was over, we decided to build luxury homes together. After our four-unit project was successfully completed and sold, again without realtors, my friend lost interest. I went on to successfully build and renovate seven luxury residences, the largest of which was over 20,000 square feet and had two elevators. A door closed on me ten years ago when I lost my eyesight and one slammed shut when I lost my wife of almost 40 years. But then another door opened in 2015, when I received my wonderful guide dog, Hercules.

My philosophy: When the door to opportunity opens, only a fool doesn't walk through it!

Memorable Moments

We all have memorable experiences in our life that we flashback to on occasion and I wanted to write some down while they were fresh in my mind.

The David

When Betty and I were traveling around Europe in our VW van one of our favorite destinations was Florence, Italy. There was a wonderful campground in Florence located on a hill overlooking the city and we could walk down the hill to the covered bridge and be in the heart of Florence. Everyone has seen pictures of the statue of David, but it was an entirely different experience to see it in person. As you enter the Accademia Gallery of Florence (Galleria dell'Accademia di Firenze) where David is on display you pass several fascinating and beautiful statues. But then you come to The David and it literally takes your breath away. Something you never forget.

Windsurfing in Panama

I have literally thousands of wonderful memories about the 12 years that Betty and I spent cruising on Expectation, but one stands out. We normally anchored in a sheltered cove, but on this occasion, we were anchored off the coast of Panama in wide open water but behind a reef that was just below the surface swell so the anchorage was quite comfortable. We were about a mile from a beautiful tropical island. The windsurfing conditions were perfect. There was enough wind to make it exciting but not enough to overpower me. Because of the reef the waves were manageable. I had one of my greatest windsurfing days and eventually landed on the beach of the deserted island and it was perfect. Undisturbed white sand backed by beautiful palm trees. I sat in the sand and realized how lucky I was to be alive.

The 9/11 attack, December 11, 2001

Betty and I had checked into the Oxford Hotel in Denver as we had a flight to catch early the next morning. She had the TV on while I was doing some work and her morning news program was interrupted when the first plane hit the New York trade center. She called me over to watch and we were stupefied to see the second plane hit and the collapse of the building. We didn't go anywhere that day—just stayed glued to the TV.

Pearl Harbor, December 7, 1941

It was Sunday and my parents allowed me to walk to the Waldo theater with two friends to see a cowboy movie. As we were passing the radio shop, we heard the news that the Japanese had bombed Pearl Harbor. Us 10-year-olds did not think it was a big deal as we were sure the little Japanese soldiers would be no match for Americans and we went on to watch the Lone Ranger and Tonto take care of the bad guys.

Roosevelt dies April 12, 1945

My friend, Richard Miller, and I were practicing the shot put in the grassy area by Ward Parkway in Kansas City when someone in a passing car stopped to give us the news. At 14 we were not too concerned about it but I will always remember where I was on that fateful day.

Kennedy assassinated, November 2, 1963

I was in my car following Joanne Lyon on our way to meet her dog groomer, as Joanne thought he would do a great job of grooming my Newfoundland dog, Priscilla. I wasn't listening to the radio but Joanne was and signal me to pull over so she could give me the bad news. We went on to the groomer who was so impressed with Priscilla that he took her to the St. Louis dog show the following week where Priscilla won best-of-breed and went on to become a champion.

My Musical Life

My musical life as a performer began and ended at my seventh-grade graduation from Hale Cook School. In those days you graduated from grade school after the seventh grade and were off to high school.

My seventh-grade class had practiced the three songs we were going to sing at our graduation ceremony for almost three months. We were all dressed up and eager to sing for the audience when my teacher came to me and said, "Don't sing, just move your mouth. You might spoil it!" I was deeply hurt but I sang anyway.

I love music, although I know I do not have what is called good rhythm. So how is it possible that I married two women who love to dance and were accomplished dancers? The only part of dancing I liked was the slow dance because that meant virtually standing still and swaying while you held your partner close. It tells you something that Robbie, after our divorce, moved back to Kansas City and married Bob Reynolds, the guy who had been her favorite dancing partner at yacht club parties.

Betty was also a marvelous and enthusiastic dancer. She tolerated me during the slow dances. However, she was a very popular partner when the tempo picked up.

Now don't get me wrong, I love music and for many years have bought season-tickets to the Aspen Music Festival rehearsals. I sometimes go to the Sunday concerts, still, I prefer the rehearsals because you hear the entire concert and also the conductor perfecting the orchestra members' performance.

I also enjoy musical theater though I recently figured out that I am paying for a ticket to watch the dancing that I cannot see. It makes more sense to ask Alexa to play the performance so I can enjoy the music without being frustrated by missing the dancing.

My musical life? Enjoy? Yes. Perform? No.

Death Penalty

Today capital punishment is legal in 30 U.S. states and over 3,000 people are on death row. More than 1,300 individuals have been executed in the U.S. 90 countries have the death penalty but as a practical matter, only 54 foreign countries actually enforce it. In other countries, it is still on the books but seldom enforced, usually only for crimes committed during wartime. The U.S. is the only Western country that routinely uses the death penalty.

I am against the death penalty and feel it should be abolished in the U.S. for a number of reasons. First, no one has proven that the death penalty is a deterrent to crime. Most murders are acts of passion or are committed in the course of another crime such as a robbery.

Death penalty trials are expensive. The American Bar Association states that death penalty trials are 20 times more expensive than trials seeking a life sentence without parole. Since 1976, California alone has spent more than $4 billion on death penalty trials. It costs far more to go through the legal process required in a death penalty case than keeping the accused in prison for the rest of his/her life.

But the most important fault of the death penalty is that once applied it is irrevocable. In recent years more than 100 prisoners who were on death row have been released because DNA or other evidence has come to light that proved they were innocent.

It is time we join the rest of the civilized world and eliminate the death penalty!

Where Was I?

Almost everyone remembers where they were when world changing events took place. Here are my memories of where I was when significant events happened throughout my lifetime.

The Bombing of Pearl Harbor, December 7, 1941

At 10 years of age, I was old enough to go to the movies by myself. On this date, I was with two friends headed for the Waldo Theater in Kansas City. On our way, we heard a radio very loudly announcing the Japanese bombing of Pearl Harbor and the fact that this surely meant war. Our reaction, and the initial reaction of most of the country, was that the Japanese were tiny people from a small island and would be no problem to defeat. We went on to see a Lone Ranger short and a western movie.

V-day, the end of World War II, September 2, 1945

The whole family was at our cabin at Lake Lotawana when the news came over the radio that the war was finally over. I was a little young to comprehend the full significance but my parents and their good friends, Edith and Candy Houston, were delirious with joy and proceeded to get quite drunk.
Assassination of John Kennedy, November 22, 1963
We were convinced it was time to have our 100-pound Newfoundland, Priscilla, groomed. I was following my friend, Joanne Lyon, on Ward Parkway Boulevard in Kansas City to a dog grooming place she knew. Joanne had heard the shocking news on the radio, put on her blinker and pulled over to tell me. We went on to the groomer who thought Priscilla looked

like a special dog and asked if he could take her to a dog show in St. Louis the following weekend. Priscilla had been bought from Little Bear Kennels in Connecticut as a pet puppy, not a show dog, but we thought it would be fun to see how she did in a show and gave permission. As it turned out she won best of breed, and we allowed her to continue to be shown and she won her championship and could be called Champion Little Bear's Priscilla. It did not change her personality one bit.

First Moon Landing, July 20, 1969

Robbie and I were living in apartment seven in the Château Chaumont, and I was hard at work building and selling the Château Roaring Fork. It was a beautiful Sunday, so we took all three kids and were off on a picnic at one of our favorite picnic spots on Independence Pass. We did not see the TV coverage until we returned late in the afternoon.

September 11, 2001

Betty and I happened to be in a hotel in Denver that morning. She was watching TV when they announced the first airplane hit the trade center. We were both glued to the TV when we saw the second plane hit and hardly left the hotel room that day as the terrible news kept coming in.

Epilogue

As I assembled these stories I have the urge to write many more: this book represents a fraction of my life's experiences. My hope is to record my many travels with grandchildren.

Stand by for more.

Nick Coates

NOTES

FAMILY HISTORY

1 The Iron Brigade took pride in its designation, "1st Brigade, 1st Division, I Corps", under which it played a prominent role in the first day of the Battle of Gettysburg, July 1, 1863. The 6th Wisconsin (along with 100 men of the brigade guard) are remembered for their famous charge on an unfinished railroad cut north and west of the town, where they captured the flag of the 2nd Mississippi and took hundreds of Confederate prisoners.[5] https://en.wikipedia.org/wiki/Iron_Brigade

2 Minié ball, or Minni ball, is a type of muzzle-loading spin-stabilized bullet for rifled muskets named after its developer, Claude-Étienne Minié.

3 Sod house. Building a House. Without trees or stone, homesteaders had to rely on the only available building material — prairie sod, jokingly called "Nebraska marble." Sod is the top layer of earth that includes grass, its roots, and the dirt clinging to the roots.

OLIVE COATES -- MY MOTHER

4 Liberace was a flamboyant pianist known for his glitz and glamor and who twice had his own TV show
https://www.biography.com/musician/liberace

HOUSE BESIDE A LAKE WITH A BOAT DOCK

5 Two beds were at the normal level with drawers underneath them and two were above, accessible by ladder. On the wall at the head of each bunk was a hand-drawn map of the lake, our cove or something else to do with Lake Lotawana. These were wonderful drawings that a friend of my parents had given them.

MY YEAR IN ENGLAND

6 http://www.thamesweb.co.uk/windsor/windsorhistory/isc.html

7 A method of going up a slope in which a skier sets the skis in a form resembling a V, and, placing weight on the inside edges, advances the skis by turns using the poles from behind for push and support.

THE PANAMA CANAL

8 The Panama Canal lies at a latitude of 9° N, where the North American Continental Divide dips to one of its lowest points.

9 Panama. Christopher P Blake. National Geographic Books, 2007. Jungle Operations closed in 1999.

ABOUT THE AUTHOR

Nick and Hercules
Photo: Kim Coates 2024

Neligh (Nick) Coates lives in a retirement community in San Antonio, Texas with his guide dog, Hercules. His favorite activity is to write about his experiences and the unique characters he has known.

Printed in Great Britain
by Amazon

c03d4899-2a64-40d4-bd3c-7b298e837c1aR01